The Live Music Business

T0299914

The Live Music Business: Management and Production of Concerts and Festivals, Third Edition, shines a light on the enigmatic live music business, offering a wealth of inside advice and trade secrets to artists and bands looking to make a living in the industry. Previously published as *The Tour Book*, this new edition has been extensively revised, reorganised, and updated to reflect today's music industry.

This practical guidebook examines the roles of the key players – from booking agents to concert promoters, artist managers to talent buyers – and the deals, conventions, and processes that drive this global business. Written by a touring professional with over 25 years of experience, this book elucidates why playing live is crucial to the success of any musician, band, or artist, explaining issues like:

- what managers, promoters, and agents do and how they arrange shows and tours;
- how to understand and negotiate show contracts;
- how to create a contract rider and how it affects the money you earn from a show;
- how to appear professional and knowledgeable in an industry with its own conventions, language, and baffling technical terms; and
- a three-year plan using live performance to kickstart your music career.

Intended for music artists and students, *The Live Music Business* presents proven live-music career strategies, covering every aspect of putting on a live show, from rehearsing and soundchecks to promotions, marketing, and contracts. In an era when performing live is more essential than ever, this is the go-to guidebook for getting your show on the road and making a living from music.

Andy Reynolds is a concert tour manager and audio engineer with more than 25 years of professional touring experience. He has worked for artists such as Maribou State, George FitzGerald, Maverick Sabre, The All-American Rejects, House of Pain, Super Furry Animals, Machine Head, and Pavement and has also worked supporting U2, Whitney Houston, and the Foo Fighters. He also teaches live sound engineering and concert tour management at colleges and universities in the UK.

The Live Music Business

Management and Production of Concerts and Festivals

THIRD EDITION

ANDY REYNOLDS

Routledge
Taylor & Francis Group

NEW YORK AND LONDON

Third edition published 2022
by Routledge
605 Third Avenue, New York, NY 10158

and by Routledge
2 Park Square, Milton Park, Abingdon, Oxon, OX14 4RN

Routledge is an imprint of the Taylor & Francis Group, an informa business

First edition published by Thomson Course Technology, 2008

Second edition published by Cengage Learning PTR, 2012

Library of Congress Cataloging-in-Publication Data
Names: Reynolds, Andy, author. | Reynolds, Andy. Tour book.
Title: The live music business: management and production of concerts and festivals/Andy Reynolds.
Description: Third edition. | New York: Routledge, 2021. |
Includes bibliographical references and index.
Identifiers: LCCN 2021027392 (print) | LCCN 2021027393 (ebook) |
ISBN 9780367894917 (hardback) | ISBN 9780367859725 (paperback) |
ISBN 9781003019503 (ebook)
Subjects: LCSH: Concert tours–Management. | Music trade–Vocational guidance. | Popular music–Vocational guidance.
Classification: LCC ML3790 .R49 2021 (print) | LCC ML3790 (ebook) |
DDC 780.23–dc23
LC record available at https://lccn.loc.gov/2021027392
LC ebook record available at https://lccn.loc.gov/2021027393

ISBN: 978-0-367-89491-7 (hbk)
ISBN: 978-0-367-85972-5 (pbk)
ISBN: 978-1-003-01950-3 (ebk)

DOI: 10.4324/9781003019503

Typeset in Avenir, Bell and Bembo
by Deanta Global Publishing Services, Chennai, India

For Eileen and Lily

CONTENTS

FIGURES AND TABLES

FIGURES

TABLES

ACKNOWLEDGEMENTS

Many thanks to all the artists and crew I have had the pleasure to work with. Special thanks to Chris Davids and Liam Ivory and the rest of the Maribou State live band and crew. Much love and respect to Noel Kilbride, Nick Jevons, Andy Dimmack, Phil Winward, and Ross Chapple. A glass raised to Noel "Rickey" Ricketts – rest in peace, dude.

Props to the promoters, booking agents, artist managers, and independent label owners. There would be no book without you. A special "yo!" to Adam "Mouj" Moujahid and Graeme Stewart.

Love and respect for fellow academics, teachers, lecturers, staff, and others – and a big shout out to Steve Meluish for championing my work.

Finally, to all students past, present, and future – thank you for letting me share my experiences with you. Best of luck for the future!

INTRODUCTION

"The top 10% of artists make money selling records. The rest go on tour".[1] *Scott Welch, manager for Alanis Morissette and LeAnn Rimes*

"We used to have a tour to promote a record, now we have a record to promote a tour".[2] *Ken Fermaglich, booking agent, Guns N Roses and Paramore.*

The statements of Welch and Fermaglich above are indicative of opinion regarding the importance of live music for artists. The common view is that artists increasingly look to revenue from ticket sales, as income from recorded music fell post-2000. This may be true, and may not be relevant for the vast majority of music artists. In the case the view is based in fact, there is also little guidance for artists on how to create revenue from performing in clubs, theatres, arenas, stadiums, and green-field, open-air festivals. The roles of the key figures, the deals, conventions, and processes, of the live music business are not widely documented. For instance, there are some aspects of the industry that operate "on a handshake" – verbal agreements for deals worth millions of dollars – and that is bewildering for the outsider.

However, the decade 2010–2020 also saw the live music business become a "real business".[3] What was previously a collection of small companies with a fragmented offering has turned into a global business, dominated by international companies who have the knowledge and financial capacity to invest in new artists, new venues, better marketing, and better ticketing systems. This investment assists artists in reaching more fans and give those fans a better concert experience.

The live music business, therefore, needs closer examination. This book will help you to appreciate the roles of the key players in the live music business and give you knowledge of the day-to-day planning of concert tours and festival appearances. The book is divided into two parts. The first, Live Music Management, looks at the people and companies who organise the concerts and make the deals. You will be introduced to the work of the booking agents, the role of the concert promoter, and the relationship of the artist manager with the two. The second part, Live Music Production, looks at the mechanics of how those deals get transformed into the concerts, festivals, and club nights. You will meet the technical and production crew and examine the six elements of concert production and get a detailed explanation of the budgeting process for a concert tour.

NOTES

1 Kafka, P., 2003. "The road to riches", *Forbes*, 7 July, 2003.
2 Rendon, F., 2018. "Q's with UTA's Ken Fermaglich: Powerhouse rock agent talks clients, industry" [WWW Document], n.d. URL https://www.pollstar.com/News/qs-with-utas-ken-fermaglich-powerhouse-rock-agent-talks-clients-industry-135722 (accessed 3.12.21).
3 Gensler, A., 2019. "Q's with... Marc Geiger WME partner & head of music on the decade and what lies ahead", *Pollstar* 39, 15–16.

DOI: 10.4324/9781003019503-101

PART ONE
Live Music Management

Live music is big business. Any examination of an industry usually includes an assessment of the worth of that industry or market segment. PricewaterhouseCoopers (PwC), a consultancy, value live music (ticket sales and related sponsorships) as being worth $30 billion by 2022 – of which over $24 billion will be from ticket sales.[1] Pollstar, an industry trade paper, reported that gross ticket sales from the top 100 tours of 2019 was $5.5 billion.[2] The forecast might be unrealistic: $22 billion worth of tickets need to be sold in the next four years if the PwC figures are to be achieved.

Whatever the predicted worth of the business, the value to an artist entering the industry must be valued using different metrics – that of the promotional possibilities and the revenue it will bring to that particular artist.

This section will introduce you to the key players in the organisation and management of the live music business – the artists, the artist mangers, the booking agents, and the talent buyers/concert promoters.[3] Figure P1.1 shows the relationship of these key players all revolving round the artist.

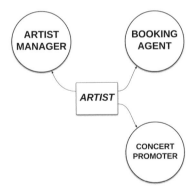

Figure P1.1 The key players in the organisation and management of the live music business

NOTES

1 PricewaterhouseCoopers, 2019. *Global Entertainment & Media Outlook 2019–2023 – Getting Personal: Putting the Me in Entertainment and Media*. PwC. URL https://www.pwc.com/gx/en/ente rtainment-media/outlook-2019/entertainment-and-media-outlook-perspectives-2019-2023.pdf (accessed 11.11.19). https://www.pwc.com/gx/en/industries/tmt/media/outlook.html.
2 *Pollstar 2019 Year End Special* [WWW Document], n.d. URL https://www.pollstar.com/speci aledition/pollstar-2019-year-end-special-142982 (accessed 9.29.20).
3 Concert promoter is the more common term used to describe talent buyers and one used from now on in this text.

DOI: 10.4324/9781003019503-1

1

CHAPTER 1
THE ARTISTS

CHAPTER OUTLINE

The three parts of the music business (recorded, publishing, and live) revolve around the artist. The artist creates the "product" – songs and performances – which generate revenue in the respective business areas. Revenue in the live music business is generated primarily from selling concert tickets for performances at one-off shows, on concert tours, and at festivals. The key players identified in Figure P1.1 will all receive a portion of the ticket sales, and some key players will be able to generate ancillary income from the artist's live activity. But it is the artist who drives the business – the ability of an artist to sell concert tickets, thus "spinning the wheel" of further income generation, is of foremost importance. Selling tickets is not only an income stream. Artists and their managers view the ability to sell tickets as an indicator of the connection between the artist and the fans. The number of streams and YouTube views for a particular artist may reach the millions but "there isn't any shortcut to selling tickets. You have to go through a process of development and building an audience", according to Harry McGee, an artist manager.[1] Artists agree. "There are a lot of artists with millions of streams worldwide because they have got on some play list", says Victoria Hesketh, who performs as Little Boots, "but they couldn't put a gig on and sell ten tickets".[2]

The views of artists and their managers may contain sweeping statements, and it is clear there are two benefits from live performance. The first is an income stream which may well exceed that from recorded music (streams, downloads, and physical sales). The second benefit is the relationship between the artist and the fan. Buying a concert ticket shows a deeper connection with the artist than that of following them on social media or adding a song to a play list. These two benefits should therefore be acknowledged in any artist's career planning. This is true regardless of the career stage the artist finds themselves. Figure 1.1 shows a timeline of an artist's career and the contribution live performance makes at each stage.

Figure 1.1 depicts the artist's career from the point they have established themselves, whether by being signed to a management company, being signed to a record company, self-releasing an album, or a combination of those milestones. The artist will still perhaps organise their own shows in year one. Depending on genre and location,

DOI: 10.4324/9781003019503-2

Figure 1.1 Time line: The contribution of live performance to an artist's career

these performances may be in bars, pubs, and function centres, hired by the artist and staged with the intention of impressing, friends, family, and industry tastemakers. A management team or record company may have become involved, and the need arises to "showcase" the artist's abilities (we will examine the concept of showcases in chapter three: Booking Agents). The artist should have progressed to selling concert tickets to the public ("hard tickets") by the end of year one.

A booking agent will have become involved towards the end of year one, and the agent will work tirelessly in year two to secure appearances at domestic green-field, open-air, summer music festivals. The artist will appear very early in the day at these events (when many festival-goers have either not arrived or are still sleeping in their tents) or on one of the many smaller stages and tents that make up a large-scale music festival. Still, these appearances are an accepted way of introducing an act to the general public and gauging the reaction from new fans. The agent will also arrange for the artist to be added to the bill by established artists (called a "support slot" or "opening up"). Opening for a well-known artist is another way of finding new fans and gauging the artist's ability to entertain a crowd.

The artist will have established themselves by the end of year two and will be booked to appear at international music festivals in year three. The artist will also commit to a tour of 1000–5000-capacity domestic venues in the autumn or winter of year three. The so-called "headline tour" is a milestone for artists, validating their hard work and the commitment from their fans.

Year four will see the artist capitalising on the foundations laid in the first three years, with them headlining domestic music festivals and moving into stadium-level touring (>5000~20,000-capacity).

THE IMPORTANCE OF LIVE PERFORMANCE

The perceived impact of performing live has shifted, since 1999, from proving ability to a revenue stream.

Pre-1999, playing live was a way of proving the ability of the artist, therefore gauging their "authenticity".[3] Ability includes both the technical nature of the craft (good singing, competent playing of instruments, decent songwriting) as well as the mysterious

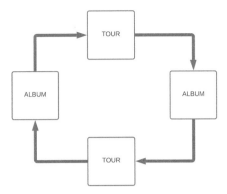

Figure 1.2 The album-tour-album cycle. An artist releases an album, undertakes a concert tour to promote the album, finishes the tour, writes, records, and releases a new album, undertakes a concert tour to promote the new album, and so on

"star quality" that successful artists have. Authenticity is a desirable asset – audiences respond favourably to artists who have "paid their dues" by starting out in grassroots venues and "can judge what they do is real".[4]

The discovery of new artists in the pre-internet era relied on teams of Artist & Repertoire (A&R) people first hearing demonstration recordings (demos) of bands. The team would then attend live performances of the bands they felt were going to be successful. An artist that could hold the interest of an A&R person attending a gig in a bar would stand a good chance of being signed to that record company. This still holds true – live sets are seen as "the best indication of the quality of an artist and their music".[5]

LIVE PERFORMANCE AS A PROMOTIONAL ACTIVITY

The music business of the "old days" (pre-1999) concentrated on getting radio play of singles that were released to promote an artist's new album. Performing live was seen as a promotional activity – playing live and touring was undertaken to alert fans to songs on the latest album. A successful artist would therefore find themselves in the "album-tour-album" cycle (Figure 1.2).

PRE-1999: "THE OLD DAYS"

It is generally accepted that the music industry has operated in two phases "pre- and post-Napster". Napster was a peer-to-peer file-sharing service that launched in November 1999 and enabled music fans to discover and keep the music they liked, without paying for it.

Napster and other file-sharing services are often blamed for the slump in recorded music sales from $36 billion in 2000 to a low of $29 billion in 2007.[6] Whether file-sharing was totally to blame is arguable; increasing competition from console gaming, DVDs, and other consumer entertainment, also played a part. What is true is that the recorded music industry has had a long, slow, climb back to the sales volumes reported in 2000. Veterans of the music business sometimes use the phrase "the old days" in speeches and reports – they are referring to the business before 1999.

The "cycle" describes the timeline of an "album campaign" – the period allocated to promoting a new album. The album-tour-album cycle involved releasing an album, touring to support the release, finishing the tour, resting, writing new material, entering a studio to record the new material (often also involving the writing of material in the studio), releasing the new album, going on tour to support the new album, and so on. The cycle was accepted as the lot of a successful artist, and the recorded music business did not have any involvement in the live side of the business – they were happy as long as the artist hit the road to promote the new album. Mick Jagger of the Rolling Stones sums up the relationship:

> Recorded music and the business of it is a totally separate subject from the road, and it has a completely different business model and, of course, one's linked to the other. But for years, they were never really linked at all. In fact, you could never get the two groups to talk to each other. It was a nightmare.[7]

The modern record company may be more invested in the live music business these days, and the album-tour-album cycle is still applicable. An artist will have other activities taking place between – or concurrent with – stages of the cycle, such as film and TV appearances,[8] product launches,[9] and collaborations with other artists. There is also sentiment regarding the value of the album in the modern streaming-led music business and that a promotional campaign will no longer feature, or even need, the album as a collection of songs at its centre.[10]

That may be the case in future; for now, playing live is a valid promotional strategy with demonstrable benefits. Artist and record companies report significant uplifts in sales for artists who perform at major music festivals,[11] such as the Coachella Valley Music and Arts Festival (US) and the Glastonbury Festival of Contemporary Performing Arts (UK). Chart-reporting company Nielsen SoundScan reported that Tupac Shakur's "Greatest Hits" album (released in 1998) saw increased sales of 571% after the rapper appeared at the Coachella festival in 2012.[12] This despite Shakur having died in 1996 and appearing at the Coachella festival represented as a hologram.

LIVE PERFORMANCE AS A MAJOR REVENUE STREAM

The A&R discovery process now includes measuring an artist's popularity on social media and music upload sites, such as SoundCloud, to gauge future success. The ability to perform live may still be counted in the A&R decision, and the earning potential from live performance is an important consideration. The introduction to this book features a quote from Scott Welch, a music manager, about artists making the majority of money from touring (the quote appeared in an article written in 2003, as revenues from recorded music were in free-fall). Regarding live performance as a major revenue stream is a common sentiment and is backed up by data. The highest-earning artists of 2018 made almost 75% of their money from touring and concert activity.[13] The list of 50 artists compiled by Billboard magazine[14] included U2, Garth Brooks, Metallica, Bruno Mars, and Ed Sheeran in the top five, who also all have respectable income from recorded music and publishing. The fact that these artists received three-quarters of the revenue from live performance is noteworthy and fuels the seemingly endless blog posts and articles about the importance of live as the major revenue source for modern artists.

Do artists outside of the Top 50 earn the same proportion from touring and concerts? Individual artist data are protected, and the data reported in the Billboard report are based on projections, using accepted industry reporting.[15] These projections have some significance when reporting on earnings exceeding ten million dollars, as a percentage change here and there still gives a convincing picture of earning proportions. However, a successful artist outside of the Billboard Top 50 earners list will make a lot less from their music, and generalisations on lower incomes are misleading. For instance, say an artist earns the equivalent of the US household income for the year, $61,000.[16] The Billboard report suggests the artist would earn 75% of this figure from live performance – $45,750 – which is a great deal to earn from performing in bars and clubs. You shall see the potential revenue an emerging artist can expect to receive in *Creating the Deals* later in this book. A take-away from this section should be that the importance of live performance as a revenue stream for artists is true at the top of the market (artists with established careers or that have capitalised on breakout success to go directly to per-forming in arenas), and that perceived importance and revenue share may not be true for emerging artists.

A SIGNIFICANT REVENUE STREAM IF COSTS ARE LOW

It should be noted at this stage that reported revenue from live performance is depend-ent on associated touring costs. Table 1.1 shows the broad categories of artist expenses when performing live. You will look at these costs in part two, *Live Music Production*; for now, you should know that touring is expensive.

An undiscovered artist will incur these costs in the same way as a stadium-filling legacy act. The costs for the emerging artist will be less in total but may be a greater percentage of the performance income. For instance, the artist may have to rent a car or van, book a hotel, put new strings on her guitar, and pay her backing musi-cians, to perform a show in the next state. A rough total for these expenses could be $400; the revenue from the show may only be $500. This is not an unrealistic scenario, and any calculation of performance income as a major revenue stream must

Table 1.1 The four categories of live performance expenses, with examples for each

CATEGORY	EXAMPLES
WAGES	Session musicians
	Musical director
	Other performers
	Technical crew
	Touring management crew
	Merchandise sellers
	Drivers
TRANSPORT	People carriers
	Sleeper buses
	Trucks
	Flights
	Freighting of equipment
ACCOMMODATION	Hotels
	Apartments
PRODUCTION	PA (sound)
	Lights
	Video
	Backline
	Set
	Stage
	Work permits and visas
	Rehearsals

factor in the costs involved. An artist who is going to make a living from live music must keep their costs down.

THE IMPORTANCE OF LIVE PERFORMANCE BASED ON GENRE

The benefit of authenticity is apparent when taking genre into account. For instance, live music is seen as the preserve of "real" musicians – those in groups playing "rock music" with other musicians, with guitars, drum kits, and vocals unaided by technology. This type of music, and the performance, can be viewed as "authentic".[17] At the same time, authenticity in certain genres may have been compromised using technology in live performance.[18] Pop music performers may lip-sync (pretend to sing while pre-recorded vocal tracks are played), for instance, and are therefore judged as inauthentic. A study of the top-grossing tours of all time would seem to confirm this sentiment, as all but four of the artists in the current top 20 highest-grossing tours chart as provided by Pollstar, a trade magazine, are groups performing guitar-led music that fits broadly into the rock genre.[19]

A genre may be deemed to be inauthentic, and historically purveyors of music in genres considered to be inauthentic would not seem to benefit from live performance, compared with artists operating in "authentic" genres. Changing audience consumption habits have seen a shift in this perception. An example is hip-hop. Although accounting for over 20% of music consumption (physical sales, downloads, and streams) in 2018,[20] hip-hop had never been considered successful in concert venues. Platinum-selling hip-hop artist Jay-Z's 2008 headline slot at the Glastonbury festival was met with criticism, with many complaining of the booking of a hip-hop artist for a festival that mainly featured rock and folk[21] artists.[22] Concerts and tours by other hip-hop artists were often affected by worries of violence at the shows and did not sell many tickets.[23] Hip-hop concerts also suffered with a lack of authenticity – sub-standard sound and lack of performer charisma also plagued hip-hop tours of the 1980s and 1990s – giving the impression the artists "could not play".

Before the pandemic, hip-hop was proving to be as successful in concert halls as in recorded music. A hip-hop fan's ability to discover new music through streaming and music upload sites, such as YouTube (a video-sharing service) and SoundCloud, has lowered the barriers to entry, especially for independent artists (those not signed to a record company), and "industry gatekeepers have become less important".[24] Hip-hop artists can gauge demand for their music by analysing the statistics provided by Spotify (a music-streaming service), for instance; concerts and tours can then be booked in cities where there is sufficient demand. (You will see more on this in "Strategy" section later in this part). The result is artists can perform in the cities where their fans live and can then use that support to justify inclusion on the bill at major music festivals. Fans have less concerns about authenticity, the removal of gatekeepers allows fans to champion music on their own terms, and the concert experience is part of that dedication to an artist.

WHO ARE THE GATEKEEPERS?

Gatekeeper is the term used to describe people who create a barrier between two sets of people. The term originated to describe secretaries and personal assistants who controlled access, either by phone or in person, to company executives and business people.

The term is used in the music business to describe creative decision makers – an example being radio stations. Traditionally, you heard music on the radio, but you did not hear all the music that had been released; you heard only the music that has been filtered through the radio show producers and presenters who decided to play it out.

Other live music business gatekeepers are the booking agents and promoters. You can only attend the concerts that have been organised by those two parties, and that arrangement used to rely on instinct and gut feeling to pick which artist would sell a good number of tickets. Analysing data from internet services such as Spotify has changed that arrangement: fans can implore an artist to perform in a certain city and back up the request with statistics about relevant views and streams. Promoters and booking agents still must work together to organise a show, but the fans have more say on what they want to see – and when.

LIVE PERFORMANCE ENABLES AN ACCELERATED TIMELINE OF SUCCESS

The discussion on hip-hop, and the removal of barriers to entry for emerging artists, is relevant to the live music business. Thanks to internet-enabled services, such as YouTube, music discovery is a level playing field, and a fan in Birmingham, England can discover and enjoy the same music as a fan in Birmingham, Alabama and Birmingham, Saskatchewan. Artists increasingly own the distribution and marketing of music, and this control has given music-makers the ability to disrupt traditional methods of promotion – concert touring amongst them. Artists are able to build an audience and give those fans what they want – including selling them concert tickets. This has always been the case – signing a record deal, touring to promote an album, releasing another album, touring in larger venues to promote the new album and so on – and now the process takes less than a year, instead of five or ten. Live Nation Entertainment (a concert promoter) proposed that the "new way" for artist development tracked a path from self-release to filling arenas in three months![25] The thinking is if 2 million people in New York state stream an artist's song, there is a good chance the artist can entice 2000 of them to attend a show in Manhattan.

NOTES

1 Ingham, T.(2018) "The thrill of finding a new act". *Music Business Week*. Q4 P12.
2 Parker, M., 2019. "Under the influence – Little Boots", *Electronic Sound One* 59, 26.
3 Anderton, C., Dubber, A., and James, M., 2013. *Understanding the Music Business*. SAGE Publications Ltd, London.
4 Frith, S., 2007. "Live music matters", *Scottish Music Review*., p13.
5 McGuiness, E., 2006. "Eleanor McGuiness – POD." Interview with Andy Reynolds.
6 IFPI, 2008. "IFPI -Recorded music sales" [WWW Document]. URL https://web.archive.org /web/20081205010520/; http://www.ifpi.org/content/section_statistics/index.html (accessed 12.23.20).
7 Serwer, A., 2002. "Inside Rolling Stones Inc." (republished 2013) [WWW Document]. *Fortune*. URL https://fortune.com/2013/07/21/inside-rolling-stones-inc-fortune-2002/ (accessed 1.8.20).
8 A Star Is Born (2018 film), 2020. Wikipedia.
9 Shop Beyoncé, n.d. "Shop Beyoncé" [WWW Document]. URL https://shop.beyonce.com/ (accessed 1.8.20).
10 Homewood, B., 2018. "'The album is the end of a campaign, not the beginning': Coda's Alex Hardee sizes up the music biz" [WWW Document], 2018. URL https://www.musicweek.com/ live/read/the-album-is-the-end-of-a-campaign-not-the-beginning-coda-s-alex-hardee-sizes-up -the-music-biz/073449 (accessed 1.8.20).
11 Riley-Smith, B., 2013. Playing Glastonbury can Increase Album Sales Twentyfold. [WWW Document]. URL https://www.telegraph.co.uk/technology/news/10331053/Playing-Glastonbu ry-can-increase-album-sales-twentyfold.html
12 Caulfield,K.(2012)"Tupac's virtual Coachella appearance spurs huge sales bump" [WWW Document], n.d. *Billboard*. URL https://www.billboard.com/articles/news/489895/tupacs-virtua l-coachella-appearance-spurs-huge-sales-bump (accessed 1.9.20).
13 Chapple, J. (2017) "75%+ of richest artists' income is from touring", 2017. *IQ Magazine*. URL https://www.iq-mag.net/2017/07/75pc-richest-artists-income-touring/ (accessed 11.1.18).
14 Billboard Staff (2018) "Billboard's 2018 money makers: 50 highest-paid musicians" [WWW Document], n.d. *Billboard*. URL https://www.billboard.com/photos/8465835/highest-paid-m usicians-money-makers (accessed 1.8.20).

15 Billboard Staff (2018) "How Billboard's 2018 money makers were determined" [WWW Document], n.d. *Billboard*. URL https://www.billboard.com/articles/business/8466168/highest-paid-musicians-methodology-money-makers-2018 (accessed 1.8.20).

16 Guzman, G.G., (2010). *Household Income: 2018*. United States Census Bureau. Washington

17 Auslander, P., n.d. *Liveness. Performance in a Mediatized Culture*. 2nd ed. Routledge, New York.

18 Auslander, P., n.d. *Liveness. Performance in a Mediatized Culture*. 2nd ed. Routledge, New York.

19 'List of the highest-grossing concert tours' (2020) *Wikipedia* Available at: https://en.wikipedia.org/wiki/List_of_highest-grossing_concert_tours

20 Leight, E., 2019. "Hip-Hop continued to dominate the music business in 2018", *Rolling Stone*. URL https://www.rollingstone.com/music/music-news/hip-hop-continued-to-dominate-the-music-business-in-2018-774422/ (accessed 1.9.20).

21 Chapple, J. (2017) "I couldn't pay Marc Bolan': Michael Eavis on Glasto's history", 2017. *IQ Magazine*. URL https://www.iq-mag.net/2017/09/michael-eavis-glastonbury-keynote-iff-2017/ (accessed 1.9.20).

22 Lloyd, A. (2019) "Glastonbury's Emily Eavis: Jay-Z backlash was out of control" [WWW Document], n.d. URL https://news.yahoo.com/glastonburys-emily-eavis-jay-z-backlash-was-out-of-control-230100152.html (accessed 1.9.20).

23 Charnas, D., 2011. *The Big Payback: The History of the Business of Hip-Hop*. New American Library, New York.

24 Robertson, D., 2019. "Urban sprawl", *IQ Magazine*, 32.

25 Live Nation Entertainment, 2010. *Investor & Analyst Day*. Live Nation Entertainment, Beverly Hills, CA.

2

CHAPTER 2
ARTIST MANAGEMENT

CHAPTER OUTLINE

An artist manager will become involved in an artist's career at a point mutually agreed by the artist and manager. An arrangement will be made as to the scope of the manager's work and responsibilities. The arrangement will last (hopefully) for the entirety of the artist's career, and even when music business specialists (booking agents and promoters) are brought on board, the artist manager will still have a huge part in the planning and execution of the artist's live performance career.

THE ARTIST MANAGER'S ROLE IN LIVE PERFORMANCE

"Managers are responsible for connecting artists with career income, and earn a percentage of the economic activity they generate for [the] artists and themselves".[1]

Paul Allen, *Artist Management for the Music Business*, 2015.

There are many definitions of the role of the artist manager (see Passman, MMF, et al), and Allen's concept of connecting the artist with income is a useful one. An artist manager will charge a percentage of artist earnings (commission) and that percentage rate varies. 15%–20% of gross earnings (before deducting expenses) is a typical range, with most managers charging 15%.[2] Gross earnings from recorded music have fallen, as fans stream music rather than buy physical copies or download digital files. The payout to the artist per stream is negligible, compared with royalty rates from physical products, and the resulting management commission amount is also low. The modern music manager must work hard to connect their clients with "career income", and live performance is seen as a major source of that income (see

DOI: 10.4324/9781003019503-3

Case study: Nick Mulvey). A report from the Music Managers Forum (MMF), a trade body, found that 64% of artist managers surveyed view "live events and tour management skills" as vital to the success of their business and, ultimately, the success of their artist clients.[3] This high percentage must be important, especially given the large proportion of solo artists in the year-end recorded and concert revenue charts (see *BBC Sounds of...*).

CASE STUDY: NICK MULVEY

The team behind English singer/songwriter Nick Mulvey used live performance to re-engage his audience and increase sales of his second album, "Wake Up Now" (2017). Mulvey, his manager, and record company Fiction Records, "developed a post-album release and live strategy that covered the musical evolution through three tours, giving so much life and new experiences for fans",[4] according to the team. The three tours featured three different line-ups. The first tour was with Mulvey's full five-piece band. The second was performed as a trio, and the last tour was with Mulvey performing solo with stripped back instrumentation. The audio for all three tours was recorded and used for different releases – the recording from the first tour being made into a "live" EP; the recordings from the last tour were issued as solo session EP.

The campaign not only provided Mulvey with performance income for the concerts, but recycled material already available on the album using new recordings, which captivated his monthly listeners, whose numbers increased from 1.7m when the album was released, to 2.5m monthly listeners some 14 months later. Mulvey's Spotify followers grew 103% in the same period, to 122,000 followers on the streaming platform.

BBC SOUNDS OF ...

The British Broadcasting Corporation (BBC), the UK's national television and radio broadcaster, presents the results of its "Sound of..." poll in January of each year. The poll takes place in November of the previous year and asks music business professionals for their predictions for talent to watch in the forthcoming year. Table 2.1 shows the results of the poll from the last three years and indicates the make-up of each act – whether it is a group, duo, or solo artist.

Managers of artists nominated in the poll should be pleased – the poll has been accurate in predicting successful talent. However, many artists nominated (and eventually successful) are solo artists. A live strategy must consider the extra costs of touring for solo artists and a plan on how to raise the necessary funds to do so. Do managers take this into account when first courting a new artist client?

Table 2.1 The BBC "Sound of..." results 2018, 2019, & 2020

YEAR	WINNERS
2018	Sigrid – solo artist Rex Orange County – solo artist IAMDDB – solo artist Khalid – solo artist Pale Waves – group ALMA – solo artist Billie Eilish – solo artist Jade Bird – solo artist Lewis Capaldi – solo artist Nilufer Yanya – solo artist Not3s – solo artist Sam Fender – solo artist Superorganism – group Tom Walker – solo artist Yaeji – solo artist Yxng Bane – solo artist
2019	Octavian – solo artist King Princess – solo artist Grace Carter – solo artist Slowthai – solo artist ROSALIA – solo artist Dermot Kennedy – solo artist Ella Mai – solo artist FLOHIO – solo artist Mahalia – solo artist Sea Girls – group
2020	Celeste – solo artist Easy Life – group YUNGBLUD – solo artist Joy Crookes – solo artist Inhale r – group Arlo Parks – solo artist Beabadoobe – solo artist Georgia – solo artist Joesef – solo artist Squid – group

THE MANAGER'S CONSIDERATIONS FOR LIVE PERFORMANCE

The temptation would be for an artist manager to rush into booking as many live engagements for their artist as possible. This would provide much-needed income (depending on the size of the venues and the resulting costs incurred) but is not a strategy a successful manager should pursue. Over-exposing an artist in this way would result in dwindling ticket sales over time, as fans became bored with seeing the artist repeatedly. The artist would also find it difficult to write and record new material, collaborate with other artists, and pursue other, non-music, activities if they are constantly on the road.

The manager should therefore assess the following to map out a campaign for their artist client:

- genre
- fan base
- artist's primary location
- previous live performance history
- recording history
- forthcoming releases
- production considerations

GENRE

You were introduced to the concepts of authenticity and genre in live music earlier in this part. While genre should not have a limiting effect on an artist's ability to play live, some consideration should be given to the artist's genre when planning a live performance strategy. For instance, promoters of hip-hop shows may be required (or feel the need) to install metal detectors at the concert venues entrances. Hip-hop concerts have been plagued by violence,[5] and the installation of metal detectors and personnel with "wands" (handheld metal detectors) is to prevent guns and knives from being brought into the auditorium. A manager representing a hip-hop artist may feel that the added cost to install the machines on each concert date, and the inconvenience to the fans (let alone the social message their use implies), outweighs any potential promotion and revenue from concert touring.

Genre may be linked to appeal. Rock, in all its forms, sells a lot of tickets, and many promoters and venues are willing to host shows in this genre. "World" music (the term given to music encompassing many different styles from other parts of the globe[6]) is less popular, thus limiting venues in which a world music artist can comfortably sell out. A manager of a world music artist may concentrate on one-off concerts in capital cities, for instance, or placing their artist on the bill at relevant world music festivals. This would be a good strategy; however, this would limit potential income from live performance compared with a rock artist.

FAN BASE

Gauging an artist's appeal in different cities and countries is easy thanks to data from the various internet services and digital service providers (DSP), such as Spotify. Managers with access to the data can see exactly where fans are streaming music and video or talking about artists on social media – and how many are doing so. This information can then be used to pinpoint cities where an artist should perhaps visit on a tour or back up assumptions about an artist's popularity in a given territory.

YouTube offers such a service as part of its "Artists" platform.[7] This part of the service is open to anyone with a browser and internet access (you don't have to be part of the artist's team to run a search) and could be used by an artist manager, booking agent, or concert promoter to gauge the "broad strokes" demand for an artist.

Of course, online activity is no more than a "click of the mouse",[8] with perhaps no further engagement by the listener. The manager's job, working with the booking agent and the concert promoter, is to work to turn these clicks into engagement in the form of sales of concert tickets. You will learn more about this in subsequent chapters, and there is no doubt that having access to this data can help with a live performance strategy.

ARTIST'S PRIMARY LOCATION

An artist's primary location (where they live or are based) can have the same enhancing or limiting effect on the potential benefits of live performance as the genre in which they operate.

The potential hindrance and benefits can be applied at a macro and micro level. Artists living in the US, UK, and Germany, have access to vibrant and lucrative respective domestic markets, according to the International Federation of the Phonographic Industry (IFPI), a trade body.[9]

Artists living in a city that has a well-established live music scene will benefit from access to venues and an audience prepared to pay for live music. Conversely, artists in large population areas such as Los Angeles or London will face competition. An artist seeking to create a fan base through constant gigging may experience difficulties in securing bookings, as many other artists are vying for the live music audience. It may therefore be advantageous for an artist to be located in a less populated area if their aim is to build up credibility, ability, and appeal through live performance. Atkins (2007) cites the numbers of artist performing in three cities – Los Angeles CA, New York NY, and Boise ID – on any given night.[10] He suggests (perhaps sarcastically) that an aspiring artist would do well to move to Boise to grow their audience through live performance, as there is less competition from other artists.

PREVIOUS LIVE PERFORMANCE HISTORY

It should be a given that an artist is ready and able to perform live. Many artists have, in fact, never performed live before being taken on by an artist manager, signed to a record deal, or to a booking agency. The route to being discovered has changed, and the verification process of "seeing the band live" (see "*The importance of live performance*" earlier) by managers and labels is not necessarily undertaken. One booking agent suggests that 20% of the artists signed to an agency have not performed live before the signing.[11] This fact would suggest that other metrics are being applied to gauge the potential of the artist to the booking agency, and you shall find out what these are in subsequent sections.

RECORDING HISTORY AND FUTURE RELEASES

An artist does not necessarily have to be signed to a record company to have a demonstrable track record of releases. The artist may have self-releases and video uploads to YouTube, for instance. The earned views and streams will have probably brought the artist to the attention of the manager in the first place, providing data on fan numbers and locations.

Future release plans are also a useful factor when deciding a strategy for live performance. As well as their own release (a new album or single), the artist may be collaborating with another artist. A typical collaboration is the "feature", where an artist (usually a vocalist) will feature on a recorded track by another, possibly more successful, artist. The manager looking to plan a tour for her artist would be pleased if such a feature is slated for the future. The feature will enable her artist to piggyback on the name and reach of the second artist.

PRODUCTION CONSIDERATIONS

The manager will have to examine the production aspects of the artist's live performance as these will impact on the artist's ability to perform regularly.

A four-piece, guitar-based band will be able to perform in any venue that has electricity. The band can use common modes of transport (a van or two cars will accommodate the band members and their instruments); the band's guitar and bass amplifiers and drum kit (collectively called the "backline") can be purchased or rented in most countries in the world; and no additional musicians are required for live performances. A venue booked for a performance by a guitar-based band does not even have to have a complicated public address (PA) system – anything that will help amplify the vocals above the sound of the backline will be adequate. Booking this type of act into repeated engagements is simple – the artist can travel easily to each show and keep the associated costs to a minimum.

Contrast that with a solo artist who creates music at home on a laptop. There are many issues to confront to make the transition of the music from home studio to stage. How will the artist present her music? Will it be enough to simply plug her laptop into the sound system and sing over top of her recorded music? Will she have to employ other musicians to help reproduce complicated parts or provide added excitement on stage? Will the sound system at the venue be capable of reproducing the necessary bass frequencies and volume? Does the artist have the charisma to keep an audience interested during the songs? Can she sing without all the audio effects (echo, reverb, pitch correction, etc.) she uses on the recordings? How much rehearsal time is needed to translate the recorded audio parts to live performance? And the list goes on...

The scenario of the solo, electronic-based artist is common. The ability to upload self-released material to Spotify and YouTube has helped many artists reach fans across the world – fans who are more than willing to spend money on concert tickets. However, staging a show for an electronic music artist will usually involve either hiring additional musicians and vocalists for each performance or renting supplementary video and lighting to provide interest, or both, to create an "authentic" performance. These ongoing costs hamper the ability to perform regularly.

A BUSINESS STRUCTURE FOR LIVE PERFORMANCE

You have seen that artists make most of their revenue from live performances – at least at the superstar and heritage level. A forward-thinking manager will look to make sure that income stream is protected in case other parts of the artist's career are not doing so well. A manager will therefore advise her artists to set up business entities that deal with different areas of an artist's business affairs. So, for instance, all live performance business-related affairs – invoices, bills, payments, and taxation, will go through the "books" and administration of a touring "company". The exact legal form of these entities will depend on the country – in the US it could be a corporation, subchapter S corporation, or limited liability corporation (LLC)for instance; in the UK a limited (LTD) company, or limited liability partnership (LLP). The business entity helps to make accounting and payment of taxes simpler – a touring LLC would only report money made and paid to do with an artist's live performances for instance. Her other income – streaming, publishing, film, and TV work, for instance – would be treated separately, possibly through different business entities.[12]

Radiohead, a UK-based alternative rock band, have several business entities.[13] They set up "Radiohead Ltd" in 1993 to administer their increasing touring turnover (that company was liquidated in 2013). The band now have many separate limited companies and LLCs, including one to administer their income from merchandise (t-shirt and other apparel) sales.

GROSS VS NETT: THE MANAGER'S COMMISSION FROM LIVE PERFORMANCE

The artist manager earns money on a gross commission rate of most of the artist's earning activity – the manager takes her percentage "off the top", before other costs have been deducted. A manager on a 20% gross commission rate would earn $100,000 from an artist's recorded music sales of $500,000 (20% of $500,000 = $100,000).

The artist and artist manager should decide early on in their relationship regarding the commission rate for live performance income, and if that rate should be on the gross or nett income. Figure 2.1 gives an example of the effect of gross commission on live performance income. Touring costs are always high, and commissioning on the gross income can wipe out any profit for the artist.

Ideally, the manager should charge a nett commission rate – only taking their percentage on whatever is left after they have paid all expenses. Figure 2.2 shows the effect of commissioning on the nett of the performance income. Using the same amounts as in Figure 2.1 you can see that 20% of the nett of $10,000 is $2000. That is not as great an amount as $10,000 gross commission from Figure 2.1, and it does leave the artist with profit from her touring activity. The manager will have to find ways to reduce touring costs if she wants her nett commission amount to rise.

Income from shows $50,000
Less expenses $40,000
Profit/loss before management commison: $10,000
Manager takes 20 % **gross commission** $10,000 20% of $50000
Total costs now: $50,000 ($40000 + $10000)
TOTAL PROFIT: **$0**

Figure 2.1 An example of the effect of gross commissioning by artist managers on live performance income. The artist does not make a profit in this case

Income from shows $50,000
Less expenses $40,000
Profit/loss before management commison: $10,000
Manager takes 20% **nett commission** $2,000 20% of $10000
Total costs now: $42,000 ($40 000 + €2000)
TOTAL PROFIT: **$8000**

Figure 2.2 An example showing nett commissioning by artist managers on live performance income. The manager makes less commission, and her artist makes some profit

POTENTIAL REVENUE FOR MANAGERS FROM LIVE PERFORMANCE

Artist managers have difficulty earning a living from their artists alone. The MMF report of 2019 cited managers reliance on other, non-music, income (such as brand consultancy) to pay the bills.[14] A successful artist may "earn 57% of their income from live",[15] but what if the manager's roster has no successful artists?

Table 2.2 shows an example of the income the manager of Farry Kisher, a successful electronic act, would receive for a year of live shows. The performances are a mix of festival performances for the live band, and DJ gigs. Farry Kisher can receive continuing live income by performing DJ shows. This is useful, as they might be writing and recording a new album this year – concert promoters might not be keen to book the live band without new material. The heavy DJ schedule must surely have an impact on the band's ability to concentrate on the album though.

Farry Kisher will earn £127,000 ($166,000) from the live band festival shows and DJ gigs this year. Their manager is on a 20% nett commission rate for live performances. We do not know the costs, and so it is difficult to work out the manager's potential earnings from the live performance. You will examine touring costs in *Part Two: Live Music Production*, and for now we can assume the fees from the six festival shows (in bold) will be halved after associated costs. Income from the DJ shows should remain

Table 2.2 The performance schedule and contract deal highlights for Farry Kisher, a successful act. How much will the manager earn from this activity?

Date	Country	City	Venue	Fee		Currency
Fri 29 Jan	United Kingdom	Bristol	The Marble Factory	2000		GBP
Fri 05 Feb	United Kingdom	London	Bermondsey Social Club	400		GBP
Fri 12 Feb	United Kingdom	Birmingham	Rainbow Warehouse	2000		GBP
Sat 13 Feb	Netherlands	Amsterdam	De Marktkantine		2300	EUR
Tue 16 Feb	United Kingdom	Reading	Purple Turtle	400		GBP
Fri 19 Feb	United Kingdom	Leeds	The Faversham	1500		GBP
Sat 20 Feb	United Kingdom	Brighton	Patterns	2000		GBP
Thu 25 Feb	Turkey	Istanbul	Klein		4000	EUR
Fri 04 Mar	United Kingdom	Liverpool	The Shipping Forecast	1000		GBP
Tue 15 Mar	United Kingdom	Sheffield	The Tuesday Club	2000		GBP
Sat 26 Mar	Ireland	Dublin	Button Factory		3000	EUR
Sat 02 Apr	Germany	Berlin	Weyde3		1350	EUR
Sat 09 Apr	United Kingdom	Manchester	Antwerp Mansion	1500		GBP
Fri 15 Apr	United Kingdom	London	Shapes	3500		GBP
Fri 22 Apr	United Kingdom	Nottingham	Rescue Rooms	2000		GBP
Sat 30 Apr	United Kingdom	Stoke-on-Trent	Keele University Students Union	2000		GBP
Sun 01 May	United Kingdom	London	Netil House	1500		GBP
Sat 28 May	**United Kingdom**	**Bristol**	**Love Saves the Day**	**4000**		**GBP**

(Continued)

Table 2.2 (Continued)

Date	Country	City	Venue	Fee	Currency
Sat 28 May	United Kingdom	Bristol	Love Saves the Night @ Motion	2500	GBP
Sun 29 May	United Kingdom	Lincoln	Lost Village Festival	1000	GBP
Sat 04 Jun	United Kingdom	Hay on Wye	How the Light Gets In	2000	GBP
Sun 05 Jun	Netherlands	Amsterdam	Amsterdam Open Air	3700	EUR
Sat 11 Jun	**United Kingdom**	**Manchester**	**Parklife**	**5000**	**GBP**
Sun 12 Jun	United Kingdom	Holyhead	Gottwood Festival	500	GBP
Sun 12 Jun	United Kingdom	Brighton	Wildlife Festival	2500	GBP
Sat 18 Jun	Netherlands	Eersel	We Are Electric Festival	2250	EUR
Sun 26 Jun	United Kingdom	Somerset	Glastonbury Festival	750	GBP
Sun 03 Jul	Spain	San Jorge (Ibiza)	Amnesia Ibiza	2000	EUR
Fri 08 Jul	Croatia	Tisno	The Electric Elephant	1000	GBP
Sat 16 Jul	United Kingdom	Glasgow	Berkeley Suite	2000	GBP
Sat 16 Jul	Spain	Barcelona		2500	GBP
Sun 17 Jul	**United Kingdom**	**London**	**Citadel**	**8000**	**GBP**
Sat 23 Jul	**United Kingdom**	**Huntingdon**	**Secret Garden Party**	**5000**	**GBP**
Sat 30 Jul	Spain	Ibiza	Zoo Project Club	2000	EUR
Sun 31 Jul	United Kingdom	Lake District	Kendal Calling	3500	GBP
Sun 07 Aug	Romania	Cluj-Napoca	Untold Festival	2800	EUR
Sat 13 Aug	Belgium		We Can Dance	2500	EUR

Date	Country	Location	Venue/Festival	Amount	Currency
Sun 14 Aug	United Kingdom	Cornwall	Boardmasters Festival	3000	GBP
Wed 17 Aug	Belgium	Hasselt	Pukkelpop Festival	2500	EUR
Fri 26 Aug	Malta	Attard	TheSoundYouNeed Festival	3500	EUR
Sun 28 Aug	United Kingdom	London	SW4	5000	GBP
Sun 04 Sep	**United Kingdom**	**Gwynedd**	**Festival Number 6**	**4500**	**GBP**
Sun 11 Sep	**United Kingdom**	**Isle of Wight**	**Bestival**	**3000**	**GBP**
Sat 17 Sep	Spain	Ibiza	Zoo Project Club	200	GBP
Fri 23 Sep	United Kingdom	Manchester	The Warehouse Project	2000	GBP
Sat 01 Oct	United Kingdom	Southampton	Rose Bowl	1000	GBP
Thu 06 Oct	United Kingdom	Liverpool	Sefton Park Palm House	7000	GBP
Sat 08 Oct	United Kingdom	Leeds	Distrikt	2000	GBP
Fri 14 Oct	United Kingdom	Norwich	UEA	1000	GBP
Fri 21 Oct	United Kingdom	Oxford	O2 Academy Oxford	750	GBP
Fri 21 Oct	United Kingdom	Exeter	Lemon Grove	1500	GBP
Sat 22 Oct	United Kingdom	Birmingham	Rainbow Warehouse	1000	GBP
Fri 28 Oct	United Kingdom	Cardiff	Y-Plas	1000	GBP
Fri 11 Nov	United Kingdom	London	Studio Spaces	2500	GBP
Fri 25 Nov	United Kingdom	Brighton	Patterns	2000	GBP
Fri 02 Dec	United Kingdom	Glasgow	Berkeley Suite	1500	GBP

INCOME   **£101,000**   **£127,000**   **€ 31,900**

TOTAL INCOME £(GBP)

as almost 100% profit, as many of the deals include transportation and hotels paid by the relevant promoter/organiser. Farry Kisher are therefore looking to bank an estimated £112,000 ($146,000) from live performances alone, and their manager will earn £22,400 ($29,500) in commission from this activity. This amount may seem high and should be viewed in context. Farry Kisher will travel to and from 56 engagements this year (Table 2.2), which will restrict their ability to engage in other revenue-producing activities, such as song-writing and recording. The manager's commission is also low compared with the average US household income of $61,937.[16]

NOTES

1 Allen, P., 2015. *Artist Management for the Music Business*. 3rd ed. Focal Press, Burlington, MA.
2 Passman, D.S., 2015. *All You Need to Know about the Music Business*. 9th ed. Simon & Schuster, New York.
3 Music Managers Forum, 2019. *Managing Expectations. An Exploration into the Changing Role and Value of the Artist Manager*. Music Managers Forum, London.
4 Musically, 2018. *Sandbox. The Year's Best Music Marketing Campaigns 2018*. Musically, London.
5 Platon, A. (2016) "Irving Plaza shooting: Patrons say metal detectors were not used" [WWW Document], n.d. *Billboard*. URL https://www.billboard.com/articles/columns/hip-hop/7385843/irving-plaza-security-metal-detectors (accessed 1.10.20).
6 *World Music* (2020) *Wikipedia*. Available at https://en.wikipedia.org/wiki/World_music
7 https://charts.youtube.com
8 Hamilton, A. (2007) "Interview with Andy Davies of Radio 1". *The Times*.
9 IFPI, 2019. *Global Music Report 2019*. International Federation of the Phonographic Industry, London.
10 Atkins, M., 2007. *Tour:Smart: And Break the Band*. Smart Books, Chicago, IL.
11 Edwards, J., (2016). *Booking Agents* [Presentation] AIM Academy Masterclass: Understanding the Live Industry.
12 Allen, P., (2015). *Artist Management for the Music Business*. 3rd ed. Focal Press, Burlington, MA.
13 Marshall, A., (2016). "Radiohead's corporate empire: Inside the band's dollars and cents". [WWW Document] URL https://www.theguardian.com/music/2016/apr/29/radiohead-corporate-structure-firms
14 Music Managers Forum, 2019. *Managing Expectations. An Exploration into the Changing Role and Value of the Artist Manager*. Music Managers Forum, London.
15 Mulligan, M., 2015. *The Music Industry's 6:1 Ratio*. Music Industry Blog. URL https://musicindustryblog.wordpress.com/2015/03/27/the-music-industrys-61-ratio/ (accessed 1.21.20).
16 Guzman, G.G., (2010). *Household Income: 2018*. United States Census Bureau. Washington.

3

CHAPTER 3
BOOKING AGENTS

CHAPTER OUTLINE

DOI: 10.4324/9781003019503-4

The artist and her manager may reach milestones early on, such as signing a recording contract, gaining a publisher, and making the first recordings. The artist will have been performing live concurrently with these activities, and the booking and organising of showcases and concerts will become too much work for the manager. The booking agent will become involved at this stage, although the manager cannot simply hire an agent: a relationship has to evolve between the artist, the manager, and the booking agent, and the agent must be assured the artist has ticket-selling potential.

You will examine the work of the booking agent in this chapter.

WHAT DO BOOKING AGENTS DO?

A talent agent is someone who finds paid engagements (film, TV, radio writing) for creative people. A talent agent who finds gigs, shows, and tours for a band, singer, or a DJ, is a booking agent; the process of securing a show or tour is known as a booking, hence the name. The booking agent does not put on shows – hire a venue, print tickets, do the marketing, etc. The booking agent works with the artist, artist manager (and sometimes a record company), to identify live opportunities for the artist – a show or series of shows – and she brokers a deal between the artist and the concert promoters (see *Concert Promoters*) who may want to put on those shows featuring that artist.

The booking agent negotiates a performance fee, based on projected ticket sales, for each concert (see *Creating the deals* later in this part). The booking agent then issues a contract between the promoter and the artist. The contract will include stipulations to do with the "engagement" (concert). One stipulation is that the promoter will pay a deposit to the artist before the concert. The deposit may well be 50% of the negotiated performance fee, and is paid to the booking agent, who holds it in an escrow account on behalf of the artist.

The role of the booking agent changes once the deals they have put together are contracted and tickets for the concert are put on sale. The booking agent now acts as an administrator for the artists, collating figures on the amounts of tickets sold, whether or no deposits have been paid, and collecting revenue due from performance fees due after each concert.

The role of the booking agent post-Napster has evolved and is no longer a simple relationship with artist clients and promoters[1]. Agents are increasingly connected with (and acting as) Artist & Repertoire (A&R), music publishers, lawyers, and publicists. Live performance may be the primary revenue source for many artists, and the importance of the booking agent has grown with the reliance on that income. Delegates at the 2019 International Live Music Conference (ILMC), a live music business event, were asked who they thought "held the power" in the business. 30% of those polled stated it was the booking agent, 35% said the artist manager the artist 20%, and the promoter 15%.[2]

HOW DO BOOKING AGENTS EARN MONEY?

A booking agent makes money by charging her client (the artist) a percentage of that artist's gross income for the performance. This performance fee is negotiated by the booking agent with the promoter; you will study this in depth in "Creating the Deals".

The percentage the booking agent charges is known as the commission, in a similar way to that of the artist management commission (see *The Artists* and *Artist Management* for an explanation of artist management commissions). This commission rate is universally set at 10% for contemporary live music – rock, pop, alternative, and 15% for DJ work. This percentage rate may be a convention that has some precedent in US regulation: the US entertainment unions – AFM (American Federation of Musicians), and SAG-AFTRA (the entity formed after the merger of the American Federation of Television and Radio Artists and the Screen Actors Guild) have set talent agency commission at 10% for all talent agents, including booking agents.

There is no official regulation in the UK concerning agency commission rates, but 10% seems to be the norm for "traditional" artists, and this is probably in recognition of the official rates set by the US unions.

The amount an agent is paid will vary based on her position and the type of agency she works for. An agent at the start of her career may work for a regional agent (see *Who are the booking agents?* later in this part). The regional agency may not represent superstars of known heritage acts and will have a roster of proven, "hard-working" acts. The agents may be able to book a respectable amount of work for these acts and with performance fees lower than for superstar acts. The commission amount the agent receives will therefore be lower and arrive sporadically, according to how many shows she has been able to book for her roster. The agency may offer the agent a "draw" – a monthly advance against commissions – to keep the agent. For instance, the agency may offer the agent $2000 a month as a draw (advance). The agent then has to book enough shows and earn enough commission to cover that advance; that would be performance fee income of $20,000 a month to cover her advance of $2000 (10% of $20000=$2000). The agent will be paid the difference when she brings in performance income that exceeds the advance amount.[3] An agent that consistently fails to earn enough to cover the advance each month will most likely be fired.[4]

At the other end of the scale, the agents who work for global full-service agencies (see *Who are the booking agents?* later in this part) are paid a salary and a bonus. The bonus may not be directly related to the amount of commission the agent brings in and will be a factor when the bonus is calculated. An agent at a full-service agency is expected to bring in three times her salary in commission each year.[5]

The agent's commission is a cost for the artist and has to be factored in when calculating touring income and costs. These costs will be explained in *Part Two: Live Music Production*. An artist can expect to pay her agent the same commission rate throughout her career. There can be no doubt that booking shows for a superstar or heritage act is

Table 3.1 An example of the booking agent's commission for a show at Irving Plaza, NY (1200 capacity)

CONCERT:	IRVING PLAZA. NEW YORK, NY.	
	GROSS FEE NEGOTIATED BY BOOKING AGENT	$5000
	BOOKING AGENT COMMISSION	$500
	(10% OF GROSS FEE)	

Table 3.2 A similar example, this time showing commission amounts for a show the agent has arranged at Arlenes Grocery, NY (150 capacity). The booking agent's commission is always on the gross performance fee

CONCERT:	ARLENES GROCERY. NEW YORK, NY.	
	GROSS FEE NEGOTIATED BY BOOKING AGENT	$500
	BOOKING AGENT COMMISSION	$50
	(10% OF GROSS FEE)	

easier than with a 'baby band' (the name given to an act that is starting out), and the potential commission for a tour of arenas will be higher than that from booking shows in bars and clubs. It might therefore be expected that an agent will reduce her commission rate for heritage and superstar acts. However, agents are not historically keen on this rate-cutting, as it would create a precedent for all acts. The artist manager may therefore negotiate a final commission-related amount with the agent ahead of large tours or festivals.[6]

Tables 3.1 and 3.2 show examples of how a booking agent commissions her client's live performance work. The commission is always on the gross performance fee.

A booking agent will have a large roster of artist clients to make sure she can earn the required commission income. The booking agent of the example in Figure 3.1 will earn $50 in commission. She will have to book a great many shows at this level to earn a living – highlighting the need to have a large, diverse roster. The roster of an agent at a full-service agency may number 30 acts.[7]

REGULATIONS FOR BOOKING AGENTS

A booking agency is an employment agency, and their business practice may be regulated. You have seen the regulations concerning commission rates above, and there are other regulations that vary from country to country.

Booking agents in the US are regulated by state legislature and the entertainment unions. Some US states require booking agents to be licensed and pay bonds, sometimes as much as $50,000, to trade as a booking agent.[8] SAG-AFTRA and the AFM will also require a booking agency to be franchised to the respective unions. Union members

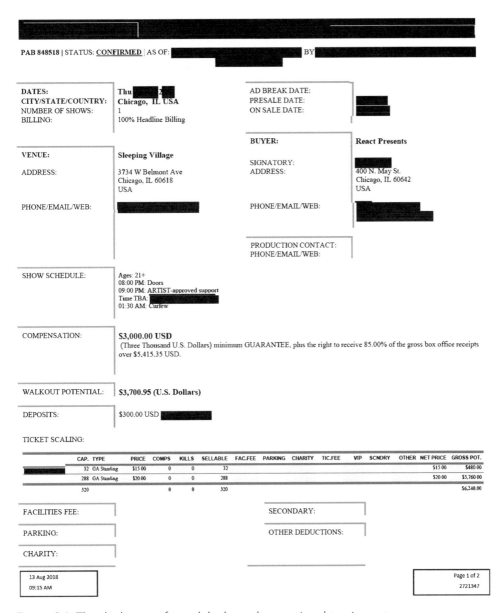

Figure 3.1 The deal memo for a club shown by a national touring act

(musicians) are not permitted to seek work from any agency that is not franchised to the respective union.

Booking agents in the UK also must work within regulations, including the "Employment Agency Act 1973" and "The Conduct of Employment Agencies and Employment Businesses Regulations 2003". This last legislation forbids, amongst other activities, agencies in the UK charging clients for photos taken on their behalf or for the prospective client to have to pay a fee to register with the agency. A booking agent should not charge an artist for any service apart from the commission amount on whatever fee they negotiate for the performances.

| TICKET FEE: | | ADJUSTED GROSS POTENTIAL: | | $6,240.00 |

| VIP: |

| NET POTENTIAL: | | $6,240.00 |

SCALING NOTES:

Ticket Scaling: GA / Walk Up

Comps (on top): 15 - TOUR / 15 - TBD

EXPENSES:

TYPE	FLAT AMOUNT	% AMOUNT	PER TICKET	MAX AMOUNT	NOTES
Advertising	$500 00				
Box Office	$60 00				
Catering	$250 00				
Insurance	$84 00		$0 24		
Other 1	$50 00				Promo
Other 2	$40 00				Insurance + Licensing
Prod Mgr	$180 00				
Security	$60 00				
Sound & Lights	$360 00				
Staffing	$125 00				
Expense Totals:	$1,709.00		$0.24		

MERCHANDISE:

Artist sells; All Merchandise: 100.00% of proceeds to ARTIST.

EXCLUSIVITY:

Artist shall not perform a publicly advertised engagement within 150 miles of the applicable Venue, for a period of 120 days prior to or 90 days after the performance of the Engagement at this applicable Venue.

BOOKING AGENT: ▋▋▋▋▋▋▋▋▋

RESPONSIBLE AGENT(S): ▋▋▋▋▋▋▋▋▋

Figure 3.1 Continued

AGREEMENTS AND CONTRACTS BETWEEN AGENTS AND ARTISTS FOR LIVE PERFORMANCE

A booking agent should set out their responsibilities and the terms of business with their clients – the music artists they represent. In general business, a contract would usually be used to set out these terms and conditions, and that is the case with most of the live music business. This is not the case for UK-based booking agents. The majority of UK booking agents do not have a contract with their artists – the scope of business, and its terms, is agreed on a handshake.

Booking agents in the US will have a contract with their clients, as the agents have to be franchised by the unions you were introduced to earlier – SAG-AFTRA and the AFM. The contract from the agency is, therefore, copies of agreements between the artist, the booking agent, and the union.[9]

The contract, or gentleman's agreement, should set out the scope of the agent's duties and responsibilities, including the following:

- commission rate and payment schedule
- territory
- term
- taxation
- work permits and visas
- travel

COMMISSION RATES AND PAYMENT SCHEDULE

A commission rate of 10% of gross performance fees is universally accepted. The agent may be responsible for other, non-performance related work for her artist (film and TV work, or brand endorsements, for instance), and an agreement should be in place as to the commission rate, if any, for that activity.

The agent may have commission targets to meet as part of her contract with the agency and so will need to ensure that any commission owed to her is collected regularly, at least in time to be included in target-reporting periods. Performance fees and deposits for performance fees, are usually paid straight to the agent and held in escrow accounts to then be disbursed to the artist. The agent can theoretically deduct her commission amount from the money held in the relevant escrow account and not have to wait for the artist to pay what is owed. This is in fact common practice, and the agreement/contract should stipulate when the agent will take commissions and other payment from the amounts held in escrow. A detailed examination of deposits and commission withdrawals can be found in *"Revenue streams from live music – artists"* later in this part.

TERRITORY

The booking agent will require exclusivity of territory – an artist cannot ask two or more agents to find her work in the US for instance. An artist would also expect that a US-based agent would be more familiar with venues and promoters in North America and less so with Europe, Australia, or Japan. It would make sense for an artist to have different booking agents in the different territories, and this is common. Territories are typically defined as:

North America & Canada
UK & Europe
Rest of the World (ROW)

Paradigm (a booking agency) lists the following territories on its website:[10]

USA
Canada
Mexico
Caribbean
South America
Europe
Asia
Middle East
Australia
Africa

A US-based agent will have that territorial exclusivity indicated in their arrangement with the artist. Confusion and conflicts may arise when more than one agent is responsible for booking an artist. For instance, a European festival organiser may approach the US-based agent of a US act regarding that act performing at their festival – when the festival organiser should have perhaps approached the UK & European agent of the US act about the same show. Having different agents for different territories may be sensible and the artist (and her manager) should be aware of the potential conflicts and issues that may arise from such an arrangement. A former booking agent says it is "impossible" to book a worldwide tour without using "sub-agents" (multiple local agents), in the different worldwide territories.[11]

TERM

Term – the length of time the contract is valid for – is not as defined in booking agent contracts as in artist management or exclusive recording contracts. It is widely accepted that the agent is in it for the long haul; "We are here to build careers", says Kirk Sommer of WME.[12]

TAXATION

The booking agent will be able to advise her client on local and foreign taxation as applicable to live performance fees. She will do this in conjunction with the local promoter, who must comply with local taxation regulations. In the UK for instance, the Foreign Entertainers Unit (FEU) of Her Majesty's Revenue and Customs department encourage concert promoters to register with the FEU. Promoters then receive a "starter pack" of information to assist in the collection of the relevant taxes. The concert promoters can then inform the booking agents of foreign artists about the artist's tax liability and possible exemptions.

WORK PERMITS AND VISAS

A booking agent should also be able to advise the time scale, requirements, and cost for arranging and obtaining work permits and visas. Obtaining such permission is necessary for their artists to perform legally in other countries. Arranging work permits and visas requires specialised knowledge, and it is in the agent's best interests to be advised of what rules and regulations are in place. For instance, applying for a US work visa is costly and time consuming. However, an artist manager may want the booking agent to arrange a US tour to capitalise on sudden success for her artist. The booking agent should be aware of the process of gaining a US visa and be able to advise the manager of the timescale required to arrange the visas plus the costs involved.

TRAVEL

Agents representing DJs will arrange travel and accommodation on a show-by-show basis. The club owner or promoter may be asked to include flights and hotels as part of the deal, or the agent will use the artist's money to pay for the necessary travel and accommodation. The agent will charge a higher commission rate – usually 15% of the gross performance fee – for doing so.

WHO ARE THE BOOKING AGENTS?

The Pollstar "Booking Agency Directory 2019 Summer Edition" lists 640 booking agencies worldwide. An agent at United Talent Agency describes these agencies as being "roughly split into two categories"[13]:

- independent agencies who concentrate on live touring and festival work for their music clients, and
- full-service, global agencies (mostly headquartered in Los Angeles) who offer their music clients opportunities in touring, festivals, film, TV, books, and advise them on branding and digital strategies.

INDEPENDENT BOOKING AGENTS

Independent agencies concentrate on concerts and touring, as described above. They may specialise in a particular genre, such as blues or electronic music, and may service a local college or university, finding and booking local and regional acts into that venue. (As well as the Pollstar directory, the smaller agencies can also be found in the "International Booking Agents Directory".[14])

An example of a small agency in the US would be Leafy Green Booking (www.leafy-green.com), whose roster favours extreme alternative bands such as Swans, Unsane, Meat Puppets, and Mudhoney. This type of alternative music is obviously a niche attraction and being able to continuously book shows for the roster will be difficult compared with booking "flavour-of-the-month" or superstar acts. Revenue from commissions may be low and not generated regularly. Independent agencies may therefore offer other live music-related services, such as artist management, consultancy, and concert promotion, to create additional revenue.

FMLY (https://fmly.agency), is an independent boutique agency, who specialise in representing DJs and electronic music artists. FMLY also offer consultancy and festival curation – finding and suggesting the talent for stages at contemporary music festivals – as part of their business.

FULL-SERVICE BOOKING AGENTS

The full-service US agents dominate concert and tour bookings worldwide. These agencies are going through a period of mergers and acquisitions, with several agencies being taken over or merging, leaving 15 or so key players. The mergers and acquisitions have not just involved larger companies acquiring or absorbing smaller ones; there has been a trend for the larger agencies with a more traditional roster buying the agencies that deal with electronic music and DJs. For instance, The Agency Group (itself recently acquired by UTA) acquired Bond Music Group (agents for Moby, Dirty Vegas, and Francois K, amongst others) in 2014.[15] Paradigm, which acquired AM Only (agents for Skrillex, Carl Cox, Hardwell, and David Guetta)[16] and Coda Music (UK), have themselves been acquired by Wasserman, a media group. Takeovers and mergers of this type reflect the commercial value of electronic/club music – estimates put the global electronic music industry at $6.9 billion.[17]

RESPONSIBLE AGENT

An artist client of a full-service agency will be assigned a responsible agent (RA) from the pool of concert booking agents working for that agency. The RA may be the reason the artist decided to work with that agency in the first place. The RA is the first contact for the artist, and the first port-of-call for any other agent within the company.

THE ROLE OF THE BOOKING AGENT IN LIVE PERFORMANCE

> "Agents build a network of promoter contacts across their territories, they find suitable opportunities for putting forward the artists they represent, they persuade the promoters to book the artists, they respond to enquiries, they route tours, negotiate deals, liaise with artist managers, confirm shows, issue contracts, and oversee the promotion of the shows"
>
> *Joe Ogden, former agent at X-Ray Touring; author, Early Stages: A Guide to Booking Gigs.[18]*

Ogden's explanation may be simplistic when describing the work of the modern booking agent. Certainly, there can be no doubt as to the increased importance of the role of the booking agent. Artists now seek more than someone to book shows and tours for them:

artists seek representation for film scoring, TV appearances, brand partnerships, and advice on digital strategy – and the full-service agencies can provide that representation and advice. The booking agent has become "crucial to the development of the artist",[19] especially for artists who want involvement in how their live performance career is presented. Successful artists are concerned with performing in the "right" venues, at the "right" ticket price, which helps "set the tone of the campaign and the perception of the artist".[20] Artists are increasingly "discovered" (presented to the general public) at a very early stage in their development.

You have studied the perceived value of live performance to the artist earlier in this part. Consumers engaging with a music artist are non-committal – there is no cost to the fan for following an artist on social media, for instance. "Hard ticket" (tickets sold for a specific artist concert, not a multi-artist festival performance) sales are therefore seen as an indicator of an artist's success.[21] Ticket sales also help with artist longevity, creating relationships with fans away from recorded music and social media; the modern booking agent needs to be considerate of this when planning an artist's live campaign. Booking tours and festivals for short-term financial gain is not an astute booking policy. Working effectively with the artist's manager, record company, public relations (PR) people, publisher, and lawyer/business manager, will help the booking agent to devise an enduring touring and live performance strategy.

IDENTIFYING OPPORTUNITIES FOR LIVE PERFORMANCE

The booking agent, the artist, and her manager, will want to devise a strategy for that artist's live performances. The plan will be discussed and refined during early meetings with the booking agent – indeed agents courting an act will be expected to have devised a plan for that artist to win them as a client.[22]

The artist manager will have already considered an artist's value proposition,[23] based on the following criteria, which the booking agent will also consider:

- genre
- fan base
- artists primary location
- previous live performance history
- recording history
- forthcoming releases
- production considerations

(Please see "*The managers considerations for live performance*" earlier in this part for detailed explanations of these criteria.)

The plan for live music performances should be adapted accordingly. An agent courting a rising "baby-band" hip-hop artist in North America for instance, may suggest a first-year campaign of performances at festivals such as JMBLYA, Dreamville, and Astroworld, as well as college shows that are "great for developing artists".[24]

Booking shows for baby bands and rising stars requires "grit and determination"[25] on behalf of the agent. Concert promoters and festivals organisers will likely not have heard of a particular act, and the agent must convince that promoter to take a chance on an unheard entity, hold a date at a venue in the calendar, and pay a substantial performance fee to that unknown artist!

Artists at the other end of the scale (superstar and heritage) will have relatively little difficulty in securing high-paying, and far-reaching, concert tours and festival slots.

Booking agents with a roster of baby artists and superstar acts will be engaged in outgoing deals (offering acts to promoters) for their lesser-known artists and examining incoming deals (offers from festival promoters) for their superstar and heritage acts.

Data is now a big part of the decision-making process for the artist team, including the booking agent. Digital service providers (DSPs), such as Spotify, can provide an artist with data about fan engagement and demand. The data are useful when considering a live performance strategy, and you shall examine data in the live music business later in this part.

We shall also examine incoming offers for artists later; the booking agent's first job for new and baby bands will be identifying the potential opportunities for live performance in these areas:

- showcases
- opening for other artists ("supports")
- headline club shows
- the college circuit in the US
- festival slots

SHOWCASES

The showcase is any live performance that is manufactured to place the artist in front of other music industry professionals and tastemakers.

Showcases were traditionally organised by the artist manager to "showcase" a new artist to a record company's A&R people. The manager would hire a room in a bar or other suitable space (many record companies had showcase rooms for hire in their basements), and simply invite as many record company and publishing A&R people as possible. The A&R people could watch the band, see what they "were all about", and hopefully arrange with the manager to talk about a record deal. Showcases were often soul-destroying affairs for everyone involved, not least because of the artificial nature of the event: no one in attendance knew (or even cared) about the music they were listening to, and the lack of a ticket-buying, drunk audience meant the artist had no reaction to respond to.

Showcases are still a common way of introducing an artist to the wider music industry, and also music fans, but it is rare for an artist to be completely unknown before a showcase. An artist should have been engaging with listeners on social media (and possibly through live performance) and should have a fan base. A record or publishing deal may already be in place because of this activity, and the artist only needs a series of performances to boost her reputation amongst the industry and beyond.

The booking agent, therefore, will look to the music industry conferences to showcase a new client to the rest of the live music business. Conferences such as South By South West (SXSW) in Austin, TX (March), and Eurosonic Noorderslag, Groningen, Netherlands (January) are attended by concert promoters, festival organisers, talent buyers, other booking agents, and artist managers from around the world for workshops, debates, keynote speakers, and showcase gigs for new and emerging talent. Showcase performances at music industry conferences are less sterile than old-fashioned record company showcases – the gigs are in established live music venues and can be open to the public, although there are usually enough delegates attending to provide a ready-made audience at each event. Crucially, the showcases mostly take place in the evenings of the event, allowing delegates to drink and relax while still working (finding new talent). Showcasing new talent in this way will put the artist in front of live music business professionals, and the booking agent should then arrange meetings with interested parties to plot out concert tours and festival performances.

OPENING FOR OTHER ARTISTS

Opening up (or supporting) other artists on their headline shows and tours is a tried and true way of breaking a new act through live performance: the headline act is the one that appears at the top of the bill and typically closes a concert; the baby band gets to perform in front of an audience far larger than the one they could draw on their own, thus gaining them exposure and vital experience on responding to an audience and developing their stagecraft (see *Case study: Dirty Honey*).

CASE STUDY: DIRTY HONEY

Dirty Honey, a rock band from Los Angeles, offer proof that opening up can help break an act – if there is a clear plan in place.[26] The band got to number one on Billboard's "Mainstream Rock" chart in October 2019, despite having no record label behind them. Manager Mark DiDia used live performance to raise awareness of the band, initially securing opening shows with Slash, the former guitarist of Guns N' Roses, a hard rock band. DiDia then brought in Ken Fermaglich, a booking agent with United Talent Agency (UTA), who is known for booking rock and heavy metal artists. Fermaglich secured opening slots for Dirty Honey with Guns N' Roses, themselves, and Alter Bridge, a hard rock band. The audiences for both liked what they heard, downloading and streaming Dirty Honey's self-released song, "When I'm Gone", in sufficient numbers to get them to the top of the charts.

The artist team may therefore consider opening slots as a strategy going forward, but there are several pitfalls to this strategy. Firstly, opening slots are difficult to secure (see *Choosing the support acts*). The potential exposure, described above, for an opener at a sold-out show creates demand for those slots. A baby band must know the headline act personally, share management with the headliner, share booking agents with the headliner, or have a very persuasive booking agent of their own to have a chance of opening for an established act. The prestige of opening slots is so great that it is possible to offer these slots to the highest bidder – a process known as the "buy-on". Buying onto a show or tour is common in the pop world, for instance, where record companies will pay the headliners to secure their new act onto the bill.

Second is the issue of cost. Presuming the deal is not a buy-on, the opening act will be paid very little for their performances. You will examine the way live performance deals are structured in *Creating the deals* later in this part; for now, you should know that any opening act fee is a cost to the promoter – one they will minimise as much as possible. The artist will have the same touring costs as if they were playing headline shows (see *Part Two: Live Music Production* for an explanation of these costs) but with very little income, considering the audience numbers. Planning a tour as an opener requires careful judgement and cost-effectiveness analysis[27] by the artist and her team.

Finally, that cost-effectiveness is difficult to measure. Beyond simply raising awareness, there is no evidence that opening for established acts automatically helps to break a baby band. The audience may not have even entered the building when the support band takes the stage! Therefore, everyone on the artist's team, especially the artist herself, must be prepared to capitalise on the exposure to a larger audience. There will be touchpoints[28] with the audience – t-shirts sales, opportunities for selfies, blogging from the road, and so on, that must be embraced to fulfil the goal of breaking the band.

CHOOSING THE SUPPORT ACTS

The choosing of support acts for a tour of large clubs or theatres is done by the headline act themselves, with help and advice from the artist manager and booking agent.

A shortlist of candidates for the tour opener is drawn up by the management and booking agent. That shortlist may include artists who have a personal relationship with the headline artist – old school friends, siblings, boyfriends, and so on. Indeed, this is the most common way to get an opening slot – know someone in the headline band!

HEADLINING CLUB SHOWS

The agent may have inherited an act (the artist may have left their previous agency), or the act may have a sufficient fan base to warrant going straight to headlining club shows (we define club shows as venues of 400–1000 capacity, and they are not necessarily nightclubs). In any case, the agency will have the difficult job of approaching venue owners and national promoters to hold suitable dates and decide on ticket price.

The artist will be unlikely to make much (if any) profit from a club tour, as expenses will be high. There must be a temptation for the booking agent to go instead for festival slots, as these can generate higher performance fees for the artist and reach more people. However, a good booking agent will want to prove her client's ability to sell hard tickets. Performing a series of sold-out club shows is proof there is a strong demand for a particular artist, and that hard-ticket success gives the artist, and her booking agent, bargaining power when it comes to securing higher profile, and higher-paying, festival slots.

Booking a headline tour for an emerging artist, even one with a strong fan base, is difficult. Concert promoters and venue owners will want to know that the online success – numbers of fans streaming, watching on YouTube, etc. – will translate to hard-ticket sales (see *YouTubers*). The booking agent may have to offer conciliatory deals, which have less risk for the promoter, and so less money for the artist. The deal may involve a lower ticket price, which limits the gross potential to all parties or a low guaranteed performance fee (see *Gross potential*). A low guarantee will mean the promoter does not have to sell that many tickets to break even, but it does limit the profit potential for the artist. You shall see more about the concert deals in *Creating the deals* later in this part. For now, you should realise that an agent booking a headline tour for a new artist has to negotiate deals that entice the national promoters to want to stage a concert and that do not financially cripple the artist.

Figure 3.1 shows the deal memo of a typical club show for a national touring artist. The deal is structured to give the artist a decent performance fee ($3000) and the ticket price is high ($20 for an emerging artist) to allow the promoter to potentially make a small profit.

Gross potential = $6400
Promoters' costs $1709
Guarantee $3000
Total promoter has to spend $4709
Break even $4709/$20 = 236 tickets

The artist guarantee is high, though, and the promoter will have to sell 236 tickets (in a 320-capacity club) just to break even, let alone make any profit.

Headlining a club tour is the concrete milestone in an artist's live music career. Closing and selling out 1000–5000-cap clubs help booking agents and managers have fruitful discussions with festival promoters down the line.

YOUTUBERS

Musical YouTube stars have been able to enter the touring market at the medium club capacity (700–1500 cap) level, supported by demand from their subscribers. Booking agents have negotiated deals with ticket prices between $29 and $50 for such

YouTubers as dodie, Poppy, and Hannah Trigwell,[29] who are often touring for the first time. Promoters can be assured of a decent profit from such tours and must be mindful of associated production costs. YouTubers are often independent artists and have no record company behind them to help with tour support. The promoters may have to allow for associated touring costs as part of the deal, as these are usually artist costs. Even so, getting YouTube stars in front of a live audience can help take the artist to the next level which ensures a lasting and profitable relationship for the promoters. Shawn Mendes, a singer/songwriter, took part in YouTube's Meet and Greet Convention (MAGCON) tours, which are a package tour of comedy and music online talent,[30] in 2013. Mendes' appeal broadened after those initial tours, and he now has agency representation through Paradigm, a record deal, and he sold over one million tickets for his 2019 world tour.

GROSS POTENTIAL

Deals for concerts start out with the gross potential:

Gross potential = ticket price x licensed capacity of the venue.

Establishing the gross potential of a concert gives the promoter and booking agent a baseline upon which they can construct the deal.

"UNDERPLAYS"

A headline tour of clubs in the early stages of an artist career is less likely to earn any serious money and is about breaking the artist and proving her potential to gain and keep an audience. There is a matter of proving prestige and the artist team may employ the "underplay" – deliberately choosing venues that are too small to cater for the demand in a particular city – to give the impression the artist has greater reach and selling power than is the case.[31] A booking agent may, as part of a strategy to break an artist, persuade a promoter to hold a concert in a 500-capacity venue, when indeed potential demand for the artist could result in 1000 tickets being sold in a larger venue. Arranging the date in the smaller venue ensures the concert will sell out, and the resulting "buzz" surrounding the show, with lines of people around the block, will help to establish the artist.

Underplays are a risky strategy which, for the promoter, could mean losing out on ticket sales.

THE COLLEGE CIRCUIT IN THE US

The booking agent may investigate the college circuit in the US as an opportunity to expose her client to an audience and to start earning performance revenue.

The US college concert "circuit" has proven itself to be good for reaching the 18–24 demographic with college shows being instrumental in growing an artist's career.[32] Travis Scott, a hip-hop artist, has played many US college tours and now has a sizeable live fan base.

Performing college shows may be a good strategy for breaking a baby band; it is not necessarily a high-revenue option, as many of the deals offered will not be based on hard-ticket sales. On-campus events tend to be free for students to attend, and the money for live acts comes from the colleges' overall annual student welfare budget or from funds and awards that are given at the last minute. However, not having to buy a ticket means that students are more likely to focus on, and respond favourably to, just the music and not have "a lot of expectations around the production".[33]

College entertainment programming departments are run by the students – these students are not experienced concert promoters and will not be conversant with the ins and outs of a modern concert deal. A booking agent at a full-service agency is "not keen on spending two hours on the phone discussing posters and contract rules with a 19-year-old student",[34] and so agents will go through a specialised division within the agency, or through "middle-men" college agencies. Paradigm, a full-service agency, has a college department that helps to ensure their artists are represented to colleges and schools, for instance. A college may have made an offer for a particular artist, who turned down that offer; it is one of the jobs of Paradigm's college division to propose another suitable Paradigm client to the college.[35] The division has had success with artists such as Jesse McCartney, a singer-songwriter and actor and T-Pain, a rapper, on the US college circuit.[36]

Artists who are perhaps facing diminishing audience numbers can also do well out of the college circuit – packaged as nostalgia attractions. One successful US college middle-man agency claims "there are always a few crowd-pleasers who still tour and crank out music".[37] The agency is offering these "crowd-pleasers" to colleges for "throwback" events and mentions artists such as the three-time platinum record-selling band, The All-American Rejects.[38]

FESTIVAL SLOTS

Open-air, green-field festivals, such as Coachella (US 125,000-cap), Wacken Open Air (DE 80,000-cap), and Melt! Festival (DE 20,000-cap), run over two or three days, have multiple stages, and feature 30–40 different artists per day (Figure 3.2). The artists appear in prearranged "slots" – stage times of between 20 minutes and two hours each. The lure of a good festival slot for an emerging artist is hard to deny. Performing at 16.30 on a sunny Saturday afternoon to a captive audience could be seen as the holy grail of a strategy for breaking a band through live performance. Managers, booking agents, and festival promoters, are therefore under increasing pressure to make the right deals and obtain the right slots for artists. Festival organisers need to make suitable offers to secure new talent, and the booking agents must secure good festival slots for as many of their clients as possible.

Figure 3.2 Open-air festivals are an important part of an artist's performance activity. The picture shows the view from the front-of-house mixing console at Melt! Festival, an open-air festival in Ferropolis, Germany. Image courtesy of the author

Supply and demand for festival slots is an industry concern. Concert promoters need proven headline talent to sell tickets yet need to be aware of emerging talent to create a unique and popular line-up. Booking agents have a great supply of talent, both headliners and baby bands, to fill the various slots and must ensure that all their clients have a chance at appearing at a decent time, on a suitable stage, to maximise their exposure to a captive audience. A well-received festival performance in the summer will lead to hard-ticket sales in that fall/winter, for instance. Organisers and booking agents are both faced with much longer "lead times" (the time from agreeing the deal to when the artist takes the stage) with headliners at major festivals being secured two years ahead of their slot. Long lead times are a risk when booking headliners, especially heritage headliners. Age-related illness, even death, may force the cancellation of a headliner's festival show, and a suitable replacement may be hard to find, especially at short notice.

The teams behind emerging talent also face a risk with long booking lead times. On the one hand, booking agents need to secure slots for their clients who, at the time of booking, may not have any other promotional activity (record release, streaming, other live shows) in place. For instance, a booking agent needs to persuade festival organisers to book her client in November for open-air festivals in August of the next year. Does the promoter take the chance, with no music in place, and no real data on audience engagement? Or do they offer slots to established artists who, although not "cutting-edge", are guaranteed to persuade fans to pay for a festival ticket? There is no right answer to this problem, and festival promoters have to go on instinct and, perhaps, historical data. The scarcity of suitable slots does create a situation where long lead times are normal. Booking agents will get their clients onto bills anyway, because there is no point in waiting.[39] Festival season may be over when the artist releases her record, for instance, and anything can happen between the deal being secured and the festival weekend itself, with "new bands who come through and explode".[40] The promoters must allow for this and leave some of their festival slots unbooked until closer to the event. Some 20% of European festival slots are available this way.[41]

Artist fees for festival appearances may be significant, even for emerging artists. Festival organisers can offer between $1000 and $5000 for a mid-afternoon/early evening slot on a festival main stage or the same for the artist to headline a smaller tent (500–2000 capacity). Those fees are well and good if an artist has a series of festival appearances over the summer, but that may not be the case for a baby band. An emerging artist will be fortunate to perform at two or three festivals over the summer unless they have a persistent agent, significant streaming numbers, and a real buzz about them. Hard-ticket sales from headline club shows are a better bet for financial stability. However, club shows in the summer are hard to promote, as there is competition from the outdoor festivals. These festivals also insist on radius clauses in their contracts with artists (see *Radius Clause*). The clauses are a type of "non-compete" clause, and stipulate that artists cannot perform at other festivals or hard-ticket shows within an agreed upon geographical, date-based, or both, radius of their performance at the particular festival. Radius clauses are not so much of a problem for baby bands, as they are unlikely to be accepted onto that many competing festivals and would not be playing hard-ticket club shows in the summer anyway. Radius clauses do affect DJs and rappers, who will be able to perform continuously at nightclubs during festival season. The team behind the DJ will have to weigh up the impact, and revenue, from one major music festival appearance, over that of a series of competing nightclub shows.

RADIUS CLAUSE

The radius clause is included to create "exclusivity" of an artist contracted to perform at the festival. There has been dispute involving radius clauses in recent years, with a case being brought against the Coachella Valley Music and Arts Festival (run by AEG, 125,000-cap), by Soul'd Out Productions, in 2019. A smaller festival (1480-cap), Soul'd Out Productions, tried to sue, claiming that many artists they had approached had declined offers to perform at the Soul'd Out Festival, as they were bound by non-compete radius clauses in their contracts with Coachella. Originally, the case was dismissed by Judge Michael Mosman, and it exposed the somewhat onerous nature of such clauses.

Some of the clauses in the 2018 Coachella event contract stipulated these exclusives:

- artists could not perform at any North American festival between 15 December 2017 and 01 May 2018. Coachella took place over two weekends in April of 2018, and "festival" was defined as "any engagement with 4 or more artists".

- artists could not perform at any hard-ticket show in Los Angeles, Orange, Riverside, San Bernardino, Santa Barbara, Ventura, or San Diego counties between the same dates, 15 December 2017 and 01 May 2018.
- artists were not allowed to "advertise, publicize, or leak" their own tours or club shows in the US, and specifically in the Los Angeles and surrounding area, until after their performance at Coachella.

Lawyers for AEG said "maintaining a unique festival line-up is crucial for Coachella to remain competitive".[42]

PITCHING AT MUSIC CONFERENCES

You read earlier that booking agents may represent their clients at the various worldwide music conferences. As well as performing at conference showcase events, an artist should expect her agent to be meeting promoters and festival organiser to pitch outgoing deals – touring and festival opportunities.

The European festival booking cycle starts earlier each "season" – headliners are in negotiation with organisers 10–12 months in advance, and those acts destined for other slots will want to be confirmed in December – or January at the very latest. Many of the larger live music conferences take place later than the start of the year, leaving precious little time for agents to pitch their new clients to the promoters.

The International Festival Forum (IFF) addresses the festival industry's need for a gathering place earlier in the season to book line-ups for the upcoming year (Figure 3.3). The IFF takes place in London, in September, and is where agents and festival organisers can meet in person to administer the finer details of artist avails[43] and offers.

Figure 3.3 The International Festival Forum takes place in September each year and is the place for booking agents and festival organisers to prepare the festival bills for the next year. Image courtesy of The International Festival Forum

IDENTIFYING TIME PERIODS FOR LIVE PERFORMANCE

The booking agent, having identified opportunities for live performance, will then look at the identifying periods of live performance for her client. These periods will be discussed with the artist, the artist manager, and the record label, if one is involved. The team will take into account the following to decide on the artist touring time line:

- availability of the artist
- availability of featured artists
- availability of appropriate venues
- timing of recorded music releases
- capitalising on other exposure
- festival season

AVAILABILITY OF THE ARTIST

The starting point in deciding the touring period is to consider the availability of the artist. More likely, this would be when the live work starts, so the artist knows to finish recording her new work, or to cease some other activity, by a certain date. The "tour-readiness" of the artist also needs to be considered. When was the last time she performed live? How much rehearsal and pre-production do the artist and her crew need?

Opening for a headliner presents another logistical issue. The opener has no say as to the routing[44] of the tour, as this has been decided by the promoters working with the headliner's booking agent. The opener may find it difficult to commit to some sections of the tour routing (called legs). An example of this would be a headliner's tour of the UK that also has some dates in Ireland. Travelling to Ireland requires ferry travel, which is expensive, and the opener may elect not to perform on those Irish dates of the tour because of the expense.

The artist must also announce tours earlier ahead of the performances to be able to secure advertising slots on social media and in the promotional calendars for the DSPs, such as Spotify, Apple, and YouTube. There is a "limited amount of inventory"[45] available for placements, and artists must secure them with form music and tour announcements which can be six months ahead.

AVAILABILITY OF FEATURED ARTISTS

An artist may have released music featuring or collaborating with another artist. The artist team may decide that there is sufficient demand for a one-off concert, or tour, with both artists. The other artist will have their own schedule and may not be able to commit to live performance in the proposed time period.

Likewise, an artist may be offered a prestigious opening slot on a tour and be unable to take up the offer as they are committed elsewhere.

AVAILABILITY OF APPROPRIATE VENUES

A venue's suitability for an artist at a certain point in her career is dictated by its capacity. An unknown artist booked to headline a show at Madison Square Gardens (20,879-cap) would not sell enough tickets for anyone to make any money from the engagement, for instance. The artist should be performing in venues that will hold enough people according to demand. Judging demand is difficult and data can help. An experienced promoter will also know where to place a particular artist, not only based on potential demand, but also considering other, non-capacity based, factors such as genre. You shall look at venues in greater detail in *Part Two: Live Music Production*.

There is a lack of suitable venues that cater to the demand for live music.[46] This scarcity creates pressure for promoters and booking agents. Planning a tour relies on suitable venues being available on dates that suit the artist, and this may not be the case, especially in the capital cities of the major music markets. Booking agents are forced to persuade promoters to commit to bookings as venues will become unavailable if the booking is delayed[47].

Seasonal factors also dictate the suitability of a venue. Nightclubs tend to do well all year round and theatres and arenas are a more comfortable for fans and performers when the weather is colder. However, arenas are often occupied with sporting events in fall and winter. Likewise, outdoor spaces, such as sheds[48] and stadiums, are more suited for warm weather, with stadiums again being used for sporting events during those times.

TIMING OF RECORDED MUSIC RELEASES

Touring to support the release of the artist's new album was considered standard practice before 1999. Tours were often named after the particular album and the live work was definitely seen as a promotional activity to create sales of a new record. Artists still tour in support of their new releases these days, but the focus has shifted – the recorded release almost serves as an excuse to go out on tour and earn money. Sales and streams of the recorded output are a nice by-product of this activity.

There is still the anticipation of a new album to entice promoters to book an act. The inclusion of new material into the setlist[49] of an established artist helps to revitalise the artist's performance, and audiences get the impression they are getting a "new" show, not the same, old songs that they paid to see the year before. As much as the concept of the album-tour-album cycle may becoming irrelevant, a booking agent will find it easier to promote an established act to concert promoters and festival organisers if that act has new material "ready to drop".

Supporting a record release is a good strategy for superstar acts looking to tour in so-called "secondary markets". A global record release, and subsequent local radio play, ensure artists such as Coldplay, an English rock band, have success with extended tours of South America and India,[50] for instance.

CAPITALISING ON OTHER EXPOSURE

The planning to identify a period of time is largely done many months, maybe even a year, ahead of the activity. The artist may also be able to capitalise on unplanned exposure or some other surge in demand, and there may not be much time to respond to this.

Typically, the artist team will be factoring in a surge in demand and will be prepared to back that up with live performance if it is relevant. For instance, a single or album release, or festival appearance, will hopefully ignite the interest of existing fans and make significant numbers of new ones who are all ready and willing to see the artist live.

Demand may surpass the expectations of the artist team, or another event may occur to ramp up interest in the artist. A booking agent may find it difficult to create an immediate, hard-ticket response to this new demand because there may be no suitable venues available at short notice. That demand can be satiated with an announcement for live dates in the future, and the booking agent must work quickly with concert promoters to secure suitable venues at the earliest opportunity.

FESTIVAL SEASON

The green-field, open-air festival season in UK and Europe runs from May until September. The US season starts earlier, with Coachella (US 125,000-cap) being the season's opener in April of each year. An artist manager who is planning a period of live performances may view festival season as an opportunity or a hindrance. It is assumed an artist will want to perform on as many festival bills as possible, but this may not be the case. The main reason – that an artist may not have new material released in time for festival season – is a common reason. The perception of a new album is still important when presenting an artist to the public, and festival organisers may pass on an artist who performed at festivals last year yet has no new material this time around.

Five months (the length of festival season in Europe) is a long time for an artist with no festival bookings. Open-air, green-field festivals take a lot of tickets out of the market (fans spend all their money on festival tickets, leaving them little money for other concerts in the season) and there are few hard-ticket options left for those months. The artist may view festival season as a time to write and record new material, especially if they were busy the previous year with festival appearances and winter touring.

INITIATING THE DEAL

"Deal" in this case means the financial and contractual terms surrounding an artist's performance. The deal is between the artist and the promoter (or festival organiser) and is initiated by the booking agent.

The booking agent is involved with initiating a deal in one of two ways:

- a promoter approaches a booking agent and enquires as to the avails (availability) of one of her artists with a view to making an offer for a performance by the artist at a venue organised by the promoter (an incoming offer)

Figure 3.4 Deals can be incoming or outgoing for the booking agent

- the booking agent, having identified a period of touring with the artist's team, approaches suitable promoters and offers the artist's services for live performances (an outgoing deal), see Figure 3.4

EXAMPLE OF AN INCOMING OFFER

The promoter for a new electronic music festival in Bali, Indonesia, wants Farry Kisher to perform at the inaugural event the following spring. The promoter initially contacts Farry Kisher's manager, who points them to the band's booking agent to secure the deal. Over a series of emails, the booking agent sounds out the validity and reputation of the festival and its organisational team and then asks the promoters to make an offer to have Farry Kisher perform. As this is a new festival, the offer from the organisers should specify:

- the date and location of the festival
- the proposed performance fee
- details of offer of travel and accommodation
- details of local taxation and possible relief
- the proposed line-up
- Farry Kishers' position on the bill, stage time, and the other artists performing at the same time
- the ticket price (and the price of equivalent local events as a comparison)
- the capacity of the festival
- the dates of line-up announcements and when the tickets go on sale
- details of festival sponsors and other investors
- the marketing plan

The booking agent would not need this much detail in the case of an offer from an established major festival such as Reading Festival (UK 105,000-cap) or Bonnaroo (US 80,000-cap). The proposed stage time, competing acts, and the fee would probably suffice in such a case.

The Bali festival in our example is more of an unknown quantity, and the booking agent must undertake due diligence to ensure the offer is bona fide and that the festival will go ahead as planned – and not be subsequently cancelled due to poor ticket sales, bad organisation, or both.

There will probably be a great deal of communication by email between the festival organisers and the agent, and eventually the terms of the deal will be agreed. The deal

at this stage does not constitute a formal agreement and may be enough for the agent
to draw up a deal memo. The deal memo itemises the points that have been agreed and
serves as a reminder for when the offer is confirmed and a contract is issued. Figure 3.1
shows an example of a deal memo.

EXAMPLE OF AN OUTGOING DEAL

It is February. Bum Gravy will have their debut album released in October, and
their booking agent has begun the process of persuading concert promoters to book
the band into venues around the UK to capitalise on the resulting marketing and
publicity.

Bum Gravy performed at festivals over the summer last year and have a number of
appearances at key festivals again this summer. However, the band have not headlined
shows before now, so the agent has to work hard to persuade promoters to take a chance
on an unproven act. The agent, along with the rest of the band's team, plotted out the
following strategy to make it easier to get good shows, and to make the touring effective
in spreading the appeal of the band:

- The touring period will be the last two weeks of November and the first week of
  December. The album (and simultaneous single release) will have been out for a
  month prior to the shows and will have hopefully been featured on relevant radio
  shows and DSP's new release charts.
- The band will perform in 300–500 capacity rooms, with a suitable 1000-capacity
  venue for the London date. There is potentially demand to be able to sell out higher
  capacity venues, but the team feel an underplay strategy will help establish the band
  as a significant live entity.
- Ticket prices should not be low. The band have significant streaming numbers, and
  their festival slots were well attended. The team is confident of demand for the
  band's own shows, and ticket prices at the top end of the scale for 500-cap club
  shows will mitigate any loss to the promoters.
- The band are signed to a major label, who have pledged some amount of tour support.[51] This will reduce the band's reliance on high performance fees.
- Bum Gravy are a four-piece "real" rock band and like to think they do not need
  extensive lighting or video effects on stage to enhance their show. The band will not
  be carrying any special equipment for visuals on the tour. Concert production costs
  for the band will therefore be low, and they can accept lower performance fee offers
  if necessary.
- Bum Gravy are good friends with another act who are tipped for great things. The
  other act has agreed in principle to open up for Bum Gravy on the November headline tour which will help sell tickets. This again mitigates the risk to promoters.
- The booking agent wants to start long-term relationships between the band and the
  regional and national promoters – reducing the risk to those promoters will help initiate those relationships.

The booking agent has approached her hit list of promoters armed with this "plot" along
with an indication of the range of performance fees the band is looking for. This may be

in the £2000–£5000 range per performance for instance. The promoters have started to respond with their counter-offers, where they specify:

- a suitable venue(s)
- a suitable date(s)
- the financial offer
- the venue capacity
- the proposed ticket price
- the gross potential
- the promoter's costs

The booking agent is currently receiving these offers and is passing them along to the artist's management for consideration. The agent is presenting the offers in the form of a spreadsheet, or via an online portal, to make it easier for the manager to absorb the information. Table 3.3 shows a typical sheet of promoter's offers compiled by the booking agent to show to the manager and the artist.

OTHER OUTGOING DEALS

The negotiation of deals for hard-ticket concerts takes time. The booking agent will leverage her expertise and experience to get the best deal for her artist clients. She will not want to alienate concert promoters and festival organisers and yet must drive a hard bargain.

The agent will also make outgoing deals for festival appearances and opening slots on tours. Pitching for festival slots takes place all year round and is a primary activity for booking agents in September each year. The International Festival Forum (IFF), serving the European festival market, takes place in London at that time, and agents have the opportunity to pitch their clients to organisers who have festival slots to fill. Negotiation is equally as time consuming for a hard-ticket show, as the agent must ensure her act is on the right stage, at the right time, on the right day – and earn a competitive performance fee. TV, internet broadcast rights, and sponsorship activities, many also need to be agreed. Many other artists and their agents are also trying to secure slots from organisers at the same time, creating a competitive "24-hour" culture amongst booking agents and promoters.[52]

Pitching for an opening slot on a tour works in much the same way for the booking agent. Artists considered for opening slots may already have some relationship with the headline artist – they may share management, or booking agent, or be friends with the headliner. Being put forward by the booking agent of the headline act is the most common way to be considered. The final choice is then usually made by the artist. There are occasions when an opening slot really is open for all to be considered, and the booking agent would then put forward suitable acts from her roster. The simplicity of an artist live performance setup is one important deciding factor when choosing an opening act. Electronic duos who use a couple of keyboards and a drum machine are easy to get on and off a stage filled with the headliner's equipment, thus making less work for the main band's stage crew.

Table 3.3 A spreadsheet detailing offers made by promoters. The sheet is compiled by the booking agent and sent to the artist manage-ment team for their approval

	COUNTRY	CITY	VENUE/ACTIVITY	CAPACITY	STATUS	FEE	DEAL	NOTES
08/11/	England	Manchester	Islington Mill – Production rehearsal					
09/11/	England	Manchester	Islington Mill – Production rehearsal					
10/11/	Scotland	Glasgow	King Tuts Wah Wah Hut	300	Headline	£1,500	vs 80% NBOR + PA, lights, and catering	
11/11/			Travel/day off					
12/11/	England	Newcastle	Riverside	400	Headline	£1,500	vs 80% NBOR + PA, lights, and catering	
13/11/			Travel/day off					
14/11/	England	Leeds	Brudenell Social Club	400	Headline	£1,500	vs 80% NBOR + PA, lights, and catering	
15/11/			Travel/day off					

(Continued)

Table 3.3 (Continued)

	COUNTRY	CITY	VENUE/ACTIVITY	CAPACITY	STATUS	FEE	DEAL	NOTES
16/11/	England	Nottingham	Rescue Rooms	330	Headline	£1,500	vs 80% NBOR + PA, lights, and catering	
17/11/			Travel/day off					
18/11/	England	Birmingham	The Rainbow Warehouse	400 (floor only – 1000-cap)	Headline	£1,750	vs 80% NBOR + PA, lights, and catering	
19/11/	England	Sheffield	The Plug	250 (B space 1440-cap)	Headline	£1,000	vs 80% NBOR + PA, lights, and catering	
20/11/	England	Oxford	O2 Academy 2	250	Headline	£1,000	vs 80% NBOR + PA, lights, and catering	
21/11/			Travel/day off					
22/11/			Travel/day off					
23/11/	England	Bristol	Fleece	330	Headline	£1,000	vs 80% NBOR + PA, lights, and catering	
24/11/			Travel/day off					

25/11/	England	Brighton	Komedia	Sold on 250 (550-cap)	Headline	£1,000	vs 80% NBOR + PA, lights, and catering	
26/11/	England	London	Village Underground	700	Headline	£4,500	vs 80% NBOR + PA, lights, and catering	
27/11/	England	Manchester	Academy 2	900	Headline	£5,000	vs 80% NBOR + PA, lights, and catering	Hold on Academy (2425-cap)
28/11/	England	Southampton	Engine Rooms	800	Festival billing	£1,000	+ PA, lights, and catering	On stage 14.00
29/11/			Travel/day off					

NOTES

1   de Lattre, J., 2016. "State of the agency business", *IQ Magazine*, 15.
2   ILMC, 2019. "The agency business 2019" [WWW Document], *ILMC 31*. URL https://31.ilmc
    .com/report/thursday/889-agency (accessed 1.24.20).
3   Dofat, T., 2016. *Become an Entrepreneur in the Music Business*, 1st ed. TDC Group Incorporated,
    New York.
4   Waddell, R.D., Barnet, R., and Berry, J., 2007. *This Business of Concert Promotion and Touring*.
    Watson-Guptill, New York.
5   Billboard, 2015. "How much do the booking agents who send artists on tour make?" [WWW
    Document]. URL https://www.billboard.com/articles/business/6605760/how-much-do-the-bo
    oking-agents-who-send-artists-on-tour-make/ (accessed 1.22.20).
6   Waddell, R.D., Barnet, R., and Berry, J., 2007. *This Business of Concert Promotion and Touring*.
    Watson-Guptill, New York.
7   Primary Talent, n.d. "Matt Bates | Primary talent international" [WWW Document], *Primary
    Talent*. URL https://primarytalent.com/matt-bates/ (accessed 1.22.20).
8   California Department of Industrial Relations, 2016. *Laws Relating to Talent Agencies. Excerpts
    from the California Labor Code and California Code of Regulations, Title 8*. California Department of
    Industrial Relations. URL https://www.dir.ca.gov/dlse/Talent/Talent_Laws_Relating_to_Tale
    nt_Agencies.pdf.(accessed 05.02.19)
9   Passman, D.S., 2015. *All You Need to Know about the Music Business*, 9th ed. Simon & Schuster,
    New York.
10 https://www.paradigmagency.com/
11 Edwards, J., (2016). *Booking Agents* [Presentation] AIM Academy Masterclass: Understanding the
    Live Industry
12 Waddell, R.D., Barnet, R. and Berry, J., 2007. *This Business of Concert Promotion and Touring*.
    Watson-Guptill, New York.
13 de Lattre, J., 2016. "State of the agency business", *IQ Magazine*, 15.
14 "International booking agents directory – Book gigs worldwide!". URL https://bookingagentsdi
    rectory.com/ (accessed 11.5.18).
15 "The agency group acquires bond music group", *Music Week*. URL http://www.musicweek.com/
    news/read/the-agency-group-acquires-bond-music-group/060068 (accessed 11.5.18).
16 "Paradigm brings AM only and Windish Agency in-house", *Music Business Worldwide*, 11 January
    2017, https://www.musicbusinessworldwide.com/paradigm-brings-windish-house/. (accessed
    12/01/2017)
17 Watson, K., 2018. *IMS Business Report 2018*. International Music Summit, Ibiza. URL https://
    www.internationalmusicsummit.com/wp-content/uploads/2018/05/IMS-Business-Report-2018
    -vFinal2.pdf. (accessed 05/02/2018)
18 Ogden, J., 2019. *Early Stages. A Guide to Booking Gigs*. Self published.
19 Roberts, D., 2018. "I find acts that play to nobody... and I convince people to book them"
    [WWW Document], *Music Business Worldwide*. URL https://www.musicbusinessworldwide.com
    /tom-windish-i-still-find-acts-that-play-to-nobody-but-who-make-amazing-music-and-i-con
    vince-people-to-book-them/ (accessed 1.23.20).
20 Hanley, J., 2019. "'Artists are being discovered earlier': A special report on live agents" [WWW
    Document], *Music Week*. URL https://www.musicweek.com/analysis/read/artists-are-being-di
    scovered-earlier-a-special-report-on-live-agents/077527 (accessed 1.23.20).
21 Music Business Worldwide, 2018. "The thrill of finding a new act, developing it, and then really
    breaking it – It's still the biggest buzz", *MusicBusinessUK Q4*, 11.
22 Masson, G., 2019. "Captain of industry", *IQ Magazine*, 45–48.
23 A value proposition is a promise of value to be delivered, communicated, and acknowledged.
    (Wikipedia)
24 Borba, R., 2018."Majoring in cooperation: Agents, middle buyers, and festivals bring the music
    to college", [WWW Document], *Pollstar*. URL https://www.pollstar.com/article/majoring-in-
    cooperation-agents-middle-buyers-and-festivals-bring-the-music-to-college-136363 (accessed
    1.23.20).
25 Roberts, D., 2018. "I find acts that play to nobody... and I convince people to book them"
    [WWW Document], *Music Business Worldwide*. URL https://www.musicbusinessworldwide.com
    /tom-windish-i-still-find-acts-that-play-to-nobody-but-who-make-amazing-music-and-i-con
    vince-people-to-book-them/ (accessed 1.23.20).

26 Rutherford, K., 2019. "How this unsigned rock band earned a no. 1 hit" [WWW Document], *Billboard*. URL https://www.billboard.com/articles/columns/rock/8543513/how-dirty-honey -when-im-gone-went-no-1 (accessed 1.23.20).

27 Cost-effectiveness analysis (CEA) is a form of economic analysis that compares the relative costs and outcomes (effects) of different courses of action. (Wikipedia)

28 "Touchpoint" can be defined as any way a consumer can interact with a business, whether it be person-to-person, through a website, an app, or any other form of communication. (Wikipedia)

29 "Kilimanjaro backs YouTube-focused talent agency", 2016. *IQ Magazine*. URL https://www.iq-mag.net/2016/02/kilimanjaro-live-backs-youtuber-talent-agency-free-focus-triple-a-media-vl ogger-events-summer-in-the-city/ (accessed 1.29.20).

30 Maggie Mendes (2017) *Shawn Mendes performing at MagCon 2013.* Jan 5, 2017. Available at https://www.youtube.com/watch?v=FoZEJzbSJdA

31 Gensler, A., 2019. "Underplays in overdrive: Why big artists are increasingly playing small venues", [WWW Document], *Pollstar*. URL https://www.pollstar.com/article/underplays-in-ove rdrive-why-big-artists-are-increasingly-playing-small-venues-141283 (accessed 12.23.20).

32 Borba, R., 2018. "Majoring in cooperation: agents, middle buyers and festivals bring the music to college", [WWW Document]. *Pollstar*. URL https://www.pollstar.com/article/majoring-in-cooperation-agents-middle-buyers-and-festivals-bring-the-music-to-college-136363 (accessed 1.23.20).

33 Ibid.

34 Ibid.

35 Borba, R., 2018. "Q's with Paradigm's Taylor Schultz: taking Jesse McCartney, Playboi Carti, T-Pain to school", [WWW Document], *Pollstar*. URL https://www.pollstar.com/article/qs -with-paradigms-taylor-schultz-taking-jesse-mccartney-playboi-carti-t-pain-to-school-136414 (accessed 1.29.20).

36 Ibid.

37 Concert Ideas, 2018. "Throwback events", *Concert Ideas*. URL http://concertideas.com/throwb ack-events/ (accessed 1.29.20).

38 Recording Industry Association of America, 2020. "Gold & platinum", [WWW Document], *RIAA*. URL https://www.riaa.com/gold-platinum/ (accessed 1.29.20).

39 Gottfried, G., 2019. "Booking madness: How the industry is keeping up with 'The 24/7/365 Siege'", [WWW Document], *Pollstar*. URL https://www.pollstar.com/article/booking-madness -how-the-industry-is-keeping-up-with-the-247365-siege-141355 (accessed 1.23.20).

40 Ibid.

41 Ibid

42 Grace, A., 2019. "Coachella radius clause lawsuit dismissed", *IQ Magazine*. URL https://www.iq-mag.net/2019/03/coachella-radius-lawsuit-dismissed/ (accessed 1.29.20).

43 "Avails" – Shorthand for availability, i.e., is the artist available for concept appearances at a given time.

44 "Routing" of a tour is the order of date and location for each stop on that tour.

45 Gottfried, G., 2019. "Booking madness: How the industry is keeping up with 'The 24/7/365 Siege'", [WWW Document], *Pollstar*. URL https://www.pollstar.com/article/booking-madness -how-the-industry-is-keeping-up-with-the-247365-siege-141355 (accessed 1.23.20).

46 "Underplays in overdrive: Why big artists are increasingly playing small venues", [WWW Document], n.d. URL https://www.pollstar.com/article/underplays-in-overdrive-why-big-artis ts-are-increasingly-playing-small-venues-141283 (accessed 12.23.20).

47 Gottfried, G., 2019. "Booking madness: How the industry is keeping up with 'The 24/7/365 Siege'", [WWW Document], *Pollstar*. URL https://www.pollstar.com/article/booking-madness -how-the-industry-is-keeping-up-with-the-247365-siege-141355 (accessed 1.23.20).

48 "Shed" – a particular type of amphitheatre designed for live performance and mostly found in the North America.

49 "Setlist" – the song titles and order in which they are to be performed at each concert.

50 Rendon, F. (2016) "Coldplay to fill Southeast Asia with 'Dreams'", [WWW Document], *Pollstar*. URL https://www.pollstar.com/article/coldplay-to-fill-southeast-asia-with-dreams-49499 (accessed 12.23.20).

51 "Tour support" – money advanced by a record company to support touring activity. Tour support is recoupable from music sales. See "Planning the tour" for more information.

52 Gottfried, G., 2019. "Booking madness: How the industry is keeping up with 'The 24/7/365 Siege'",' [WWW Document], *Pollstar*. URL https://www.pollstar.com/article/booking-madness -how-the-industry-is-keeping-up-with-the-247365-siege-141355 (accessed 1.23.20).

4

CHAPTER 4
CONCERT PROMOTERS

CHAPTER OUTLINE

DOI: 10.4324/9781003019503-5

Figure 4.1 The concert promoter hopes to put an artist in a suitable venue, sell tickets, and make a profit. Image by Jason Fertig/Unsplash

The concert promoter sees the potential from the right artist, in the right venue, for the right ticket price. However, concert promotion is affected by many external forces, and the concert promoter's role is financially risky. You will examine the role of these actors in this chapter.

WHAT DO CONCERT PROMOTERS DO?

Concert promoters are a form of "talent buyer" – an organisation or person who pays an artist to perform in concert.[1] By strict definition, a concert promoter's primary business is to profit from hard-ticket sales (see *Food and beverage*). Other talent buyers may sell tickets for an artist's concert, but their primary business is not to profit from those ticket sales. Certain talent buyers may offer the artists' performance to the public for free, for example. However, any examination of the contemporary music business uses the term "concert promoter" to describe all talent buyers, and that convention is continued here.

The promoter, then, hopes to create a profitable event by putting an artist into a suitable venue, in a suitable place, on a suitable date, marketing the event to the public, and selling tickets. The promoter also agrees to pay the artist for her performance. This payment will be a percentage of the proceeds of the ticket sales, a flat performance fee, or a mixture of the two. The promoter will make a profit after paying the performer and other costs (Figure 4.1).

FOOD AND BEVERAGE

This book will not include sales of food and beverage (FNB) and other concessions (car parking, etc.) associated with concert-going when discussing the financial deals (Figure 4.2). Examples of revenue will be based on hard-ticket sales. Exceptions to this, for green-field festival and night-club events for instance, will be explained at the relevant points.

Figure 4.2 Sales from food and beverage will not be counted when explaining the concert deals. Image by Edward Franklin/Unsplash

WHO ARE THE CONCERT PROMOTERS?

Concert promoters can be the talent buyers for a venue or organisation or are individuals and companies that profit from concert promotion as an activity.

SMALL VENUE OWNERS AND BUYERS

The grass roots of the live music business, small venues (<300-cap) will have an in-house buyer (confusingly often called the "booker") who may also be the owner of the venue. Small club buyers deal directly with the talent which is often local artists who contact the club to get a gig there. Booking agents who represent baby bands will also approach small venue buyers for regional dates on a national tour.

NIGHTCLUB BUYERS

Nightclubs are like small live music venues in that they often have a dedicated in-house booking team. The buyers work with booking agents to secure suitable DJs for weekend nights. Nightclub buyers will also deal directly with local DJs to promote homegrown talent.

CONCERT PROMOTERS

The majority of live music talent buying is done by the concert promoters. These buyers will rent a suitable venue for a concert or may even own the venue themselves, as is the case of Live Nation (see *Live Nation Entertainment*). Venues can range from 200-cap clubs to 70,000-cap stadiums and everything in between. The promoter then promotes the concert to the public through paid advertising and social media marketing, which hopefully encourages the public to buy tickets.

LIVE NATION ENTERTAINMENT

Live Nation Entertainment (LNE, or Live Nation for short), formed in 2005, is considered the world's leading concert promoter. Live Nation promoted 40,000 concert events in 2019, generating income of $9.4 bn, which was nearly 82% of their revenue for that year[2]. LNE positions itself as the "world's leading live entertainment ticketing sales and marketing company"[3] and concentrates its efforts in these areas:

- concerts – one off shows, concert tours, and festivals. LNE owns five festival sites outright, and operates a further.
- ticketing – Live Nation merged with Ticketmaster (a ticketing giant before the merger) in 2010 to form Live Nation Entertainment. LNE now sells tickets on behalf of its clients (for which it charges a fee), as well as tickets for its own events, through websites, apps, and mobile services. Ticketing accounted for $1.5 bn of total revenue in 2019, with 220 million tickets sold.
- sponsorship and advertising – besides traditional media placements for clients, LNE offers naming rights to their venues and other sponsorship opportunities for its partners. These activities brought in nearly $600 million for LNE in 2019.[4]

Artist Nation, a part of the concerts division, owns or operates artist management[5] companies representing Shania Twain (a Canadian singer and songwriter) and Paul McCartney (a former Beatle).

NATIONAL AND INTERNATIONAL TOUR BUYERS

Established concert promoters may see advantages in buying a whole tour by an artist. All dates on the tour are promoted and administered by the one buyer. The buyer will have calculated the gross potential of the tour, considering that certain dates on the tour will sell less well than others. However, as the revenue from every show count towards the profit, the buyer is able to "cross-collateralise" profit and loss from each date. This cross-collateralisation means that the buyer (and artist) will not lose money on a poorly selling show in one city, as other high-selling shows in other places will make up any shortfall.

COLLEGE BUYERS

Schools, colleges, and universities, are keen buyers of talent, especially artists who appeal to the demographic of their students. College shows are not necessarily hard-ticket shows and are often free for students to attend. Nonetheless, college buyers have access to funds to make reasonable offers to artists usually through a booking agent. Many colleges also negotiate with agents through a third-party, professional talent buyer, who will help guide the student team around the complexities of concert promotion.

PERFORMING ARTS CENTRE BUYERS

The buyers at performing arts centres (PACs) will be in-house and will have a remit to present diverse talent that will appeal to niche audiences yet still sell lots of tickets. PACs are often funded by local government or arts charities who will expect the buyers to spend their endowments wisely. Music, being popular, may therefore make up the majority of a PAC annual programme. A show at a PAC can be a good fit for an artist routing a tour of secondary or regional markets in the US or in Europe. PAC buyers will work with booking agents to secure talent, and full-service agencies have agents who specialise in placing their roster into PACs (Figure 4.3).

FESTIVAL BUYERS

You shall examine festival buyers in detail in *Part Three: Festivals*; for now, you should know that festival buyers operate hard-ticket sales to the public and will offer flat performance fees to artists. These offers are negotiated through the artists' booking agents.

The term "festival" is usually associated with open-air, green-field, multi-act events, but this is not always the case. Multi-act, themed, cruise ship-based, events are now popular, and the buyers for such events have a similar remit to those of their land-based equivalents.

Figure 4.3 Performing arts centres (PACs) offer mixed programming, and music is the most popular. Image of Chan Centre for Performing Arts in Vancouver, Canada, by Sean Lee/Unsplash

CASINO BUYERS

There has been increased popularity in music-related activity held in casinos in recent years. Artists, such as Celine Dion, a Canadian singer of ballads, and Brittany Spears, a troubled pop singer, have starred in casino residencies – appearing daily in Las Vegas casinos for months at a time. Casinos are also buying DJ talent with new venues offering exclusive residencies by DJs, such as Steve Aoki, an American DJ/producer, and Calvin Harris, a DJ and producer from Scotland. These residencies are almost certainly negotiated through a booking agent, as the complexities of the deal (accommodation, living expenses, honouring previously booked commitments) differ enormously from a regular, one-off concert deal.

CORPORATE EVENT BUYERS

Corporate and private events are also more popular, and, again, the full-service agencies have divisions that represent their clients to corporate buyers. The buyers themselves are trade conventions, awards shows, sports half-time vents, or political gatherings, and all require (and can pay for) an exclusive performance from a superstar artist at their event. These event buyers will go through a third-party to the responsible agent, in the same way as college buyers. Billionaire business people are also buyers – requesting superstar talent to appear at a daughter's birthday party, for instance.

THE ROLE OF THE CONCERT PROMOTER IN LIVE PERFORMANCE

The role of the concert promoter is to identify and decide on artists, venues, time periods, expenses, and ticket prices and piece those elements together to create an event. The promoter then needs to market that event to the public and hope they buy tickets.

Unfortunately, "hope" is still an often-used word in concert promotion. Unlike the other players in the live music business – the artist manager and booking agent – the concert promoter is vulnerable when it comes to predicting the number of tickets that will sell for any given concert or festival. You shall examine the conditions that create the vulnerability later.

Concert promotion is based, to an extent, on opportunity, and a good concert promoter will always be looking to build relationships with the artist, the management, and the booking agents, to ensure that there is sustainable, repeat business for everyone involved. The other players should be mindful of the fact that, without concert promoters willing to risk their money to promote shows and stages, there would be no live music business.

IDENTIFYING CONCERT OPPORTUNITIES

You saw previously in "*The role of the booking agent in live performance*" how the booking agents seek out performing opportunities for their clients. Some of these opportunities are not headlining slots – the artist they represent would not be the main attraction – and this is a key difference between the role of the booking agent and the promoter. The promoter's incentive to work with an artist is usually informed by that artist's ability to sell a lot of tickets, thus making both the artist and the promoter money. Concert promoters are therefore usually only concerned with seeking out headliners (except for organising multi-artist bills at festivals, where hot talent needs to be present throughout the line-up to attract more customers).

The in-house booker at a small venue will therefore be keeping an eye on emerging local talent, for instance. She needs to know which artists are gaining fans and when those artists are ready to perform at the venue, bringing with them numerous ticket-buying, beer-drinking, customers (food and beverage sales are important to a small venue operator).

At the other end of the scale, festival organisers will be looking at the artists they consider to be the headliners of the future. These artists may be selling good numbers of tickets for their regional shows and may also have significant streaming numbers at the moment. This evidence of strong fan interest makes the decision to place the artist in a popular time slot easy; the artist may not have quite the fan support yet to justify a 16:30 main stage slot on a Saturday, and taking a chance this year may ensure a headliner next year. If there is enough support to ensure that a good number of people will form a crowd to see the artist at that 16:30 slot, then it is likely other festival-goers will also see the artist and become fans. This boost in fan support will help ensure the artist can return next year as headliner, or at least a lot further up the bill.

In any case, the concert promoter's role is to seek out opportunities to stage a concert and to sell tickets for that concert.

VENUES

"Try to put the right act in the right venue on the right date for the right ticket price, and it will be successful". These are the words of John Scher, a concert promoter, referring to creating a sold-out concert.[6] His inclusion of the venue in the list of factors is significant – what exactly makes a "right" venue? You shall look at specific venue types in *Part Two: Live Music Production*; there are a number of factors when deciding on a suitable venue for a concert.

CAPACITY

The concert promoter wants to maximise the gross potential by selling as many tickets as possible. Deciding the potential ticket sales will dictate the capacity needed for a suitable venue. Experience, and now data, should help guide the decision. Mistakes can be made. The venue may be half-empty if the promoter guesses high and rents a venue that holds twice as many people as eventually buy tickets, for instance. Likewise, a venue may sell out quickly after the tickets go on sale, leaving the promoter knowing she could have made more money by selling a greater number of tickets in a larger-capacity venue.

The promoter would probably try to move the event to another, larger-capacity venue on the same date in this case, but this is not always possible.

Suitable venues are in short supply in most major music markets.[7] There has been much building in the large-capacity venue sector – arenas and stadiums – and smaller venues have closed in many cities.[8] Closures are due to many reasons and a cause for concern is of venues being forced to close because of building development (see *Music Venue Trust and the agent of change*). Such development either causes rents to increase beyond the financial means of the venue owners, or sees venues being bought up and demolished to make way for new apartments blocks and office complexes.

MUSIC VENUE TRUST AND THE AGENT OF CHANGE

Anyone studying or working in the live music industry should be aware of the Music Venue Trust (MVT) in the UK and its work to save venues from closure (Figure 4.4). MVT is part of the Music Venues Alliance (MVA), and the two work to help support and maintain small venues throughout the UK; their work serves as a blueprint for similar organisations in other countries.

The MVT works with grassroots music venues (GMVs) and argues that emerging talent would be restricted without GMVs giving these new artists their first chance at performing live. Much of the work of the MVT stems for the rapid closure of GMVs in the UK (35% have closed in the last ten years),[9] often for non-commercial reasons. The Music Venues Trust has scored some impressive changes to legislation and outlook regarding small venues and grass roots music in the UK. The most notable of these is the introduction of the "Agent of Change" principle into a UK government policy called the National Planning Policy Framework (NPPF). The principle says that new building developments must make sure they "can be integrated effectively with existing businesses and community facilities, such as places of worship, pubs, music venues, and sports clubs"[10] – residents of new buildings sited next to existing music venues cannot have the venue closed if they don't like the noise! This principle will not stop developers attempting to build near pubs and bars in the UK, but those venues under

Figure 4.4 The website of the Music Venue Trust showing an endorsement from Sir Paul McCartney

threat of closure now have a framework to fall back on in their defence, and the MVT works with local councils to make sure developers meet their obligations under the NPPF.

MVT also helped the Arts Council to research and launch a £1.5 million fund for GMVs in 2019 and encouraged live music companies, such as Live Nation, Ticketmaster, and AEG, to pledge support for the "Pipeline Investment Fund". This echoes work done in Germany, where the "Digitalisierung der Aufführungstechnik von Livemusikspielstätten in Deutschland" (Digitization of the Performance Technique in Live Music Venues) initiative was set up to equip all qualifying venues in Germany (<2000-cap and >24 live music shows a year) with standardised, upgraded, digital FoH and monitor consoles, digital lighting fixtures and desks, and DJ equipment. Four hundred venues qualified for the first round of upgrades, with some venues receiving as much as €10,000 for new equipment from a €1 million fund.[11]

PRODUCTION

You shall examine what is meant by the term "production" in *Part Two: Live Music Production* and how the term applies to the technical infrastructure of the venue – the sound, lighting, staging, access, and other facilities needed to stage a concert.

The venue's production should be suitable for the artist's performance, and the suitability is dictated by the genre. Singer/songwriters accompanied by an acoustic guitar will be performing in small-capacity rooms (<200-capacity) and require little in the way of sound and lighting equipment to be available in the venue, for instance. A singer/songwriter with an acoustic guitar can be seen and heard by the audience as long as she is sited on some kind of raised platform and the vocals are amplified. Vocal amplification at this level of concert is achieved with a simple self-powered (<300w RMS), two-speaker public address (PA) system, with the speakers mounted on tripod stands on either side of the performance area. This type of "vocal PA" is so-called as it is suitable for amplifying vocals only and would not have enough power to amplify bass guitars or the sub bass frequencies emitted by drum machines (Figure 4.5).

The lack of power to properly amplify bass frequencies in small venues is an issue for emerging artists and their promoters. Music production has evolved, and many artists create music using electronic sources – synthesisers, drum machines, and computer-based programs called soft synths – all of which emit full-range audio with an emphasis on bass frequencies. An artist looking to reproduce her music live will therefore need a venue PA capable of amplifying the full range of audio, including the bass frequencies; otherwise, the music will not make sense to the listener.[12] However, the promoter may have difficulty finding a venue with capacity relevant to an emerging artist – one that has a more-powerful PA than the standard associated with small venues.

Figure 4.5 The two speakers on stands in this image are typical of a "vocal" PA system. This system is suitable for <200-cap venues. Image by Dmyto Panchenko/Adobe

POPULARITY

Concert-going is an experience based on emotion (the fans like the artist), and those emotions extend to the audience's interaction with the venue (and promoter) before, during, and after, the event.

The location of the venue itself can be a factor in the success of show. Some venues are known for being difficult to reach – either by public transport or car, and this can affect the decision to buy a ticket for a concert. Similarly, the venue may be well-served by public transport, but that transport stops running at an inconvenient time for the concert-goer – they can get there but can't get home.

Other venues have a bad reputation based on concert-goers previous experiences or, thanks to social media, word-of-mouth. "Bad sound" and exorbitant prices for drinks, coat check, and car parking, are all popular reasons for fans to complain about a venue when, unless they are regular attendees at the venue, they are basing their views on the particular concert they paid to see. Audience members rarely appreciate the factors that cause sound problems or that hike prices, and one fan's experience at a concert may be the polar opposite to another fan's take on her night out, at the next concert, in the same venue.

The experienced promoter may not give these audience views much attention, but it would be unwise to promote a show by an emerging artist who cannot guarantee a significant draw into a venue that has a bad reputation with music fans.

TICKET PRICES

The promoter can control the ticket price, and this is an area of controversy within the live music business and amongst concert-goers.

The promoter will want to maximise the gross potential by selling the largest number of tickets at the highest price. The number of tickets that can be sold is dictated by the capacity of the venue, which must be suitable for the stature of the artist; thus, ticket prices are decided by anticipating the following factors:

- artist popularity
- history
- venue
- competition
- promoters' costs

ARTIST POPULARITY

The popularity of the artist is an obvious benchmark when deciding the price to charge for tickets. Usually, the more popular an artist, the more money the promoter can charge for concert tickets. This is not always the case, however. An emerging artist, although popular (perhaps as a YouTuber) may appeal to a young demographic which relies on parents to purchase tickets. The promoter must price the offer to appease the purchaser – that is, parents who can't see what all the fuss is about.

HISTORY

Does the artist have successful history of sold-out shows and tours? Have there been cancellations or no-shows in the past? These are some of the questions the promoter will be asking themselves to gauge the right ticket price. An artist with a history of shows that sold well should be able to command a similar or higher ticket price for their next run of shows. Promoters of shows by emerging artists (who have little or no touring history) will have to gauge ticket price based on other factors in this list.

VENUE

The choice of venue has a part to play in the perceived value of the concert tickets. Audience expectations of the concert setting have grown enormously thanks, in part, to promoters such as Live Nation, who have tried to elevate the fans experience at concerts to get repeat business.[13] Concert-goers no longer tolerate sticky carpets, smelly urinals, and flat, warm beer at shows.

Developers have been busy building new arenas (5000–20000-capacity) in many cities. New arenas are designed to host many activities – sports, family shows, etc. – and music is always the most popular format.[14] Certain venues are associated with certain genres of music, or types of events. Ensuring the audience feels comfortable with buying a ticket should take into account the suitability of the venue.

COMPETITION

Concert tickets cannot be discounted to create demand, as two separate concerts are not similar. A concert-goer faced with the choice of two events will not decide to attend one of the events just because the ticket is less expensive. The fan will respond to her tastes and preferences by choosing one concert or attending both.

PROMOTERS' COSTS

The promoter will incur costs – hiring the venue, paying an audio engineer, etc. – and she will want to make sure she makes enough money from ticket sales to cover those costs plus a profit. One major cost is the artist's performance fee. Promoter and artist must agree to keep costs (including the fee) low, or charge a higher ticket price to cover those increased costs. You shall look at promoters' costs in more detail in *Creating the Deals* later in this part.

TIME PERIODS

The concert promoter can only have an artist perform in concert if that artist is available. Although the days of artists being unavailable due to spending months recording in a studio are rare, artists may have other commitments that create touring "windows" – time periods when the artist can commit to performing live. These periods will be decided by the artist, the artist manager, and booking agent, and the promoter will be informed of the months that are allocated to touring.

The international live music business has a touring "season" – the period when most touring takes place. Most of the concert touring of the US and Europe takes place between April and September. Opportunities to tour outside of that period exist, and the promoter should be aware of the lull caused by holidays. The period between Thanksgiving (A US holiday on the fourth Thursday of November) and Christmas (another holiday period from late December to early January, associated with high spending on gifts and travel) is a poor time for concert touring, especially club shows that have a large "walk-up" (buying tickets on the day of the show) audience. Music fans have many financial and social obligations during this time and may not be inclined to attend a concert on a whim.

Concert tickets must be put on sale at a time that will maximise initial sales, and the role of the promoter is to work with the artist and management to decide when to announce a concert or tour. This activity is called the "on-sale" (or "going up") and the promoter should consider when fans are more likely to respond to the announcement of the tour or concert. Announcing between Thanksgiving and Christmas, for instance, would be a bad move for the reasons described above.

The standard practice for on-sales today is to make an announcement some three or four months in advance of the first date of the tour. The announcement will tell fans the cities and dates of the tour, and the date (usually a week later) when tickets go on sale. The on-sale date will usually be at the end of the week or month (both being paydays for workers), and strong sales on that day are an indicator that the show will sell out.

On-sale dates and festival "radius clauses" (see *"Identifying opportunities for live performance"* in Chapter 3) create tension for artists and promoters. An artist may be planning a tour following their performance at the Coachella festival (US), for instance. However, the radius clause from the Coachella organisers stipulates that, although the artist can sell hard tickets for their own shows, they are not allowed to "advertise, publicise, or leak"[15] details of the shows until after their performance at the festival. The ban on publicity would make it difficult to have a successful on-sale event, with a short lead time between the on-sale and the concerts. Fans may have other financial commitments in the short lead time and be unable to buy concert tickets.

Promoters and artists must anticipate the effect that radius clauses may have on their own tours and on-sale activity.

THE FINANCIAL OPPORTUNITY

"We do it for the love of the music, and unfortunately that does not pay the bills" is a common refrain amongst small venue owners and bookers. The sentiment may be based in truth and unfortunately economics dictate that a lower ticket price for a show in a small-capacity room is never going to make anyone rich.

There is money in concert promotion, though, and you have seen an example of it in Live Nation, a concert-promoting behemoth, who have been able to monetise other activities that take place when attending a concert, such as car-parking and food and beverage concessions.

Most western concert promoters operate in the range between Live Nation and the small, sub-150-capacity venues that make up the "grass roots". These middle strata of promoters do make money from concert promotion and sometimes must leave their musical taste out of the equation when looking at opportunities to stage a concert and still make money.

Still, the financial opportunity is there. A promoter staging a show in a 2500-capacity room at $25 a ticket looks to gross $62,500 for that one event. A proportion of this money will be paid to the artist, and some will be spent on the staging and marketing of the concert. The shrewd promoter will be able to make a profit of 2–5% of the gross of this type of concert. An established promoter, such as Goldenvoice (US) or CTS Eventim (European-wide) should be able to repeat this business many times per year, often many times per night, thus ensuring a healthy, sustainable business.

THE FINANCIAL RISK

The concert promoter takes a financial risk when agreeing to promote a show. The deals for concerts stipulate the artist must be paid the agreed performance fee (the "guarantee") even if the tickets do not sell. Unfortunately, the reasons for a show not selling out are varied.

LACK OF DEMAND

The artist, her management, booking agent, and the promoter, may misjudge the appeal of the artist. Fans then do not buy tickets and the promoter will lose money. An experienced promoter will avoid such situations by reviewing the opportunities list you saw earlier; it may be the case that a booking agent persuaded the promoter to take on a show, despite the promoters "gut instinct".

Another scenario may see the profit from adequate sales eaten away by high costs. The artist may insist on large-scale production elements for her show, with a deal stipulating the promoter paying most of the bill. The show may sell out, but the costs are great, leaving the promoter with a loss.

COMPETITION FROM OTHER EVENTS

Direct competition based on ticket price is unlikely. Competition from similar, mass-attendance events is more likely. Festival organisers have a full-time job trying to differentiate their offering from other open-air, green-field events taking place at the same time, for instance. Sporting events are also competitors and are hard to anticipate in progress-based sports such as football. Here the fixture dates are announced in advance and there is no indication of which teams will compete on the night. The national team getting to a competition final may be great for sports fans and can have consequences for the promoter of a concert on the same night, who cannot know if the team would reach that stage.

WEATHER

Abnormal weather conditions are common and concerts, especially outdoor festivals, are cancelled or postponed. Concert promoters may be insured which will mitigate their risk. The promoter may not have to pay the artist's performance fee and may already have sent a deposit (a percentage of the total performance fee) to the artists. The major loss in the event of a cancellation will be that of the marketing costs, which will be considerable.

Weather can also affect concerts at the club, theatre, and arena levels. Fans may be unable to attend due to snowstorms or floods. The fans are unlikely to be able to apply for a refund, and their non-attendance will have an impact on sales of food and beverage at the venue, and sales of artist-produced merchandise ("merch") – t-shirts and hoodies for example.

Re-arranging postponed events is expensive. Promoters may offer refunds to fans who cannot attend the alternative dates and the refunds are an expense for the promoter. The surplus of tickets now available for re-sale for the new date may not sell as the concert is now too far in the future, the "buzz" for the artist has gone, or there is competition from other events at that time.

TRANSPORT

Strikes by public transport staff cause similar problems to that of inclement weather. Strikes are often called at short notice, and fans are probably unlikely to be eligible for a refund if they cannot attend the concert. Transport disruption is more likely to effect bar and club venues (<1000-capacity) who rely on walk-up custom.

ILLNESS AND ACCIDENT

"The show must go on" does not seem to apply to the modern live music business. Concerts and tours are regularly postponed due to "illness", leaving both the promoter and the artist out of pocket. The shows may be rescheduled, but the associated costs can be considerable, as you saw earlier. Insurance taken out by both promoter and artist may mitigate some of the expense, but the payments from any policy will take months to arrive. The promoter and artist will have bills to pay in the meantime. In the meantime, the booking agent and promoter will organise the replacement date and will work out a deal that reflects the costs incurred by the promoter for the original date. One form of compensation (apart from the insurance cover pay out) is for the artist to take a lower performance fee or less of the ticket spilt for the new show.

INDUSTRY ISSUES AND CHALLENGES FOR PROMOTERS

The live music business may be buoyant at the moment – more people are paying higher ticket prices to see more shows. Concert promoters still face challenges, but unlike their recorded music colleagues, one of these challenges is not the threat of new technology. The threat is part of nature – ageing.

A 2019 report found that the average age of artists' responsible for the top ten concert grosses was 53 – and rising.[16] There is no doubt that heritage acts, such as The Rolling Stones, The Eagles, and Fleetwood Mac (British, American, and British, rock bands that formed in the 1960s), are a considerable concert draw. The personnel of those acts are all over 60, with some members now over 70 years old. Concert promoters (and fans) are faced with the fact that those bands will stop touring within the next five years, either through voluntary retirement, or death of key members.

The generation of artists following the heritage headliners are also dealing with nature. U2 (an Irish rock band), The Red Hot Chilli Peppers (a US funk-metal band), and Slipknot (a US alternative rock act), still have considerable ticket-selling potential but are also getting old. The band members may feel the need to cut down (or stop touring) in the next ten years, at the same time as their fan's attraction starts to fade. The topic of "finding the headliners of tomorrow" is always a feature of the live music business conferences held each year.

Bars, clubs, and grassroots venues (<500-capacity) continue to face uncertainty. You have looked at the threat from property development and the owners of small venues are increasingly hampered by their inability to grow with an artist. The owner/booker of a 250-capacity venue may encourage a local artist to perform all her shows in that venue and help grow that artist to the point where she can sell out that venue. However, it is at that point of success that the artist will need to move to larger, higher-capacity rooms, and the original owner/booker loses her business. A national promoter, such as Live Nation, is likely to make a move on the artist at this point, promoting subsequent shows by that artist in one of their own 700–1000 capacity venues. The owners of sub-700 capacity clubs and grassroots venues can never grow with the artist and are reliant on a steady supply of local and emerging talent to sell concert tickets. At the same time, the nature of music production, from groups of musicians and singer/songwriters, to artists employing electronics, means that grassroots venues are unsuitable for emerging talent. Bars and pubs don't have sound systems capable of reproducing the range of frequencies (read: bass below 80Hz) generated by modern music. There could be a time soon when grassroots venues simply don't appeal to either the talent or the live music fans.

SECONDARY TICKETING

Secondary ticketing, the reselling of concert, theatre, or sports tickets, is a problem for concert promoters. The resale market was worth €2.7 bn in 2019,[17] and the money made from the resale rarely makes its way back to the promoter or the artist. While many tickets are resold for legitimate reasons – the original buyer cannot now attend the concert, for instance – there is now an industry that encourages ticketing arbitrage. Online portals, such as StubHub, make the reselling of tickets easy, with the potential of big profits for the seller. This may have led to the use of robotic ticket-buying systems ("bots") and ticket-"sniping" software to buy large quantities of tickets for popular events and offer them on resale sites almost immediately after the tickets have gone on sale in the regular markets (see *The Hannah Montana incident*).

THE HANNAH MONTANA INCIDENT

A 2007 tour by Hannah Montana, an American singer-actress now known by her real name, Miley Cyrus, was the first to highlight the emerging secondary ticketing market. Fans (or rather the parents of the singer's young audience) were struck by the fact that although the tickets for the tour had just gone on sale, the performances were often sold out within minutes, and tickets were available for inflated prices on the secondary ticketing sites within minutes of the official "on-sale" time. How could this be?

Several concert tickets were always pre-allocated by promoters, as part of the deal struck with the artist and their booking agents. These pre-allocations usually honoured long-held arrangements with venues and brokers, and included:

- season ticket-holders
- ticket-buying clubs
- fan clubs

- venue holds
- production holds (seats or floor space that may be required for sound and lighting equipment on the night of)

These pre-allocated tickets are often the "best in the house" with proximity to the stage or good sight lines. They may not necessarily be issued and can, in fact, be sold to the general public, usually for a higher than face-value price.

Subsequent investigation into the Hannah Montana incident found that, yes, many of the tickets being offered for resale were originally pre-allocated tickets. That fact alone would not explain the scarcity of general access (GA) tickets. Investigations also uncovered the use of sniping software and automated bots. To work at scale and make serious money, brokers use bots or sniping software. The capabilities of such software enabled ticket touts to make tens of thousands of ticket request per day, which could then be resold on secondary sites. (Ticketmaster reported that on some days 80% of its ticket requests were generated by bots.[18]) After the Hannah Montana debacle, a variety of legal actions and technological advancements have attempted to solve the problem of ticket-sniping. For instance, Ticketmaster sued RMG Technologies (RMG), a company that developed and marketed sniping software specifically aimed at Ticketmaster.[19]

Unfortunately, this pattern of scarcity for face-value tickets and concurrent availability on secondary sites has not changed. The face value of tickets for the Hannah Montana tour of 2007 were $21 to $66 and were resold on StubHub for an average of $258, plus StubHub's 25% commission.[20] StubHub reported that ticket sales from reselling Hannah Montana tickets accounted for $10 million of its sales in 2007, the most for a single act in the company's history.[21] The premise is clear – reselling tickets can make someone other than the promoter and artist a lot of money.

INCREASED COSTS ASSOCIATED WITH HEALTH AND SAFETY.

The pandemic of 2020-21 has created extra costs for doing business in all areas, and that includes the live music business.

Promoters face reductions in saleable venue capacity to comply with social distancing regulations (venues operating at 10% capacity, for instance), and at the same time, extra costs for on-site testing, hygiene, sanitising, signage, and medical facilities.

NOTES

1 Waddell, R.D., Barnet, R., and Berry, J., 2007. *This Business of Concert Promotion and Touring*. Watson-Guptill, New York.
2 Live Nation Entertainment, Inc., (2020). *Live Nation Entertainment Annual Report 2019*. Beverly Hills. Live Nation Entertainment, Inc.
3 Ibid.
4 Ibid.

5   Securities Exchange Commission, n.d. "Exhibit 21.1Subsidiaries of Live Nation Entertainment, Inc" [WWW Document]. URL https://www.sec.gov/Archives/edgar/data/1335258/0001335 25819000024/lyv-20181231xex211.htm (accessed 1.5.21).

6   Ibid.

7   Weiszfeld, D., 2019. "Insiders EP04: Interview with Tom Windish on the Live Industry | Soundcharts Blog" [WWW Document], *Soundcharts*. URL https://soundcharts.com/blog/tom -windish-interview (accessed 1.24.20).

8   Hann, M., 2019. "Live venues are the lifeblood of the music industry".[WWW Document] URL https://www.ft.com/content/dbb098ea-4be1-11e9-bde6-79eaea5acb64 (accessed 23/03/2019)

9   Ibid., 2.

10 "National planning policy framework" [WWW Document], n.d. GOV.UK. URL https://www .gov.uk/government/publications/national-planning-policy-framework--2 (accessed 9.5.19).

11 POP RLP, 2019. "Digitalisierung der Aufführungstechnik von Livemusikspielstätten in Deutschland", [WWW Document]. URL https://translate.google.com/translate?hl=en&sl=de &u=https://pop-rlp.de/news/2019/programm-zur-digitalisierung-der-musikclubs-geht-die-dri tte-foerderrunde&prev=search (accessed 9.4.19).

12 Small self-powered speakers cannot reproduce bass frequencies, especially sub-bass frequencies below 80Hz. Listen to the track 'LFO' by the UK artist LFO on laptop speakers and then on a large hi-fi or concert sound system to see how the lack of sub-bass affects the perception of music. You will notice the bass line motif in 'LFO' disappears when the track is played on laptop speakers. Unfortunately, the sub-bass in that track is the main part!

13 Live Nation Entertainment, Inc., (2020). *Live Nation Entertainment Annual Report 2019*. Beverly Hills. Live Nation Entertainment, Inc

14 The tables in European national Arena Yearbook show music dominates the charts of tickets sold, and revenue per event. National Arenas Association, 2017. *European Arena Yearbook 2017 (Yearbook)*. ILMC, London.

15 Grace, A., 2019. "Coachella radius clause lawsuit dismissed", *IQ Magazine*. URL https://www.iq-mag.net/2019/03/coachella-radius-lawsuit-dismissed/ (accessed 1.29.20).

16 Ingham, T., 2019. "The average age of the world's biggest live artists is 53 -- and rising", *Rolling Stone*. URL https://www.rollingstone.com/pro/features/average-age-biggest-live-artists-53-ri sing-863337/ (accessed 1.5.21).

17 Music Week,2021. "FEAT issues guide for tackling Europe-wide ticket touting" [WWW Document], *Music Week*. URL https://www.musicweek.com/live/read/feat-issues-guide-for-ta ckling-europe-wide-ticket-touting/082400 (accessed 1.22.21).

18 New York Attorney General, 2017. *Obstructed View – What's Blocking New Yorkers from Getting Tickets?* New York Attorney General, New York.

19 Queue-it, 2020. "Ticket bots: Everything you need to know", [WWW Document], *Queue-it*. URL https://queue-it.com/blog/ticket-bots/ (accessed 1.6.21).

20 Loewenstein, A., 2010. "Ticket sniping", *Telecommunications & High Technology Law*, volume 8. Page 5-13

21 Ibid.

5

CHAPTER 5
CREATING THE DEALS

CHAPTER OUTLINE

You have now seen the work of the artist manager, the booking agent, and the concert promoter. These participants work together to organise concert and festival appearances for artists. There is a financial motivation in creating these events, the terms of which are laid out in a "deal". The form of the deal will vary depending on factors including the perceived appeal of the artist, the type of venue, whether the artist is headlining or performing in a support slot, and so on. At a basic level, the deal centres around four factors: the gross potential of the concert, the ticket price, the promoter's costs, and the profit-share between artist and promoter (Figure 5.1).

DOI: 10.4324/9781003019503-6

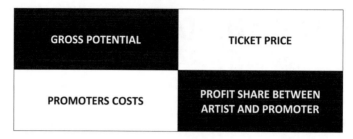

GROSS POTENTIAL	TICKET PRICE
PROMOTERS COSTS	PROFIT SHARE BETWEEN ARTIST AND PROMOTER

Figure 5.1 The four factors that determine the deal

100 PEOPLE IN A BAR

A simplistic explanation of concert deals is "100 people in a bar". In this scenario, a bar owner has invited a local band to perform a show at her bar. The bar holds 100 people legally (the capacity), and the owner is going to charge $1 a ticket. The gross potential of the show is therefore $100 (capacity x ticket price).

DOOR SPLIT/BACK-END DEAL

The simplest deal is the door split, or "back-end deal". General admission (GA) tickets are sold for the show, and the revenue from those ticket sales is added up at the end of the night. This amount is the "box office receipts" (BOR). The promoter (bar owner in this case) deducts her expenses to give the net box office receipts (NBOR), and the remaining money is split between the band and the promoter (Table 5.1).

The split of profits is usually 80/20 in favour of the artist. Promoters' expenses (costs) are agreed to beforehand to make sure the artist receives all the money they are due.

THE GUARANTEE DEAL

The owner in our example wants to offer the band a flat fee for their show in her bar. She will work out a deal based on the gross potential minus her costs for putting on the

Table 5.1 The promoter deducts her expenses before splitting the profits with the artist to give a straight "door split/back-end" deal

VENUE CAPACITY	100
TICKET PRICE	$1
BOX OFFICE RECEIPTS (BOR)	**$100**
PROMOTERS EXPENSES	$40
NET BOX OFFICE RECEIPTS (NBOR)	**$60**
ARTIST SHARE (80% OF NBOR)	**$48**
PROMOTER SHARE (20% OF NBOR)	£12

show (she excludes sales from food, beverage, and coat check from the calculations) and pay the band a guaranteed amount from the potential profit. Common costs for promoters are venue rental/operation, wages for venue sound and lighting technicians, ticket printing, and marketing. You shall examine the promoter's costs in detail later in this part. The gross potential minus the promoter's costs will show a potential profit which can then be split between the owner and the band. The gross potential is hypothetical as no one knows how many tickets will eventually be sold. However, the costs can be calculated accurately based on the owners' experience of putting on other shows in the past (see Table 5.2).

The bar owner calculates the potential profit as being $45.00 ($100.00 gross potential minus $55.00 anticipated costs) and offers the band $20.00 for their performance. She offers this, stating that the amount will be paid, regardless of how many tickets are sold on the night of. The band are obviously dismayed at this offer, as they envisaged the gross potential of $100.00. They demand at least 80% of the profit as in a door split deal ($36.00). The bar owner counters their objections by explaining that it is unlikely the band will sell 100 tickets. Ticket sales could be as low as 50, which would leave no profit and therefore no payment to the band (see Table 5.3). The bar owner insists that the $20 guarantee is the best deal for the band, and they should take it.

The deal in Table 5.2, a flat guarantee deal, is common for hard-ticket concerts. The booking agent and promoter will negotiate a guaranteed performance fee for the artist based on the gross potential, the ticket price, and the promoters anticipated costs. The promoter will be keen to keep costs as low as possible to make sure there is still profit if tickets do not sell well. The artist's contract rider is a cost to the promoter, and we shall discuss the impact of riders on show deals later in this part. The booking agent

Table 5.2 The promoter will have costs, examples of which are shown here

VENUE CAPACITY	100
TICKET PRICE	$1
GROSS POTENTIAL	**$100**
VENUE HIRE (MANAGER, BAR STAFF, CLEANER ETC)	$20
TICKET PRINT	$5
POSTERS AND FLYERS,	$10
SECURITY PEOPLE	$10
SOUND ENGINEER	$10
PROMOTERS COSTS	*$55*
NET POTENTIAL (GP-PROMOTERS COSTS)	$45
OFFER TO ARTIST ("GUARANTEE" or "FEE")	**$20**

Table 5.3 The artist might not sell all 100 tickets. In this case they only sell 50, resulting in a loss for the promoter

ACTUAL SALES	50
TICKET PRICE	$1
BOX OFFICE RECEIPTS	**$50**
VENUE HIRE (MANAGER, BAR STAFF, CLEANER ETC)	$20
TICKET PRINT	$5
POSTERS AND FLYERS,	$10
SECURITY PEOPLE	$10
SOUND ENGINEER	$10
PROMOTERS COSTS	$55
PROMOTER LOSES	-$5

will be looking to get the highest guaranteed fee they can without causing the promoter to go broke.

The deal for a hard-ticket concert is negotiated with the promoter making an offer to the booking agent of the artist. The offer should present the guarantee, along with a breakdown of the anticipated costs, and a proposed ticket price. The artist may have some preference regarding the ticket price – keeping prices affordable is a concern for many artists – and the promoter will have to work within those stipulations. The promoter will also want to know what she can expect in terms of production costs – supplying sound and lighting equipment to the artist specifications – to accurately predict her costs. Information about these specifications, and other stipulations from the artist, should be found in the artist's contract rider, and this may not be available at the time of the negotiations for the show.

RIDER COSTS

The bar owner in the "100 people in a bar" example may receive stipulations in the form of a contract rider for the show she is organising (you will examine the contract rider later in this part). These stipulations are a cost to her, so she includes them in her calculations. Unfortunately, the show cannot make a profit, even on a sell-out (all tickets are sold), with these additional costs. The owner can either refuse to honour the requests in the rider or raise the ticket price. Table 5.4 shows the impact of the rider costs and adding an opening act on the initial deal. Table 5.5 shows how raising the ticket price to $2 affects the gross potential. This increased gross potential will allow the owner to offer a new deal that will cover her costs. She will not offer all of the potential profit as a guarantee in case the show does not sell out. A fee offer to the artist of $80 would be appropriate in this case.

Table 5.4 The promoter will lose money when she supplies all the items listed in the artist's rider

VENUE CAPACITY	100
TICKET PRICE	$1
GROSS POTENTIAL	**$100**
VENUE HIRE (MANAGER, BAR STAFF, CLEANER ETC)	$20
TICKET PRINT	$5
POSTERS AND FLYERS,	$10
SECURITY PEOPLE	$10
SOUND ENGINEER	$10
OPENING BAND 1	$10
CATERING	**$15**
PROMOTERS COSTS	*$80*
NET POTENTIAL	$20
OFFER TO ARTIST ("GUARANTEE" or "FEE")	**$20**

Table 5.5 The promoter can break even, and supply all the items specified in the artist rider, by raising the ticket price. She will be able to raise the fee offer to $70 and still have some protection if the show does not sell out

VENUE CAPACITY	100
TICKET PRICE	**$2**
GROSS POTENTIAL	**$200**
VENUE HIRE (MANAGER, BAR STAFF, CLEANER ETC)	$20
TICKET PRINT	$5
POSTERS AND FLYERS,	$10
SECURITY PEOPLE	$10
SOUND ENGINEER	$10
OPENING BAND 1	$10
CATERING	$15
PROMOTERS COSTS	*$70*
NET POTENTIAL	$120
OFFER TO ARTIST ("GUARANTEE" or "FEE")	**$70**

SOFT-TICKET SHOWS

Guaranteed or flat fees are also paid for "soft-ticket" shows, such as open-air festivals and college events. Admission to these types of events is discounted or free (in the case of college shows) or includes many artists, in the case of festivals. DJs are also paid flat fees for nightclub and festival performances.

The amount of the guarantees for these types of events is negotiated based on the attraction of the artist and the tenacity of the booking agent.

THE GUARANTEE VERSUS PERCENTAGE DEAL

The guarantee versus percentage deal ("versus deal") allows for the artist to receive the guarantee, or instead share in the increased profits if the show sells out. Look again at figure 5.5. A sell out show based on this new ticket price would leave a potential profit of $120.00. The bar owner has offered $70 as a guarantee to the band, leaving her with $50.00 in profit – almost as much as the band. The band therefore ask for a "versus deal" of $70.00 vs 80% of net box office receipts (NBOR). This guarantee versus percentage deal states that the band will receive the guarantee of $70, or 80% of the profits, (after the promoters' costs have been deducted), whichever is the greater amount.

The payment of the percentage amount as opposed to the guarantee is triggered when ticket sales are greater than the sum of the costs and the guarantee. Reaching this point is called "breaking percentage" or "overage". Table 5.6 shows the calculations if the show in the bar sold 95 tickets on the night. The guarantee is less than 80% of the resulting NBOR and so the artist walks away with $88.00 (80% of $110.00)

Versus deals allow promoters to make offers to artists who may not have a stellar ticket-selling history or who are looking to move up in venue capacity. There might be uncertainty about how many tickets the artist will sell. The promoter can make a "versus deal" with a low guarantee offer to the artist. The guarantee may be based on potential ticket sales of three-quarters or half of the gross potential. The promoter will still cover her costs and be able to pay the guarantee to the artist, in the event ticket sales are actually that low. The artist will receive a greater amount on the versus deal if the show does then sell out.

THE GUARANTEE PLUS BONUS DEAL

The guarantee plus bonus deal sees the artist being offered a low guaranteed fee, with bonus payments being made at certain ticket sales points. For instance, bonus payments could be triggered for a deal at a 1000-cap venue when 500 tickets are sold, then 600, then 700, and so on. The final bonus level should be at the full-capacity level – 1000 tickets in this case.

Table 5.6 The calculations for "guarantee vs percentage" deal, in this case the guarantee
of $70 vs 80% NBOR. The artist "broke percentage" and so walked away with
the 80% of the NBOR – $88.00 in this case

ACTUAL SALES	95	
TICKET PRICE	**$2**	
BOX OFFICE RECEIPTS	**$190**	
VENUE HIRE (MANAGER, BAR STAFF, CLEANER ETC)	$20	
TICKET PRINT	$5	
POSTERS AND FLYERS,	$10	
SECURITY PEOPLE	$10	
SOUND ENGINEER	$10	
OPENING BAND 1	$10	
CATERING	$15	
PROMOTERS COSTS	*$80*	
NET BOX OFFICE RECEIPTS	$110	
OFFER TO ARTIST	$70	VS 80% NBOR
AMOUNT PAID TO ARTIST ON NIGHT	**$88**	

CROSS-COLLATERALISED DEALS

Cross-collateralisation of deals takes place if a single promoter stages multiple dates by the same artist. The deal offered may be for one guarantee for all the performances. Table 5.7 shows how a cross-collateralised tour may work. The concert in venue C has high costs and is unlikely to sell out. The promoter would lose money if the deal for this concert was arranged as a standalone deal. However, by cross-collaterising the guarantees, the promoter can spread their costs across the multiple dates and mitigate the loss incurred from a poor-selling concert. Conversely, the artist does not benefit from "breaking percentage" on high ticket sales and may be offered slightly lower guarantees than for the equivalent standalone concert. The artist will benefit from a co-ordinated marketing and promotion effort for the tour.

THE PROMOTER'S COSTS

The deal negotiated between the booking agent and the promoter will allow for the promoter to deduct or claim back certain expenses (costs) from the final ticket sales. Some of these costs form part of the promoter's offer to the artist; others are the costs of staging the show and are presented along with the offer to the booking agent. The following is a list of the most common expenses for a promoter and apply to hard-ticket and soft-ticket shows in varying degrees of importance.

Table 5.7 A cross-collateralised deal for three concerts

STAND ALONE DEAL	VENUE A	VENUE B	VENUE C
TICKETS	$10	$10	$10
CAPACITY	100	200	100
GROSS POTENTIAL	$1,000	$2,000	$1,000
COSTS	$400	$900	$500
NET POTENTIAL	$600	$1,100	$500
GUARANTEE	**$400**	**$750**	**$350**

Total promoters' costs (guarantee + expenses)   *$3,300*

CROSS-COLLATERALISED DEAL	VENUE A	VENUE B	VENUE C
TICKETS	$10	$10	$10
CAPACITY	100	200	100
GROSS POTENTIAL	$1,000	$2,000	$1,000
COSTS	$400	$900	$500
NET POTENTIAL	$600	$1,100	$500
GUARANTEE	**$500**	**$500**	**$500**

Total promoters' costs (guarantee + expenses)   *$3,300*

PA, LIGHTS, AND CATERING

"PA, lights, and catering" (or sound, lights, and catering – SLC) is a contract term. The promoter agrees to supply, at her own cost, sound and lighting equipment to the artist's specification (although this is rarely the case, as we shall discuss in *The Contract Rider* later in this part). "Catering" refers to food and drink the promoter also agrees to supply, again at her sole cost. Stipulations for sound and lighting equipment, as well as the food and beverages required, will be detailed in the artist's rider. Most deals include this clause.

VENUE HIRE

The promoter may need to hire a venue to stage the concert. Promoters such as Live Nation (US) own venues and may be holding the concert in a venue they operate. The deal will therefore not stipulate venue hire (as the promoter owns the venue) but some day-to-day operational cost will be set out as a cost.

PROMOTER'S REP

The promoter's "rep" (representative) is the person employed by the promoter to be present in the venue on the day of the concert. The rep acts as a liaison between the incoming touring party, the venue, and the concert promoter themselves. The major concert promoters, such as AEG (US), employ reps on a freelance basis; the cost of employing them for the night is included as an expense.

SECURITY STAFF AND EQUIPMENT

The cost for hiring the venue may include the provision of security personnel, or the promoter may have to hire them independently. Door staff and stewards are not permanent members of staff and are hired to work on a casual basis concert-by-concert. Local or national regulations may dictate the number and positioning of security and stewarding personnel for a concert and increased numbers of staff are an added expense for the promoter. Stewards are posted to undertake the following activities:

- prevent vandalism and theft of artist's equipment and transport
- restrict access to artist dressing rooms, backstage production offices, load-in areas, and artist transport parking lots
- prevent theft from merchandise stalls (stock and money)
- assist with crowd direction and flow

Genres like hip hop and grime have a reputation for violence involving guns and knives. The promoter may feel the need, or be required as part of a licence, to install temporary security equipment such as walk-through or hand-held metal detectors. Particularly contentious events may also see the need for uniformed police officers. The police charge their services to concert promoters, and the resulting bill can erode potential profit.[1]

Likewise, emergency medical technicians (EMT) may be required to have a presence at the event and will charge accordingly.

Installing a barrier between the audience and the stage is common practice in clubs. The barrier is not intended to stop audience members getting on stage during a show (although that is a bonus); rather it is designed with safety in mind. The barrier should be able to alleviate injuries caused by crushing if an audience surges forward. A venue may have a purchased a barrier, and would charge the promoter a fee for its use; or the promoter will have to source and rent a suitable barrier if none is available in the venue.

STAGE HANDS

An artist touring with rented sound and lighting equipment in trucks will require stage hands (also called "local crew") to help unload, set up, dismantle, and load out the equipment (Figure 5.2). Stage hands are hired locally in each city on the tour route. The crew are hired for a duration called a "call", which may be two, four, or six hours long each. The concert day will start with a call for the load-in and end with another call for the load-out. Stage hands work in pairs, and a call for a 10,000-capacity arena show would involve 20 stage hands.

Figure 5.2 Stage hands ("local crew") are hired for the duration of the concert to assist with unloading, assembly, tear-down, and loading of the visiting production's equipment. Image courtesy of the author

TICKETING

The concert promoter needs a mechanism to sell tickets – either physical paper tickets or electronic vouchers and codes that admit entry. Physical tickets need to be printed and distributed and or electronic ticketing services need to be initiated. Both ticket types need to have robust numbering, sales monitoring, and distribution mechanisms.

Ticketing companies such as Ticketmaster (part of Live Nation Entertainment), and See Tickets (UK) offer full service to event organisers. They make money by adding a small charge for printing and distributing the tickets – this charge is added to the price the fan pays for her ticket.

Promoters may have to pay a "box office commission" to venues that offer their own ticketing system (although this is rare). The small charge on each ticket helps to pay for the real, live human beings who sit in the box offices, selling tickets.

DYNAMIC PRICING

Concert promoters have recently become vocal about the price of concert tickets – saying they are too low.[2] However, the perception of value makes automatic raising of prices difficult. The average ticket price was $91 in 2019 – these tickets were for the Top 100 tours as defined by Pollstar, an industry trade magazine.[3] Concerts at that level can offer exceptional value for money, combining the music the fans love with eye-popping audio-visual content, dancers, and set pieces. Charging more for this level of experience may not stop fans from putting their hands in their pocket to pay for more expensive tickets. But what of concerts at >500–<5000-cap venues? Would fans be deterred by higher prices?

Concert promoters have experimented with dynamic pricing to answer this question. The price of concert tickets is set by computers and fall or rise based on demand, similar to that in the airline and hotel industries. Taylor Swift (a US singer/songwriter) used dynamic pricing for her "Reputation" world tour in 2017.[4] Although criticised for confusing fans, dynamic pricing paid off, with the tour grossing $345.7 million and breaking the record for the highest-grossing concert tour in the US.[5] This despite poor early sales.

Again, this pricing may be accepted at >10,000-cap venues but may not work in smaller capacity rooms. Fans are often penalised for buying early (when prices are high) at any venue capacity level. An alternative may be more pricing tiers for concerts, where the best seats or spaces closest to the performance area are priced accordingly. This practice is common, and a wider range of pricing is seen as one way of increasing the value of concert tickets. "Catching the top end allows you to subsidise the bottom end", says Michael Rapino, the CEO of Live Nation Entertainment.[6]

MARKETING AND ADVERTISING

Marketing the performance (including the advertising) will be a cost to the promoter. The accepted industry figure for concert advertising is 3–5% of the gross potential. The promoter must decide on a budget for marketing and advertising and the hope the show sells out quickly, thus minimising the need to spend the full budgeted amount. We look at marketing, advertising, and promotion later in this part.

PERFORMING RIGHTS ORGANISATIONS PAYMENTS

Performing rights organisations (PROs) such as PRS (UK), ASCAP (US), and GEMA (Germany) exist to protect the rights of their songwriter and composer members. The organisations, amongst other activities, collect a fee on behalf of their members whenever a composition by that member is performed live. The fee is deducted from the gross box office receipts (GBOR) and is usually deducted by the promoter and passed onto to the PROs. Collecting the license fee on a song-by-song, concert-by-concert, basis would be a bureaucratic nightmare so instead the promoter agrees to deduct and forward a percentage of the GBOR for each concert. The PROs then distribute this income amongst its members proportionally. The percentage of the PRO's levy varies and is currently 4% of GBOR in the UK for contemporary live music, for instance.[7]

INSURANCE

Two types of insurance are applicable to concert promoters – cancellation and public liability.

CANCELLATION INSURANCE

A concert can be postponed or cancelled for several reasons, as you saw in "The financial risk" earlier. Postponing a concert to a later date still has a cost – refunding the ticket price to fans who cannot make the new date can run into thousands of the local currency. The promoter should be insured against such an eventuality.

PUBLIC LIABILITY INSURANCE

Public liability insurance (PLI) covers the promoter in the event of distress, injury, or death to a member of the public or staff during the concert. PLI should also cover the build and tear down of any event, especially one involving a temporary space, such as an open-air, green-field festival.

TRANSPORT

Overseas festival shows are not accessible by the road transport commonly used by artists, so the band and crew must fly to these shows. DJs also fly a great deal as their itinerary is far more spread out than that of a touring act with equipment. "Fly dates", as they are known, form a large part of a touring artist's schedule, especially during the summer festival season. The cost of the airfare may be borne by the promoter as part of the deal made with the booking agent. Air fare is commonly included in deals for DJs, for instance.

The promoter may also be required to provide transport to and from the airport to the club or festival. Ground transport ("grounds") is a regular expense for promoters of festivals and involves the renting of multi-seat passenger vans (with trailers for luggage and equipment) plus reliable, sober, drivers for the duration of the event.

ACCOMMODATION

Promoters may also be obliged to provide accommodation for the artists they book. Deals for DJs include accommodation plus airfare and "grounds". A promoter will make deals with local hotels in order to minimise this cost.

WELFARE

The organisers of concerts and events are morally obliged to look after the welfare of their customers and anyone who may be impacted by the concert – local residents for instance. Some countries now enforce that obligation as part of granting permission for the concert or event to go ahead. Local licensing requirements may stipulate the installation of urinals at public transport stops nearest to the venue to prevent fans urinating in the gardens of residents for instance. Welfare infrastructure such as this is expensive and will erode potential profits.

SUPPORT ACTS

Convention dictates there will be opening, or "support", acts on the concert bill. The additional value this creates is open to debate and one thing is certain – opening acts are another expense for the promoter. The "band as a cost" explains why artists opening up in arenas (10,000–20,000-capacity) are still only paid $50–$500 for their performance. Unfortunately for the act, the promoter sees them as just another bill that needs to be paid, and looks to get away with as little cost as possible.

GUEST LIST

The guest list refers to the provision of free, or reduced-price, tickets given to friends, family and other guests of the artist, promoter, or booking agent. The names of each guest are compiled on a list (hence the name) and the named people are allowed cut-price, or free, entry.

The guest list is not a direct cost for the promoter, and each ticket that is given away eats into the GBOR. Unfortunately for promoters, most deals stipulate those artists receive ten, sometimes twenty, guest list tickets. A significant loss of revenue for the promoter if the tickets are $50.00 each!

FINANCIAL WASTE

Concert promoters work on small profit margins. Profitability on performances in sub-5,000-capacity venues is difficult – the promoter cannot sell enough tickets at a price the market deems fair to be able to offset the costs involved. Having said that, the live music business can be accused of financial waste. It would appear that not every penny is counted, and concert promoters and artists alike could make more money from each performance.

Items supplied in contract riders are a prime example of financial waste (see *The Contract Rider* later in this section). Promoters spend too much money on the supplying items in a rider, often simply allocating a set amount of money in their budget for a show. A successful national promoter will be receiving riders from different artists on a regular basis – there is little time to calculate the actual cost of the food and drink each artist is demanding. Instead, the promoter will use her experience and skill to set a fixed amount to spend on satisfying the demands of the rider.

Allocating money in this way is all well and good, but what if the artist's rider does not contain so many items to add up to the budgeted amount in the promoter's proposed costs? The rider total would still be added to the costs for the show and affect the bottom line.

TOWELS

Towels play a big part in live music production. Artist riders ask for towels for showering before load-in, for use in the dressing room areas, for use on-stage, and for showering after the show and after load-out. Riders for performances at the large theatre and arena level stipulate the need for 100 or so towels per day. At the club level, a mid-level artist may still request 20-odd towels throughout the day. The promoter is expected to provide these items, at her cost, if she agrees to them as part of her signing the artist's contract rider.

Financial waste lies in the costing of these items. A successful concert promoter will have stocks of these towels that can be washed and used again for subsequent shows. The

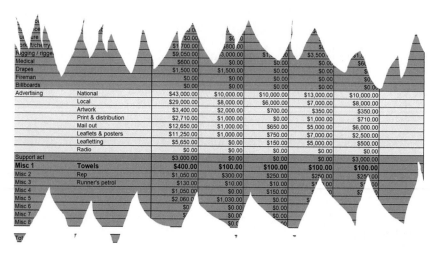

		$0.00	$0.00			
...ure						
...ork /t/cherry		$1,700.00	$800.00	$1,...	$3,500...	$1,...
Rigging / rigge...		$9,050.00	$3,000.00	$1,...	$3,500.	
Medical		$600.00	$0.00	$0.00	$0.00	$6...
Drapes		$1,500.00	$1,500.00	$0.00	$0.00	$
Fireman		$0.00	$0.00	$0.00	$0.00	$0...
Billboards		$0.00	$0.00	$0.00	$0.00	$0.0...
Advertising	National	$43,000.00	$10,000.00	$10,000.00	$13,000.00	$10,000.00
	Local	$29,000.00	$8,000.00	$6,000.00	$7,000.00	$8,000.00
	Artwork	$3,400.00	$2,000.00	$700.00	$350.00	$350.00
	Print & distribution	$2,710.00	$1,000.00	$0.00	$1,000.00	$710.00
	Mail out	$12,650.00	$1,000.00	$650.00	$5,000.00	$6,000.00
	Leaflets & posters	$11,250.00	$1,000.00	$750.00	$7,000.00	$2,500.00
	Leafletting	$5,650.00	$0.00	$150.00	$5,000.00	$500.00
	Radio	$0.00	$0.00	$0.00	$0.00	$0.00
Support act		$3,000.00	$0.00	$0.00	$0.00	$3,000.00
Misc 1	**Towels**	**$400.00**	**$100.00**	**$100.00**	**$100.00**	**$100.00**
Misc 2	Rep	$1,050.00	$300.00	$250.00	$250.00	$250.00
Misc 3	Runner's petrol	$130.00	$10.00	$10.00	$...00	$...00
Misc 4		$1,050.00	$0.00	$150.00		
Misc 5		$2,060.0	$1,030.00	$0.00		
Misc 6		$0	$0.00	$0.00		
Misc 7		$	$0.00	$0.00		
Misc 8			$0.0	...00		

Figure 5.3 The settlement sheet for a tour showing the promoter spent $400 on towels. Did they really?

cost to purchase and launder towels is negligible, yet concert promoters often inflate the cost of supplying towels. Figure 5.3 shows a cost of $400.00 for towels for a five–date tour of large theatres and arenas. A quick look on Google indicates four bath-sheets can be bought for $8.00 – the promoter can buy 200 bath-sheets for that $400.00!

SEAT KILL

"Seat kill" refers to the amount of space taken up by any production element in the audience area. For instance, front-of-house (FOH) audio and lighting control is set up on the floor in a venue (Figure 5.4). Audience members cannot stand in this space, so

Figure 5.4 A large area is used for the front-of-house (FOH) sound, lighting, and video control desks. This space contributes to "seat kill" – tickets that cannot be sold due to reduction in the licensed capacity. Image courtesy of the author

the amount of people who can legally be allowed to stand in the arena is reduced, thus "killing" the number of tickets that can be sold. Sight lines affected by speaker stacks and other production elements are also an example of seat kill. A promoter cannot sell tickets for seats with an obstructed view in this case.

The size and nature of production elements is one of the discussions the artist and promoter need to have when discussing deals for concerts of production venues. The artist may be envisaging an advanced production, with many elements that will block the view or take up lots of floor space in the auditorium. Such elements will result in significant seat kill which will in turn affect the gross potential. The promoter will therefore want an indication of the proposed seat kill – a FOH control area that potentially "kills" 50 tickets at $100 a ticket will be a source of great concern to a promoter.

LANDED DEALS

A landed deal indicates that the deal is "all in". Any extra costs, such as accommodation, are borne by the artist. Landed deals are common for festival performances and DJ gigs.

The artist may require the festival organiser to arrange accommodation, supply backline equipment, or rent in extra lighting for the sole use of the artist. A landed deal would see the promoter making such arrangements and deducting the resulting costs from the landed fee.

A typical, non-landed, deal for a DJ performing at a festival may be:

> *"$1000 plus PA, lights, and catering plus airfare, grounds, and accommodation".*

The promoter is agreeing to supply all the items, at their own expense, and the DJ will walk away with the $1000 (before paying her own income tax, of course). This type of deal is also called a "plus, plus, plus" deal.

A landed deal for the same show would be:

> *"$1000 plus PA, Lights, and catering, landed"*

The DJ will have to pay for her own plane ticket, pay for taxis to and from the show, and spend her own money on a hotel in this case. She may ask the promoter to organise the necessary arrangements, and the costs will be deducted from the $1000 fee.

THE DEAL MEMO

Negotiations for a show or festival slot may take place months before the date in question. Negotiated points will flow back and forth between the booking agent and the promoter and certain points may be specific to the individual agreement. Successful booking agents and concert promoters work on multiple shows at the same time and the details of individual shows may be lost or forgotten in a blizzard of emails. This is especially true in the negotiation stage for summer festivals. This work is done before the winter holiday break and the fine points can be confused when returning to work in January.

"Deal memos" are therefore a vital piece of documentation. The memo is exactly that – a simple outline of what has been agreed in principle between the booking agent and the promoter regarding the performance fee, stage time, number of guest tickets, production expenses, and so on. The deal memo is available for inspection after the initial negotiation and can be amended if further discussion takes place. The contract will be drawn up with reference to the deal memo when the time comes.

The full-service agencies such as CAA (US) and Paradigm (US) use computerised systems for the creation, storage, and retrieval, of deal memos. See back to Figure 3.3 for an example.

SETTLEMENT

"Settlement" (or "show settlement") is the activity that takes place during the evening of the concert. The activity relates to concerts with hard-ticket sales and is a term that encompasses any meeting to discusses the success (or otherwise) of a concert.

Settlement sees the promoter (or their representative), and a representative of the artist (usually the artist's tour manager) tallying the sold tickets and calculating any overage (percentage) due to the artist.

Concert deals are made two to nine months in advance of the concert itself.[8] A deal memo will be put together at the time the initial deal is made, and later a contract is issued (see *The Contract* later in this part). A deposit will be paid by the promoter (more on this later) and it is unlikely that the deal memo or contract would be reviewed until settlement on the evening of the concert.

The performance fee and any percentage deal will be stated on the contract, along with a figure indicating the agreed promoter's costs. The promoter will have prepared a report, usually in the form of a spreadsheet, that breaks down the actual costs, the number of tickets sold, guest list attendees etc., to show the artist exactly how much the show grossed, what expenses are liable for deduction, and whether the artist is due a percentage of the profit. Figure 5.5 shows a typical settlement statement.

REGIONAL AND SUB-PROMOTERS

The person who makes the deal and signs the contract is not always the same person who deals with the concert on the day of.

Let's use the example of a Farry Kisher, a UK artist, who is touring the Germany, Austria, Switzerland (GAS) territories. A German promoter, Konzert Fantastik, will

TKN CONCERTS
Office 212, Stanic Mill M3 4HB

SETTLEMENT

FARRY KISHER				
VENUE	**ORANGE TANG**			
DATE	**30/09**			
VENUE HIRE	£650.00		ADVANCE TICKET PRICE	£11.50
			ADVANCE TICKET SALES	520
P.R.S.	£149.50			
STAFF	£125.00			
			ADVANCE	**£5,980.00**
ARTWORK	£50.00		TOTAL TICKETS SOLD	**520**
ONLINE ADVERTISING	£100.00		GROSS	**£5,980.00**
POSTERS AND LEAFLETS PRINT	£55.00			
DISTRIBUTION	£132.00		NET	**£4,983.33**
NAT ADS	£100.00			
LISTING FLYERS	£50.00			
CATERING	£0.00			
RIDER	£86.76			
BOX OFFICE	INC		TOTAL COSTS	£1,635.79
EXTRA DRESSING ROOM RIDER	£37.53			
SUPPORT ARTIST(S)	£100.00		BALANCE	£3,347.54
			GUARANTEED FEE	**£2,000.00**
		80%	VERSUS 80%	£2,678.03
			% PAYMENT DUE	£678.03
			TOTAL NET PAYMENT	**£2,678.03**
		1	VAT (1=VAT, 0= no VAT)	£535.61
			GROSS PAYMENT	£3,213.64
			DEPOSIT	£1,200.00
	TOTAL COSTS	**£1,635.79**	**BALANCE DUE**	**£2,013.64**

Figure 5.5 A settlement statement. The deal was £2000 vs 80% of NBOR. The artist sold 520 tickets, thus "breaking percentage", and so walked out with an extra £678.00

make a deal with the Farry Kisher's booking agent, and arrange concerts in five German towns and cities:

Heidelberg
Stuttgart
Koln
Berlin
Munich

Taking the Heidelberg concert as a further example, Konzert Fantastik have in fact done a separate deal with a sub-promoter there who has organised a one-day festival in the Heidelberg town centre. Konzert Fantastik are operating as a talent scout and curator in association with the Heidelberg promoter, who in turn has rented a nightclub in the town to host the evening's performance of the one-day festival. Konzert Fantastik is the contract signatory, yet it is the local promoter and the venue who will be dealing with Farry Kisher and the other artists on the day. The local promoter is unlikely to have seen the contract rider or been party to the deal made between Konzert Fantastik and Farry Kisher's booking agent. The local promoter will have a deal with Konzert Fantastik and not with Farry Kisher. Konzer Fantastik will have made a similar arrangement with the venues and local promoters on the other four German dates.

Farry Kisher's concert tour manager (CTM) will want to advance the Heidelberg concert and will first reach out to Konzert Fantastik. Staff there will point the CTM to the local promoter, who will in turn point the CTM to the venue's operational management and technical team. These people will have no previous knowledge of the financial deal between Farry Kisher and the national promoter – simply how much money has been allocated to provide the requirements listed in the catering rider from the artist.

Sub-promoting concerts in this way are common practice, enabling national promoters to become involved early in an artist's career. The national promoter will make very little from the initial concerts they sub-promote, but they are then associated with that artist as national promoter in the future. Hopefully, the artist will grow their fan base the second time around, and the promoter will be able to book them into larger-capacity venues with increasing gross potential.

NOTES

1 Music Week, 2010. "Row erupts over police costs" [WWW Document], *Music Week*. URL https://www.musicweek.com/news/read/row-erupts-over-police-costs/042510 (accessed 1.5.21).
2 Bary, E., 2019. "Are concert tickets too cheap? Ticketmaster thinks so", [WWW Document], *MarketWatch*. URL https://www.marketwatch.com/story/are-concert-tickets-too-cheap-ticketmaster-thinks-so-2019-12-26 (accessed 2.4.21).
3 Shaw, L., 2019. "Concerts are more expensive than ever, and fans keep paying up" [WWW Document] URL https://www.bloomberg.com/news/articles/2019-09-10/concerts-are-more-expensive-than-ever-and-fans-keep-paying-up (accessed 2.5.20)
4 Knopper, S., 2018. "Taylor Swift's ticket strategy: brilliant business or slowing demand?", *Rolling Stone*. URL https://www.rollingstone.com/pro/news/taylor-swifts-ticket-strategy-brilliant-business-or-slowing-demand-630218/ (accessed 2.14.21).

5 Frankenberg, E., 2018. "Taylor Swift's reputation stadium tour breaks record for highest-grossing U.S. tour", [WWW Document], n.d. *Billboard*. URL https://www.billboard.com/articles/colum ns/chart-beat/8487606/taylor-swift-reputation-stadium-tour-breaks-record-highest-grossing-us -tour (accessed 2.14.21).

6 Cookson, R., 2016. "Live Nation calls for more aggressive ticket pricing from artists" [WWW Document] URL https://www.ft.com/content/d37c634c-e777-11e5-a09b-1f8b0d268c39 (accessed 2.5.20)

7 Live performance royalties, [WWW Document], n.d. URL https://www.prsformusic.com/royalti es/live-performance-royalties (accessed 1.5.21).

8 Live Nation Entertainment, Inc., (2020). *Live Nation Entertainment Annual Report 2019*. Beverly Hills. Live Nation Entertainment, Inc..

6

CHAPTER 6
THE CONTRACT

CHAPTER OUTLINE

You are urged to seek legal advice before entering into legal agreements. The subject of this chapter is for information only.

The concert contract is a written document relating to a specific show on a specific date. It sets out the terms that have been agreed between the artist (via her booking agent) and the promoter for that concert. Artists do not have a contract with a promoter for the lifetime of their relationship. The bar owner from the *Creating the Deals* chapter may issue a contract to the band in the example, and it would be for that one show. (See Appendix 1).

Contract law varies from country to country, and no examination of contracts here could include all the international variations. The US has considerable influence over the live music business and many contracts are issued by US-based companies. The language used in contracts is therefore US English, and many of the terms peculiar to US performance contracts have become worldwide standards. An example is the use of the term "producer" to indicate the artist or artist's production company, and "purchaser" to indicate the promoter. In any case, the contract should bind the two parties (artist and promoter) into an agreement to "produce" a concert and agree on a performance fee,

DOI: 10.4324/9781003019503-7

at the very least. Modern concert production requires consideration of many factors, so contracts for concerts include the following clauses and information:

- the parties in the agreement
- rider and addenda attached
- the venue
- date of the engagement
- billing
- services
- compensation
- details of deposits
- special provisions
- payment terms
- additional terms and conditions (in addendum)

THE PARTIES IN THE AGREEMENT

Any contract is a "written or spoken agreement intended to be legally binding",[1] so, we must declare the names of the parties involved. As discussed, a common description is that of the "producer" and "purchaser", with the addition of "artist", where necessary.

THE PRODUCER

The producer in a live performance contract is the entity that provides the services of the artist. An artist may have a company set up to deal with all her touring activity (Farry Kisher Touring, LLC for example). Invoices and payments are addressed to that company, and it is that company that is then "furnishing the services of" the artist to the promoter. The artist may not have a legal entity, and so the stage name, or the artist's individual birth names would be indicated as being the producer.

THE ARTIST

The stage name of the artist would be indicated as being "furnished" by the producer, as in "Farry Kisher Touring LLC (the PRODUCER) furnishing the services of "Farry Kisher" (the ARTIST)".

THE PURCHASER

The purchaser is the named person or organisation who is undertaking the activities named in the contract. The purchaser is the promoter ("Goldenvoice LTD"), the name of the venue ("Blah Blah Corp trading as The Venue"), or an individual ("Paul Romoter"). Open-air festivals and other large events often employ a third-party event producer who is responsible for booking the talent; that third-party would be named as the purchaser here, as they are responsible for securing and paying the artists.

Performance contracts are drawn up and issued by the booking agent and the agent; the agency is not named in the contract. The booking agent acts as "broker", facilitating the deal and with no legal responsibility in the event of dispute. The contract may go on to explain the role of the agent in a separate section, stating that they assume no liability and cannot be named as a party in any "civil action or suit" that may arise relating to the concert in the future.

"RIDER AND ADDENDA ATTACHED ..."

You shall look at contract riders in more detail later on, and you already know that complying with the stipulations in an artist rider is a cost for the promoter. The rider should therefore be available to the promoter when the deal is being negotiated, as this will give her a picture of the artist's requirements and the resulting expenses.

The reality is that artist riders are constantly evolving throughout the touring lifetime of the artist. New stipulations may be added to reflect changing elements in the show; personnel may be added (dancers and backing vocalists, etc.); or catering tastes may change. The artist may be performing in different formats according to the nature of the booking – concert hall, DJ slot, open-air festival appearance, and these changes in format have different production and personnel requirements, thus necessitating a different rider. It is common for a busy touring artist to have three riders in circulation – one for their own headline shows in clubs, theatres, and arena; one for open-air, green-field festival slots; and another for promotional events or other soft-ticket shows, such as corporate event concerts. Not only are there several riders, but those riders also need to be updated for the reasons above.

Back to our promoter. Having a copy of the relevant rider is vital when making an offer on a show – the promoter must know the anticipated costs for complying with the stipulations in the rider. This may be difficult as riders are being updated. The promoter may have made an offer based on what she saw in a rider three months ago. She now receives a contract for that concert (the offer was agreed) with the heading:

"ARTIST RIDER AND ADDENDA ATTACHED HERETO HEREBY MADE A PART OF THIS CONTRACT".

The wording states that any rider attached is part of the contract; the promoter agrees to comply with the stipulations contained in the (probably updated and expanded) rider when she signs on the bottom line. Who knows what extra expenses are now detailed in the attached rider?

THE VENUE

The name and address of the venue is indicated in this section. A separate entry may indicate the load-in address (if different from the street address of the venue). The load-in for a venue may be at the rear of the venue which technically may be for a different street, for instance.

Festival addresses would include the name of the stage or tent where the artist will perform, as well as the street address of the festival. Including a street address for a large capacity (>50,000 per day) is probably pointless. For instance, the street address for Glastonbury festival (UK) is a farm in a village called Pilton which, although technically the heart of the festival, is impossible to navigate to during the days that the event takes place. An "artist gate", "production entrance", or stage, would instead be indicated on the contract (see Figure 6.1).

THE DATE OF THE ENGAGEMENT

A performance contract is specific to a particular concert on a particular date. That date is indicated in this section. The contract may be for a series of concerts, especially in the case of cross-collateralised deals, and the dates and venues of all the concerts in the deal would be listed here.

The schedule of the day will also be listed here. Times for equipment load-in, soundcheck, stage times, and curfew, although listed here, are usually stated as a guide and are subject to change. The exception for this would be billing on festivals where the booking agent will have negotiated long and hard to get the right slot for their artist. The time periods of these slots are decided by the promoter/organiser of the festival in the very early stages of planning – the promoters work out the slots to plan how much talent they will need for each day of the festival. Promoters can then offer slots to the booking agents and certain slots on certain stages become more attractive than others. Once an agent has secured a favourable slot for her artist, it is important that position on the festival bill is confirmed by the promoter – the wording on the contract is that confirmation. Wording such as "line-up, set lengths, and performance times to be approved in writing by [agent name]" may be inserted after any schedule information to prevent promoters changing a festival slot after the fact.

BILLING

Billing refers to the position the artist will have on the "bill" – the order of artist performing on the day. The headliner is the top of the bill, the main attraction who usually closes the show. There may be a co-headliner in certain situations. Opening or support positions would be indicated for an artist who is performing lower on the bill, along with a number to indicate their position. The numbering is in reverse of the position on

MAJOR FLAIR INTERNATIONAL

An agreement, number **12345-987**, dated: **Monday, 16 November**

Between **PAUL ROMOTER** on behalf of **TKN CONCERTS** (the Promoter) and **NOTMANY LTD PP FARRY KISHER LIVE SET** (the Artist)

Whereby the Promoter engages the Artist and the Artist accepts the engagement, to present the Artist:

FARRY KISHER LIVE SET

To appear at the venue(s) on the date(s) and upon the terms set out below:

Main Stage, The Secret Garden Party Festival, Huntingdon, England - Saturday, 27 July

---

SALARY

The Artist agrees to appear for a total of 1 performance for a total fee of:

GBP £6,000 (£5,000 Artist fee plus £1,000 VAT)

Payment

The Promoter agrees to pay the sum of GBP £3,000 (50% of the Artist's guaranteed salary) by telegraphic transfer to Major Flair International to the credit of their **Sterling client account**:

A Bank Plc Media
Soho Round London
19X3 2CB United
Account Name: Major Flair International Client Account
Account Number: 2088001
Sort Code: 40-15-65

Swift Code: LUMBYB22
IBAN No. GB40LUMBC200263663665

To arrive at least two working days prior to 24 June to allow for bank settlement. N.B. Should it be necessaryto make the deposit with a cheque, the cheque should be received by Major Flair International (payable to Major Flair International Client Account) five working days prior to deposit due date to allow for settlement.

The balance to be paid as follows:

GBP £3,000 by Swift 2 weeks before the Artist's performance to credit the above account.

It is imperative that the Promoter advise Major Flair International of the Swift number on day of transfer to facilitate the tracing of monies.

Percentage Details

NONE

Figure 6.1 The contract for a festival show, indicating the stage as the address

the bill, with "first" being the act that immediately precedes the headliner. "Third support" is the bottom on a three-act bill, and the first on stage.

The billing clause for festival appearances would indicate that all advertising should list artists alphabetically, except for the headliner, who get their own line on the poster.

General Clauses

BILLING & PROGRAMMING

1. The Promoter agrees that the Artiste will be billed as FARRY KISHER LIVE in all publicity and promotion pertaining to the event of which the performances herein is a part.

Please contact Major Flair for the FARRY KISHER LIVE Press Pack.

2. The Artist's Press Pictures shall be used in all advertising and promotion for the performance.

ARTWORK

3. All artwork must be approved by Artist Management / Major Flair before general release.

ANNOUNCEMENT

4. The announcement of the Artist's appearance must be done in conjunction with Major Flair and Artist Management.

TRAVEL

5. N/A

6. N/A

VISAS

7. N/A

ACCOMMODATION

8. N/A

CATERING & RIDER

9. Promoter agrees to supply at their own expense meals and refreshments as detailed in FARRY KISHER LIVE contract rider (see attached)

TECHNICAL RIDER

11. The attached rider shall form an integral part of this agreement. The Promoter agrees and understands that it is the responsibility of the Promoter to provide and pay for all the provisions stated in the Rider. Failure to comply with any said provisions, unless specifically agreed in writing with the Artist, will be in breach of the agreement and may result in the cancellation of the engagement. Any such cancellation will in no way exclude the Promoter of their financial commitments to the Artist and the Promoter will be liable for payment to be made to the Artist of the contracted fee and any related expenses that the Promoter was required to cover in relation to this engagement.

Please contact Andy Reynolds - <andy.reynolds@livemusicbusiness.com> for any queries regarding advancing or logistics.

PERFORMANCE TIME

12. The Artist will play a maximum set length of 60 minutes. Set Time: 19:30 - 20:30

Capacity: TBC
Ticket Price: TBC

Figure 6.1 Continued

SERVICES

The promoter may have negotiated that the artist performs for a particular amount of time ("90 minutes plus encore") or that a minimum length of time on stage is required.

COMPENSATION

Performance contracts use various wording for this clause that sets out how much the artist will be paid for the concert. "Salary", "fee", and "guarantee" are also used.

Running Order:

22:30 - 23:30 A HEADLINER
21:00 - 22:00 TBC
19:30 - 20:30 FARRY KISHER
18:00 - 19:00 TBC

GUEST LIST

13. The Artist is to have a guaranteed guest list of a minimum of 10 people.

SPONSORSHIP

14. The Promoter will ensure that no sponsorship of any sort or description shall be made without specific written agreement of the Artist. If sponsorship is agreed the sponsorship monies will be split with the artists in a manner to be agreed with the artists representative dependent on type of sponsorship.

RADIO, TELEVISION & PHOTOGRAPHY

15. The Management will ensure that no audio or visual recording or photography of any kind for any purpose is made of the Artiste's performance, without written permission from the Artiste.

SECURITY

16. The Management shall guarantee proper security at all times to ensure the safety of the Artiste, auxiliary personnel, instruments and all equipment, costumes and personal property during and after the performance. Particular security must be provided in the areas of the stage, dressing rooms and all exits and entrances to the auditorium and the remote mixing console. Security protection to commence upon the arrival of the Artiste on the premises.

ITINERARY

17. The Promoter to provide a full itinerary with names, addresses and phone numbers of hotels and venues, also arrival and playing times. The itinerary to be with Major Flair one month prior to show date.

CANCELLATION

19.1 In any of the circumstances set out below the Artist may in its entire discretion cancel the appearance(s) in which event the Artist will not be liable for any direct or indirect loss including without limitation any consequential loss damage expense or liability which may be suffered by the Promoter due to such cancellation.

19.2 The Artist shall have the right without prejudice to any other rights the Artist may have, to cancel the appearance(s) under this Agreement if:

(a) the Promoter becomes insolvent or has a receiving or administration order made or threatened against any part of its undertaking or makes any arrangement with its creditors or passes a winding-up resolution; or

(b) the Promoter fails to provide any material part of any equipment, facilities, accommodation, information, services or finance which the Promoter is required to provide under the terms of this Agreement. For the avoidance of doubt the Artist shall have the right to cancel if all or any part of any sum required by this Agreement to be paid by the Promoter is not paid in full on or before the date(s) due hereunder for payment, time being of the essence for each such payment; or

(c) the condition of any equipment or facilities to be provided by the Promoter under this Agreement renders it inadvisable in the reasonable opinion of the Artist to present any appearance hereunder in its entirety; or

(d) any occurrence or factor (such as unsafe staging or disruptive elements in the audience) makes it likely in the reasonable opinion of the Artist that all or any part of any appearance(s) cannot be performed without risk to the health or safety of the Artist or of any musicians or road crew engaged on behalf of the Artist in relation to the Artist's appearance(s) or the audience; or

(e) there is any actual or threatened breach by the Promoter of any material term of this Agreement; or

(f) the illness or incapacity of the Artist (or of any member of the Artist's band or entourage or any member of the Artist's immediate family) makes it inappropriate in the reasonable opinion of the Artist for the Artist to perform; or

Figure 6.1 Continued

"Compensation" is relevant, as the deal will include the supply of sound, lighting, and other staging equipment, as well as catering, transport, and accommodation, all paid for by the promoter. The clause should dictate the amount the artist will receive, the currency the money will be paid in, as well as stipulations regarding taxation.

(g) any of the technical, security or administrative staff at any venue(s), the stage hands, or any road crew are
prevented for any reason from performing their duties relating to any appearance(s) to the reasonable
satisfaction of the Artist; or

(h) the breakdown or failure of the transportation of the Artist and/or of any musicians, road crew or equipment
required by the Artist for the Artist's appearance(s) renders it impossible in the reasonable opinion of the Artist to
satisfactorily present (an) appearance(s) hereunder; or

(i) any order or instruction of any public authority, bye-law or venue regulation renders it impossible in the opinion of
the Artist to present any appearance(s) in its/their entirety; or

(j) any act of god force majeure and/or natural causes including but not limited to climatic conditions, terrorist acts or
the anticipation thereof, fire, flood, disease or epidemic, riot or public disorder, substantial interruption in or
substantial delay to or failure of any facilities or transportation renders it impossible in the reasonable opinion of
the Artist for any appearance(s) hereunder to be presented in its/their entirety to the satisfaction of the Artist or
may endanger the safety of the Artist or any persons engaged to appear with the Artist hereunder or the
audience.

19.3 In the event of cancellation pursuant to sub-clauses 19.2(a), (b), (c), (d) or (e) of this clause, the Artist shall
retain any payment(s) made on account of the Salary and any other payments due from the Promoter hereunder
and the Promoter shall remain obliged to pay and shall immediately pay to the Artist any monies owing to the
Artist including without limitation any unpaid balance of the full amount of the Salary together with all other sums
due from the Promoter hereunder.

19.4 In the event of cancellation pursuant to sub-clause 19.2(f) of this clause the Artist shall return any part of the
Salary paid to the Artist relating to the cancelled appearance(s) and the Promoter shall not be obliged to make
any further payment to the Artist and the Promoter and the Artist shall use their reasonable commercial efforts to
mutually agree (an) alternate performance date(s) for such cancelled appearance(s).

19.5 In the event of cancellation pursuant to sub-clauses 19.2(f), (g), (h), (i) or (j) of this clause the Promoter and the
Artist shall use their reasonable commercial efforts to mutually agree (an) alternate performance date(s) for such
cancelled appearance(s). The Artist shall retain in the interim all funds which have been received into the Artist's
designated bank account(s) prior to such cancellation pending such agreement (and thereafter until the newly
arranged appearance(s) has/have taken place in accordance with the terms of this Agreement) but if such an
alternate date(s) cannot be agreed to the satisfaction of both parties [within three (3) months after the date of
such cancellation and in time for all of the necessary arrangements for such performances to be put in place]
then the Artist shall promptly return to the Promoter all such funds received into the Artist's designated bank
account(s) at the date of such cancellation less the amount of all costs or expenses incurred by the Artist in
connection with such cancellation.

19.6 Where cancellation affects less than all of the scheduled appearance(s) and where the fee breakdown per
performance is not specified in the Agreement then for the purposes of calculating the balance payable or
returnable (as the case may be) the Salary shall be divided equally between all the scheduled appearance(s).

Please sign the signature block below

I/We the undersigned acknowledge that I/We have read the above contract and clauses and agree that they will be
adhered to in detail.

Signed (the Promoter) _____ __

Address _____ _

Signed (Artist) _____

Address _____

Figure 6.1 Continued

The deal may be for a guarantee plus percentage deal, and the exact terms of the deal's
structure should be included here. For instance:

> "$5000 US Dollars (Five Thousand US Dollars) vs. 80% of nett profits after costs of
> $2000.00, whichever is the greater".

The promoter's expenses are the costs and will have been set out in the negotiation of
the offer.

Promoter Details:

PAUL ROMOTER
TKN CONCERT
Unit 55
A Business Centre
London England

Phone: 44 (0)20 876542
Mobile: 07787652
Email: promoter@tknconcert.com
VAT: 837312391

Artist Details: FARRY KISHER

Tour Manager Details:

Venue Details:

The Secret Garden Party Festival
Grange Farm, Mill Hill Field
Abbots Ripton
Huntingdon PE28 2PH
Cambridgeshire
England

Venue Date: Saturday, 23 July
Times
Get In:
Sound Check:
Act 1:
Act 2:
Act 3:
Act 4:
Curfew:

MAJOR FLAIR INTERNATIONAL, THE MAJOR BUILDING, 10-11 HORSE YARDS, LONDON W1 4HB
TEL: +44 (0)20 4700 FAX +44 (0)20 4700

This agency is not responsible for any non-fulfilment of Contract by Proprietors, the Promoter or Artists, but every reasonable safeguard is assured.

Figure 6.1 Continued

The artist is providing a service and may be able to charge a service tax on those services. The UK, for instance, has Value Added Tax (VAT) of 20%, and a UK artist who is eligible (they have a turnover of $>£85,000$ per year[2]) will charge VAT to the promoter on top of the guarantee. The contract will therefore have wording such as:

> *"If applicable, and immediately upon presentation of invoice, PURCHASER shall pay Value Added Tax (or equivalent for the applicable territory) on the GUARANTEE and all other monies payable hereunder".*

that obliges the promoter to include the service tax when paying the guarantee and any percentage of profits.

The compensation indicates any non-financial contribution as follows:

> *"$5000 US Dollars (Five Thousand US Dollars) vs. 80% of nett profits after costs of $2000.00, whichever is the greater, plus sound, lights, backline, catering, and other production, all as required by ARTIST and to ARTIST specification".*

This clause may also list specific, contracted, arrangements to do with production, such as specific flight origin and destination airports for instance.

PAYMENT AND DEPOSITS

A promoter is unlucky to want to hand over thousands of dollars in cash to an artist at the end of the night. She will therefore need instructions on how payment is to be made to the artist. The booking agent will also want the promoter to make a payment to the artist some time before the show. The details for these activities are detailed in the sections "Payment" and "Deposits".

PAYMENT

Payment details will list the currency of payment (Pounds sterling, US dollars, Canadian dollars, etc.), the accepted form (cash, certified check, cashier's check, or inter-bank transfer) and the name and address of the artist's bank account, in the case of inter-bank transfer. The bank account will be that of the booking agent's client account – a special account that is used to receive and hold payment and deposits from promoters on behalf of the booking agent's clients. All money is transferred ("wired") to that account and the booking agent forwards the money to the artist, either on request, or monthly or quarterly (see Table 6.1). Common practice is for 50% of the guarantee to be wired to the artist (via the booking agent) with a small amount being paid in cash on the night. Cash payments are useful to the artist on-the-road (to pay per diems and other expenses, for instance), and the artist does not want to be walking around with thousands of dollars earned from performance income, as this may make her a potential robbery victim.

DEPOSIT

Paying a deposit for a concert is an accepted part of the live music business and the terms of that payment are set out here. A standard contract calls for 50% of the fee being payable on signing of the contract, with the remaining 50% being transferred to the

Table 6.1 An artist booking agent account statement, showing the amount held by the agent and the payments made. The promoter of the Paris concert has not wired the remaining half of the guarantee, and the booking agent must chase that up

ACCOUNTING STATEMENT FROM BOOKING AGENT

LOCATION	PROMOTER	FEE exc VAT £	% BREAK £	VAT £	TRAVEL SHARE £	TOTAL FEE £	LESS BALANCE TO FOLLOW (Settlement Due) £	RECEIVED BY AGENT £
A VENUE, MANCHESTER	White Dove Ltd	£ 4,000.00		£ 800.00		£ 4,800.00		£ 4,800.00
A venue, Paris	Allo Henri	£ 450.00		£ –		£ 450.00	£ 225.00	£ 225.00
A venue, Amsterdam	Mojo Concerts	£ 1,000.00	£ 1,115.00	£ –		£ 2,115.00		£ 2,115.00
A venue, York	WhiteBag	£ 1,500.00		£ 300.00		£ 1,800.00		£ 1,800.00
A venue, London	GoldenVoice	£ 1,500.00	£ 1,158.58	£ 531.72		£ 3,190.30		£ 3,190.30
A venue, Bristol	GoldenVoice	£ 250.00	£ 239.14	£ 97.83		£ 586.97		£ 586.97
A venue, Brighton	GoldenVoice	£ 600.00	£ 471.11	£ 214.22		£ 1,285.33		£ 1,285.33
		£ 9,300.00	**£ 2,983.83**	**£ 1,943.77**	**£ –**	**£ 14,227.60**	**£ 225.00**	**£ 14,002.60**

artist on the morning after the concert. These deadlines are set out in the contract, and a promoter that does not adhere to them risks breaking the contract and cancelling the concert.

Having 50% of the fee paid as a deposit up front is wonderful for the cash flow of the artist (and booking agents), as the contract may be drawn up and signed several months before the concert. Paying deposits is a financial burden to concert promoters who are already exposed to the most risk in the transaction. The promoter must pay the deposits to secure the show and a busy promoter may be paying out thousands in local currency months before any concerts take place.

The payment and deposits clause will set out how any money earned from percentage deals is to be paid – cash or transfer and a deadline for making those payments.

TICKET PRICING AND SCALING

A concert promoter may have decided on a ticket price during the offer negotiations, and that price is indicated here. The venue may be a club (<1000-capacity) and only one type of ticket is on offer – the general admission (GA) type. GA allows everyone to stand wherever they like in the venue to watch the artist perform. Larger venues have scaled admission – different prices for sitting or standing in certain parts of the auditorium. An example of scaled ticketing would be that of sheds in the US. These part-open-air auditoria have a large grass section outside of the covered area and are scaled as GA. Tickets to stand or sit under the roof are scaled differently, as they afford the fan better sightliness and clearer sound. The price of these tickets is therefore higher (Table 6.2).

Different scaling for ticket prices, and the amount of available tickets in each tier, is included in the contract. The total of the ticket prices at each tier, along with the capacity, gives the gross potential of each tier, and the GP for the concert.

Table 6.2 A table of scaled tickets prices for a concert at St. Joseph's Health Amphitheater at Lakeview, Syracuse, NY 2021

Santana/Earth, Wind & Fire: Miraculous Supernatural 2021 Tour	
AUG 18 2021	
St. Joseph's Health Amphitheater at Lakeview, Syracuse, NY	**OFFICIAL PRICING**
Lawn	$40
Third row seating	$80
Second row seating	$80-$150
First row seating	$200
VIP	$259–$600

SPECIAL PROVISIONS

This section of the contract highlights specific points for this deal. The number of guest list places the artist stipulates in her rider, for instance, may have been contested by the promoter and the new agreed number of complimentary tickets would be included in the special provisions section. Information about press and publicity materials, artist touring production crew contact information, and specific stipulations on sponsorship and branding of the event are the types of activities that are detailed in the special provisions section.

NOTES

1 Oxford University Press, 2012. *Oxford English Dictionary*, 7th ed. Oxford University Press, Oxford.
2 VAT registration thresholds [WWW Document], n.d. GOV.UK. URL https://www.gov.uk/vat-registration-thresholds (accessed 1.5.21).

7

CHAPTER 7
THE CONTRACT RIDER

CHAPTER OUTLINE

The contract rider "rides" with the contract and sets out the stipulations and requirements of the artist for any performance she undertakes. The contract is specific to the concert, the contract rider applies to every concert. The artist will be performing in different concert settings – clubs and theatres, open-air festivals, perhaps even arenas and stadiums, and so a different contract rider may be produced to include requirements relevant to the different formats.

Typical rider formats would include:

- club/theatre rider
- festival and fly-date rider
- shed/arena/stadium rider
- promotional activity rider
- DJ rider, for both touring DJs and also for when artists undertake DJ gigs

At the very least, the contract rider should specify the technical requirements (sound and lighting) the artist may have, the number and mode of travel of the artist's touring

DOI: 10.4324/9781003019503-8

party, and the catering and hospitality requirements of the artist and her crew. The rider is created by the artist in conjunction with her tour manager and technical crew. The contract rider then gives the promoter an overview of what she is "buying" – the production requirements, the size of the touring party, etc.

An example contract rider can be seen in Appendix 3.

ELEMENTS OF A CONTRACT RIDER

The following indicates the sections of a standard contract rider:

COVER PAGE

A contract rider can be 10–50 pages. The front page should be a cover page with a "contents" section that gives the title of the relevant section and a page number. The rider should have a version number and expiry date (see *Version numbers*)

Contract riders are distributed as Microsoft Word or Google Docs documents, with the majority being converted to Adobe PDF format. There may be an occasion where the rider needs to be printed out onto paper. In this case the sections that need to be detached (to be forwarded to suppliers for instance) should be placed at the back of the document to make them easier to separate and distribute. An example would be the audio input list for the artist. The input list is a one-page document used by the venue's audio team. The list will be easier to detach and give to the right people if it is included as the last sheet in the rider.

VERSION NUMBERS

The live music business generates lots of documents. Documents associated with concert production contain information that is time-sensitive or is likely to change without notice. Live music business professionals adopt versioning of documents to ensure all relevant people are viewing and acting on the correct, up-to-date, version of documents (Figure 7.1). The practice is similar to that of versioning for software, where

FARRY KISHER - LIVE BAND FORMAT
TOURING INFORMATION SPRING/SUMMER 2017 V1.1
EXPIRES JUNE 01st 2017

Contents:

1) Cast & crew	Page 2
2) Hotel rooming list	Page 2
3) Transport	Page 2
4) Tour and venue accreditation	Page 3
5) Set length	Page 3
6) Merchandise	Page 3
7) Catering & hospitality	Page 4
8) Audio	Page 5
9) Lighting	Page 7
10) Stage plan and riser requirements	Page 8

Figure 7.1 The front page of a contract rider, showing version numbers and dates. Versioning ensures all recipients are working from the latest version of the document

each release is named in a "x.x" format e.g., version 2.1. The first number usually indicates major changes in the document, and the second number (after the period) reflects major adjustments. An artist's contract rider could be labelled version 3.2 for instance, and after a minor tweak to some element in the document, be then renamed version 3.3.

CONTACTS

The next page in the rider should include a comprehensive contacts section. The rider will be sent to the promoter/talent buyer of the concert. The promoter may then forward the rider to suppliers and other relevant people and those people will have no formal contact with the artist, the booking agent, or the manager. Including contact information for those parties is therefore standard practice.

Other people listed would be the artist's audio, lighting, and video technicians, as well as the artist's tour and production managers.

CAST AND CREW

"Cast" refers to the performers, "crew" to the technicians and other support staff on the road with the artist. All touring personnel should be listed here, including the artists. Many of today's top-selling acts are individuals and will tour accompanied by session musicians. Even tours of venues at the 500-capacity level will see ensembles of four or more musicians onstage with a "solo" act, and they should be listed in the "cast and crew" section.

The artist technicians should also be listed, along with the other touring personnel as relevant – drivers, caterers, wardrobe assistants, stylists, close protection personnel, and merchandise sellers.

TRANSPORT MODES

Much of an artist touring will be accomplished using road transport – sleeper buses or splitter vans. The transportation of rented sound and lighting equipment may necessitate trucks as well. The vehicles will require parking spaces and, in the case of sleeper buses, electricity to be supplied at each venue. The rider should therefore itemise the number of buses and trucks and the requirements for each.

The transport section of the rider will also indicate what ground transportation ("grounds") are needed for fly-dates (a gig that requires the artist to fly to). In this case, the rider will stipulate how many people will need picking up from the airport and what types of transport are acceptable. A clear indication should be given as to the amount of personal luggage (excluding musical equipment) that will arrive with the passengers. Suitcases and carry-on bags being forced into inappropriately sized vehicles is a common site at airports serving festival sites in the summer; promoters and organisers need to be told in advance how much luggage will accompany the band and crew.

CATERING REQUIREMENTS

A standard live music contract sees the promoter agreeing to supply catering (meals, snacks, and beverages) as part of the deal. The promoter will have allocated a set cash amount to cover the cost of the artists' requirements, and they should have been made available in the contract rider before the promoter agreed the deal.

The concept of the catering rider is known to the public thanks to stories involving Van Halen (US), a heritage hard rock act, and a proliferation of artist's riders being posted online. The term "rider" has become synonymous with the items – food and drink – and not the document. A website, The Smoking Gun (ww.thesmokinggun.com) has several pages of artist riders and seeks to point out what the site's editors feel are the most ridiculous demands.[1] (Figure 7.2) Whether the stipulations in the rider featured on the Smoking Gun are ridiculous or not is a matter for the reader to decide. One thing is apparent from reading through the uploaded riders: the total cost of supplying the requirements of some of the riders is disproportionate to the gross potential of the concert (see *Buy out*).

The catering rider should be presented as a way of making sure the dietary needs of the touring party are met, and perhaps more importantly, letting the promoter know what she is "buying" in terms of numbers of people to feed. Every item listed in a contract rider is a potential cost for the promoter. Listing expensive wines and demanding fresh copies of the latest console games may be common practice for baby bands putting together their first rider and showing ignorance as to how the deals are constructed and

Figure 7.2 Thesmokinggun.com. The website owner has obtained catering riders from famous music artists

how much of their own money (in the form of back-end percentage deals) the artist is wasting.

An appropriate rider should indicate how many people are in the cast and crew, and what (if any) dietary requirements (vegan, vegetarian, gluten-free, etc.) the touring party members have.

BUY OUT

Supplying "home-cooked" hot food is not always easy or appropriate at some venues. Clubs of <500-capacity do not have kitchens or food preparation areas for instance. It will therefore be difficult for the promoter to arrange the cooking of a meal. The promoter will then give the touring party a "buy out", a set cash amount per person that will enable the artist and crew to go out to a local restaurant or take-away food shop to get a meal. The amount of the buy out per person is indicated in the contract rider and usually varies between $10 and $30 per person in the touring party.

Supplying a buy out is easy for the promoter (they do not have to shop, cook, and serve food) but is not cost-effective. A buy out for an artist with four band members and three crew (seven in total) at $10 per person will amount to $70. The ingredients to make a tasty, nutritional, meal for seven would cost far less than that!

HOSPITALITY REQUIREMENTS

The hospitality section sets out the drinks and food that is to be made available for non-touring personnel, usually guests and VIPs.

Performing live can serve as a networking event for the artist. Inviting journalists, radio station personnel, local record shop owners, and other VIPs to a concert is stand-ard practice. The invitation may extend to join the artist after the show in her dressing room (sometimes known as green room, or backstage). Offering a drink to guest is only polite, and these will come from the artist's drinks provided as part of the rider stipula-tions. There comes a point in an artist's career where (hopefully) there are significant numbers of people who are invited backstage. An artist may run "meet and greet" competitions for its fan club members, for instance, and the lucky winner gets to go backstage and meet her idols. VIP tickets may also include an organised meet and greet event where 30–40 fans are given access to a dedicated meeting area where the artist is available to sign merchandise and pose for selfies. Serving drinks from the supplies provided as part of the catering rider is not appropriate at this scale – no artist would list enough beer to serve 40 people on their standard arena rider. They would, however, create a separate section that specifies requirements for such meet and greets.

The promoter may agree to these extra hospitality demands as they often share in the kudos of such events. The promoter will have their own guests beyond friends and family and will want to treat those guests well. They may also be sharing in the revenue for VIP meet and greet packages, and it is in their interest to supply adequate refreshments.

ACCOMMODATION REQUIREMENTS

The promoter may have agreed to supply accommodation, at her cost, for the touring band and crew. This section of the rider should therefore set out how many rooms are required and a list of the names of each person in each room.

Hotel rooms are a common deal point for DJ contracts but not so much for other artists. Accommodations are generally considered to be an artist cost. An exception seems to be for baby bands performing in Europe. Concerts at <500-capacity venues are structured on an "all-in" deal where the promoter can supply inexpensive accommodations as well.

MERCHANDISING

Selling merchandise, or "merch" – t-shirts, hoodies, beanie hats, and other apparel – as souvenirs of a concert is a significant revenue stream for touring artists. You shall examine merch in greater detail in *Revenue Streams from Live Music – Artist* later in this part; for now, you should know that revenue from merch can be significant, and the artist should exert some control as to the conditions of its sale.

The merchandise section of the contract rider will indicate to the promoter any stipulations the artist has in terms of selling its own merchandise, in particular any fees that need to be paid. For instance, venue operators will often charge the promoter, and any visiting artist, a concession or merchandising fee. This fee is a percentage or per-head amount of the income from the sale of merchandise and is payable to the venue. The payment can be a significant amount, and the artist will want to minimise this fee where possible.

The artist will set out their terms for the selling of their merchandise in the "merchandise" section of the rider and this will include:

- language to set out the artist's right to sell exclusive merchandise
- the promoter's responsibilities in tackling bootleg or counterfeit merchandise
- a clause setting out a "most favoured nation" rate for the merchandise fee. Although the promoter does not set the merch fee (or receive any of the cash, unless they are an owner/operator, such as Live Nation) this clause stipulates the promoter must negotiate the lowest possible rate with the venue
- physical inventory – stands, tables, lighting – that the promoter must supply for the artist to sell merch

Merch clauses in riders are often wishful thinking on behalf of the artist. It is unlikely a promoter will be able to negotiate a favoured nation rate with a venue unless that promoter has many concerts at the venue. However, with such large amounts of revenue being paid to the venue operators, booking agents are increasingly having to spend considerable time negotiating deal points involving merchandise concession rates.

TECHNICAL RIDER

The technical rider should be written by the artist in consultation with her technical team; this will often be the sound engineer who has been hired on and may also include input from lighting designers. (An example technical rider can be found in Appendix 4).

The contents of the technical rider evolve over the career of the touring artist. In the artist's early days, the rider will include an input list and stage plan (see below for explanations of both) and these are useful documents to promoters and venues at that stage. The artist will be performing in non-production (<1000-capacity) venues that have sound and lighting equipment installed. The in-house technicians at these venues need to know how many microphones, stands, and cables they need to supply for the artist's concert that evening, and the input list and stage plan will supply that information. You can read more about non-production venues in *Part Two: Live Music Production*.

Convention, and perhaps ignorance, will also see emerging artists specify a particular mixing console brand or loudspeaker brands in their technical rider. As mentioned, the rider is written in consultation with a sound engineer, and that person may be inexperienced. An artist at the start of her career is unlikely to be able to afford a sound engineer with experience of the live music business, and the sound engineer she does hire may be a friend just starting out themselves. In any case, the sound engineer may have read some other riders on The Smoking Gun and decided that they also should be asking for certain mixing consoles and audio gizmos to be supplied. However, a promoter is not going to replace the speaker system in a club to accommodate the stipulations of an artist's rider, no matter how much she wants to do business with that artist.

The artist will move into production venues as their career progresses (>1000-capacity), where there is no existing sound and light equipment installed. Artists touring production venues will hire and transport sound and lighting equipment for the duration of the tour. It is not necessary for input lists and other documents to be included in the technical rider for this type of touring, as they are bringing all their technical infrastructure with them. It will be necessary, though, to inform the promoter about the size and scope of the equipment being brought into the venue, including the weight of any "flown" (suspended) equipment and the total power needed for all the equipment. Again, the promoter is not going to pay for the electricity supply to be upgraded and will be in a position to flag up the issue with power as soon as they read the rider.

INPUT LIST

"Input" in this case refers to the sound sources that need "inputting" into the sound system (also known as "PA" for public address). Providing an accurate input list will ensure that the venue's audio team will know how many sound sources there are onstage, how many inputs need to go to the PA, how many direct injection (DI) boxes and microphones are needed, and the order they should appear on the mixing console. The input list can also specify the outputs – those sound sources that need to be routed back out of the mixing console to wedge monitors on-stage, or to performers' in-ear monitors (IEMs).

The input list is created by the artist's audio team, usually the front-of-house (FOH) engineer, from an inventory of the artist's stage instruments taken in the rehearsal room. Table 7.1 shows an example input list.

The input list should show the separate audio sound sources. Everything that needs to be heard through the PA needs either a microphone or a DI (direct injection) box. For each sound source there should be:

- a channel number. Having a channel number makes troubleshooting a sound-related problem easier. "There is a buzz on channel 13", is easier to diagnose than "There is a buzz on the bass booms". The artist's engineer may know what the "bass booms" are but the in-house audio team will not.
- the position of the instrument or source. SR for stage right and SL for stage left helps to indicate the position of the sound source onstage.
- Notes. Any notes about the sound source go in this column. A drummer may use two pairs of hi-hats for instance (most drummers use only one pair), and that would be indicated in the Notes column in case the house audio team think the inclusion of two pairs of hi-hats is a mistake.

STAGE PLAN

The stage plan is a diagram that indicates the positions of equipment and performers onstage, relative to someone standing onstage (see *Stage left and stage right*). The plan is useful to the in-house audio crew; they can use it to locate instruments that are listed on the input list quickly. The stage plan for a baby band may also indicate the positions of wedge and side fill monitors (if any) and where power should be supplied.

Stage plans become necessary for artists performing at green-field, open-air, festivals where the artist equipment is built on rolling riders behind the stage. The festival audio team have limited time to plug up the input and output cables, microphones, and DI boxes, and having an accurate stage plan will help them do their job.

STAGE LEFT AND STAGE RIGHT

The live music business borrows terms from theatre when describing the position of an item onstage. The position is expressed from the viewpoint of standing onstage and looking at the audience with stage right being to the right of the person onstage. Similarly, downstage (front, nearest the audience) and upstage (rear of the stage), see Figure 7.3.

Table 7.1 An example of an input list showing the sources on the stage, and the order in which they should be connected into the sound system

CH.	INSTRUMENT/ SOURCE	MIC/DI	INSERT	MON CH.	MON INSERT	NOTES
1	KICK DRUM	SHURE SM91	GATE	1	GATE	
2	KICK DRUM	BETA 57A	GATE		GATE	
3	SNARE TOP	WE SUPPLY		2		
4	SNARE BOTTOM	SHURE BETA 57				
5	HI HAT 1	AKG C451		3		STAGE LEFT
6	HI HAT 2	AKG C451		4		STAGE RIGHT
7	RACK 1	WE SUPPLY	GATE	5		
8	FLOOR 1	WE SUPPLY	GATE	6		
9	FLOOR 2	WE SUPPLY	GATE	7		
10	RIDE	AKG C451				
11	OH SR	AKG C414				
12	OH SL	AKG C414				
13	BASS BOOM	DI		8		FROM LAPTOP ON DRUM RISER
14	BASS DI	XLR		9		DIRECT OUT
15	BASS MIC	SENN MD 421				
16	GUITAR SR DI	WE SUPPLY		10		XLR FROM RED BOX
17	GUITAR SR	AKG AT4050				
18	GUITAR SL DI	RED BOX		11		XLR FROM RED BOX
19	GUITAR SL	AKG AT4050				
20	VOCAL SR	WE SUPPLY	COMP	12		
21	VOCAL CENTER	WE SUPPLY	COMP	13		
22	SPARE MICROPHONE	SHURE BETA 58	COMP	14		JUST IN CASE

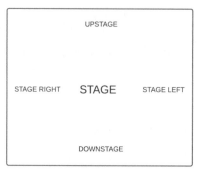

AUDIENCE

Figure 7.3 Stage directions used in concert production

AUDIO INFORMATION

The input list and stage plan are related to the audio element of the artist's performance and are contained in the "audio" section of the technical rider.

A club/theatre rider (where the artist is not touring with any of their own production apart from backline) may also include information and notes on:

- the preferred make and model of console
- the preferred make and model of the loudspeaker system
- notes on firmware updates for consoles – are the consoles at the venue up-to-date?
- the number, make, and model, of any UHF wireless equipment, such as microphones and IEMs
- provision of console use for support/opening acts
- any equipment needed for walk-in/walk-on music, such as a CD player routed to the FOH console, etc.
- contact names, telephone numbers, and email addresses of the artist's audio crew

An artist touring large theatres, sheds, and arenas will be travelling with their rented production and the shed/arena/stadium rider acts as a production document. The document does not stipulate provisions in the same way as the catering rider or club/theatre technical rider. The production document contains information specific to each department (sound, lighting, video, set, stage, and transport) and serves to let everyone associated with the concert know exactly what the artist is bringing into each building. The audio department will therefore list:

- the make, model, size, and weight of the audio system
- the power requirements
- the provision of use of the audio equipment for support/opening acts
- the contact names, telephone numbers, and email addresses, of the artist audio crew

The tour will also have a production manager, and their contact information would be included on the cover of the production document. The production manager is the first point of contact for anything to do with the technical infrastructure of the concert.

The technical riders for DJs will list the accepted types of CD or vinyl player, mixer, and firmware versions where necessary. DJ riders can also include detailed requests for specific booth monitor loudspeaker brands, the amplifiers that power them, and even the height and angle of the high-frequency cabinets.

BACKLINE

The artist with travel with their own backline – drums kits, guitar amps, MIDI controllers – whatever it is that they use to make music. Some situations occur where it is not possible to travel with any equipment – flying to a festival on another continent for instance. Such shows are called "fly-dates" and create a unique set of logistical issues. Although small, light, equipment, such as guitars, laptops, and MIDI controllers, will fit in the hold of a commercial flight, larger and heavier equipment will either not fit or be too expensive to be flown with the artist. The promoter will then be asked to supply equivalent backline equipment either at their own cost, as part of the deal for the concert, or supply it with the artist footing the rental bill.

The technical rider will therefore list the required makes and models of suitable backline equipment for fly-dates. This list will be included in the audio section of the technical rider.

LIGHTING INFORMATION

Information about the artists lighting requirements will follow a similar format to that contained in the audio section. The information listed in a club/theatre rider will be a list of stipulations for lighting equipment and the location of fixtures. However, as with audio, a promoter is unlikely to hire in, or even change, the lighting fixtures in a club for one act.

The rider/production document for sheds and arenas will detail the equipment that the artist is renting and bringing with them. The most critical information will be the rigging plots. These schematic diagrams indicate the position and type of chain hoists that are used to suspend ("fly") lighting and audio equipment above the crowd. The rigging of the chain hoists is done by riggers who work at height to create rigging points, with the chain hoists being attached to these points. Convention dictates that the promoter pays for the installation of the points, with one point being needed per chain hoist. An average arena show can use up to 200 chain hoists, which at an average installation fee of $75 a point, is not a small investment for the promoter. The promoter will therefore want to see the rigging plot early in the negotiations of the deal.

VIDEO INFORMATION

The video section of the technical rider follows a similar format to that of the audio and lighting sections.

DJ riders for festivals include stipulations for access to the video infrastructure on the stage. You will read more about the video element of modern concert production in *Part Two: Live Music Production*; for now, you should know that video in concerts has two elements: image magnification (IMAG) and projection. Any DJ performing at festival will want to differentiate their performance from that of other DJs on the bill, and the use of bespoke visuals is one way to do this. The projection element of a video production is not necessarily obtained using projectors but does involve the display of content (motion graphics or film). LED panels are commonly used, and these have different characteristics of scale, pixel density, and configuration. The artists' visual team will want to know the configuration of the proposed festival screens ahead of time, so they can design the artist visuals to fit on the supplied area. The technical section will therefore request the promoter send the artist computer-aided design (CAD) drawings of the screens as soon as possible before the concert date.

IMAG is the use of motion cameras to capture what is happening onstage and projecting/displaying those images onto large screens. The festival organiser typically uses IMAG to show pictures of the audience enjoying themselves and to serve sponsorship and advertising announcements. The DJ's team will want access to those cameras and screens during their set, as they can be used to enhance the performance. This request will be made in the technical rider.

STAGE AND BARRIER REQUIREMENTS

Specifying the size and construction of the stage and performance area is a pointless inclusion in a club/theatre rider, yet it does happen.

Staging specifications are more commonly included in production documents. Artists do not tour with the stage, even if they are renting and travelling with the rest of the production. The stage for an arena show is supplied locally and built on the morning of the show to the specification in the artist's production document.

Safety barriers (barricades) are also supplied locally, and the technical rider/production document will advise the promoter on the requirements for this. A simple request may be for an anti-crush barrier to be placed across the front of the stage, with a gap sufficient for stewards and medics to stand between the stage and the barrier. Barrier requirements for arena and stadium shows are more complicated, with some artists seeking to create second and third performance areas in the crowd standing areas. The walkways from the main stage to these other performance areas will need barriers, as well as the stages themselves. The length and construction of the barrier required will all be contained in this section of the technical rider/production document.

PERSONNEL REQUIREMENTS

Staging a concert of any size requires additional labour besides the artist, their crew, and the venue's administrative team. An artist touring non-production (<1000-capacity) venues may still be travelling with equipment other than their backline. The artist's crew will be less tired and enjoy their work more if they have help when loading in and out of the venue. Similarly, the artist's crew will not be familiar with the sound and lighting equipment at each venue, so technicians should be on-hand to assist them.

These are two examples of the extra personnel required to work on a concert, and these requirements should be noted in the technical rider.

The first example above is that of using stagehands (also called "local crew", or "locals") to assist the touring crew; two people is a conventional minimum requirement at the non-production venue touring level. You will read more about stagehands in *Part Two: Live Music Production*.

Tours of sheds, arenas, and stadiums, require many more stagehands at each concert, and the nature of their work goes beyond just unpacking trucks. The supply of the local crew is a cost to the promoter, and they will want to see the number of local crew the artist is requesting ahead of finalising the deal for the show. The artist's production team will be keen to have as many hands on-deck (especially for the load-out); at the same time, the promoter will be looking to minimise this local labour cost as much as possible.

A common local crew requirement for concerts at all levels is that of the runner. A runner is a local person with access to reliable transport who can be tasked with going on errands outside of the venue – shopping for replacement musical parts, saving the artist's crew from having to leave their work for instance. A cub tour rider will specify one such person, an arena show may ask for four runners.

CATERING AND PRE-SHOP

You have seen an example of a catering rider in the previous section. This type of rider is applicable to club and theatre touring and will differ for tours involving sheds, arenas, and stadiums.

Catering is a cost to the promoter, and she will arrange the buying, cooking, serving, and of the food, as well as cleanup. Catering for the cast and crew of a large theatre or arena tour involves producing three meals (breakfast, lunch, and dinner) as well as ongoing snacks and refreshments throughout the day. Hopefully, the promoter is busy running the promotion side of her company and does not have time to work in a kitchen for 18 hours. She will therefore hire in a local catering company who will cook and clean for the visiting artist.

The local catering company will serve a date on the tour; the cast and crew will be eating food prepared by different people for every show date on the tour. The catering rider for a production tour should take this situation into account and organise the requirements with different themes for different days of the week. For instance, the rider could specify that Thursdays are to be Italian-themed, Fridays are fish-based, Saturdays US-themed foods, such as hot dogs and hamburgers with fries, and so on.

Setting out the rider in this way discourages every outside catering company serving up the meals that are the most cost-effective – i.e., pasta-based dishes. There is nothing wrong with this, but a band and crew will quickly get bored if they are eating the same food type each day.

Artists who tour at production level in Europe, especially the UK, will hire a catering company who tours with the artist, cooking and serving at each venue on the tour. The promoter still agrees to supply catering as part of the contract, and the promoter pays the catering company to supply food to the specifications of the artist. It is nearly always the case that the artist's demands exceed the budget set out in the promoter's show costings, and so the artist ends up paying towards the catering bill.

The production document will specify the equipment needed in the kitchen at each venue and what equipment (if any) the catering company are bringing into each venue. Visiting chefs typically bring in refrigerators, drinks dispensers, coffee-making machines, hotplates, as well as all the cutlery and flatware.

The chefs touring with the artist will shop locally for produce and shops may not be open early enough to cater for breakfast on the morning of the show (the load-in for an arena show is usually 6 am). The catering rider will therefore include a "pre-shop" list that instructs the promoter as to what to buy the day before for the breakfast and/ or cash to enable the chefs to go shopping themselves. Pre-shop items typically include eggs, bacon, bread, milk, and orange juice. The promoter will buy these items and store them in the venue ready for the chefs to start cooking as soon as they can in the morning. Figure 7.4 shows a typical pre-shop requirement.

LAUNDRY

"Laundry day" is a particularly welcome event on any tour. This is the day when the cast and crew can get their clothes washed or dry-cleaned. Laundry day on a tour of clubs is a self-managed affair – the tour manager will arrange with the promoter's rep to find a local laundrette or other clothes-washing facility, get the clothes sent there, and hopefully returned before the end of the day when the band and crew leave town.

Laundry at production-level touring has an extra dimension. The performers will have stage clothes that will need cleaning, probably after every performance, depending on

---

9.3   CATERING ASSISTANTS

The Purchaser agrees to pay for and provide 2(two) catering assistant to be put at the disposal of the Artist's caterers. This assistant must have previous experience of food preparation and will work with the caterers until released by the Production Manager.

9.4 PRE SHOP

Catering pre-buy list
Please supply the following breakfast shop to be available at load in time. It is important that the runner is available at load in time to take us for our main shopping, so this must have been bought in advance.

2 x kilo English style Bacon
1 x kilo English style Sausage
1 x packet vegetarian sausages
1 x kilo butter
12 tomatoes
1 kilo mushrooms
3 x loaves toast bread (2 x white/1 x brown)
2 x loaves whole (unsliced) bread
4 x baguettes
16 x bread rolls
24 assorted pastries (danish/donuts etc)
12 litres fresh milk

Figure 7.4 The pre-shop requirement for promoters, set out in the contract rider

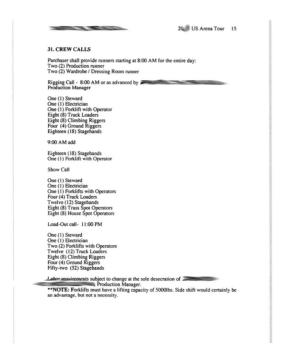

Figure 7.5 Typical plant, machinery, and crew requirements list for an arena-size production

the genre of music. The tour will have wardrobe department who oversee performers stage clothes and costumes. Cleaning these garments is a big part of the job and the wardrobe assistants will therefore need access to reliable washing facilities at the commencement of load-in. Early access is vital if they are to clean and dry costumes and stage wear ready for the concert that evening.

The requirements for washers and driers will be specified in this section of the artist production document.

PLANT AND MACHINERY

Production-level touring of sheds, arenas, and stadiums, requires extra machinery as well as manpower (see "Personnel requirements" above). Suspending audio and lighting equipment requires lifting equipment, such as forklift vehicles and cherry pickers (hydraulic personnel platforms for raising workers to height). Concert deal convention dictates that the cost for renting plant and other machinery is borne by the promoter. The anticipated requirements for plant are therefore set out in this section of the contract rider/production document. Figure 7.5 shows the plant requirements and crew call times for a typical arena concert.

NOTE

1 You should visit www.thesmokinggun.com/backstage to see catering and hospitality artists of all genres and success levels.

8

CHAPTER 8
REVENUE STREAMS FROM LIVE MUSIC – ARTISTS

CHAPTER OUTLINE

Performing live is not a business or marketing activity for many artists. The very reason they pursued a career in music in the first place is to be in front of an audience. To equate live performance as another (and significant) income stream may be distasteful for successful artists, and yet that is the fact. The revenue is not just from the selling of concert tickets, though, as you shall see in this section.

TICKET SALES

Revenue from ticket sales will be the primary live performance income source for most artists. The artist will either be performing their own, hard-ticket shows, where a deal has been negotiated to set the ticket price and a share of revenue after the promoter's costs are deducted, or soft-ticket shows, such as festivals or college performances.

The nature of the modern concert deal means better cash flow for the artist. Consider a pay-on-the-door, cash only, concert. The audience pays when they arrive for the concert, and the artist and promoter collect the money, splitting according to whatever deal they have negotiated between themselves. The artist may have spent money before the show on rehearsals, transport, marketing etc., and would have seen no income from the show until after the box office had closed and the ticket sales were counted.

Compare that with a guaranteed fee deal where the promoter agrees to pay a deposit on signing the contract. The deposits can be required two to nine months in advance of the concert itself.[1] The promoter will pay this money to the booking agent, who holds the amount in escrow for their client (the artist). An artist that has a string of concerts and festival shows in the next nine months may have large sums of money sitting in their agent's escrow accounts – money that they can request from the agent to pay ongoing bills. Refer to Figure 6.1 for an example of an artist's statement of account with their booking agent.

SCOPE OF INCOME

The scope and range of income that artists receive for performances is particular to each deal and is easy to determine. The gross potential of a concert is based on the ticket price multiplied by the legal capacity of the venue. You can ascertain the capacity of nearly any venue through an internet search or data from Pollstar, a live music business trade magazine. For instance, the Madison Square Garden presents concerts with the main space converted to hold 20,000 ticket holders. Ticket prices are scaled, and the average price is usually $65. This gives a gross potential of $1,300,000. You have no idea as to the deal that has been made, or the cost involved with staging this event, and a rough guide would be that costs are a third of the ticket price. In this case, the remaining profit would generally be split 80/20 in favour of the artist. The calculations mentioned are general, but you can determine that a sold-out show will net the artist nearly $700,000.

These calculations are useful to gauge the artist's share of revenue from hard ticket concerts but give no indication of the guaranteed fees paid to artists for festival shows or DJs for club and open-air events. The fees payable at such events are negotiated on the potential "pulling power" (ticket-selling potential) of the artist and bear no relation to gross capacity. Festival organisers and nightclub owners will take food and beverage sales into account when costing out an event and can offer more for talent fees as a result.

Table 8.1 shows the amounts for contemporary festival and nightclub shows.

An artist with a full touring and festival calendar can look forward to a lucrative year's work, providing they keep their own touring costs under control.

Table 8.1 A table of guarantees ("fees") paid to contemporary touring artists

STATUS	STAGE	FEE/GUARANTEE
Headline	Main stage	$1,000,000 – $5,000,000
Headline	Second stage/arena	$50,000 – $100,000
16:00–18:00 slot	Main stage	$50,000
Midday/opening slot	Main stage	$1000 – $5000
Midday/opening	Second or other stages	$500 – $1000

MERCHANDISE

Merchandise ("merch") can provide significant revenue for an artist. The popular view that an emerging artist can fund her touring from sales of merch at her concerts does not stand up to scrutiny though – the cost of manufacturing the items, creating a hospitable point of sale (merch table), paying sales people, and the venue merchandising fee, will erode the profit from sales.

The erosion of profits should not deter an artist from producing a merchandise product line though. The type, pricing, and distribution of the items require consideration just as when launching any product. Indeed, some basic business planning can go a long way to ensure an artist sees a healthy return on investment (ROI) for their merchandise.

Merch provides income and, perhaps more importantly, serves as a marketing device for the artist. There can be no greater endorsement than that of a fan paying money to wear the name of an artist on her chest. Merchandise is not restricted to apparel, and a forward-thinking artist team will be able to apply the artist's name and likeness to a considerable, and desirable, range of products that will sell – and sell well.

MERCHANDISING FOR EMERGING ARTISTS

The simplest form of music-related merchandise is the t-shirt and is usually the first item the emerging artist will produce. The name or logo of the artist is printed on a plain-coloured (usually black) t-shirt. These shirts are sold on each night of a tour from a merch table in the particular venue. The cost to produce t-shirts like this is low – an order of 50 printed shirts can cost as low as $2 a shirt. Selling these t-shirts at concerts for $10 each will result in a good profit – if the shirts sell. Unfortunately, many artists return home from touring with boxes full of unsold t-shirts. Why?

Fans and concert goers do and do not buy band merchandise for the following reasons:

Design. "Design" refers to the words, logo, or picture, printed on the t-shirt. T-shirts are garments to be worn. A fan is unlikely to buy a t-shirt she considers unflattering or ugly. "Good design" is unquantifiable, and careful consideration of the size and position of words and logos can make a difference.

Colour and sizing. The standard artist t-shirt is black in a medium size. A brave artist may print their t-shirts on other colours and may fall afoul of a change of taste – this season's on-trend colour may be out of fashion by the start of their tour. Printing a design on t-shirts in all the sizes from "girls fit" through to XXL may also be a waste of money. A YouTube artist's audience will be predominately young girls – not many will need (or want) to buy a t-shirt sized XXL.

Genre. Heavy metal fans buy merchandise. Likewise, fans of indie/alternative rock show their appreciation by buying t-shirts at shows. Emerging artists in other genres do not traditionally sell lots of merch at concerts – hip-hop, for instance (although that is changing thanks to superstar hip-hop artists, such as Drake (Canada) and Travis Scott (US)).

Choice. Choice inhibits decision-making when buying. (An experiment by two scientists using jam proved this in 2000[2].) Emerging artists have too many designs, on too many sizes, in too many colours. The potential customer will be bewildered by the choices (especially when also being pressured to leave the venue as quickly as possible by the venue stewards) and will leave empty-handed, making no purchase.

Scarcity. Fans can be encouraged to buy t-shirts by creating scarcity. Limited edition T-shirts featuring the dates of the tour is an example of creating scarcity (and community). Fans generally understand that such t-shirts are only available for sale at the concerts on that tour and they need to buy there and then – or else miss out.

Price and payment options. Pricing of concert t-shirts is not a factor in the purchase decision. A fan is invested in the artist and taking design, sizing, and scarcity into account, will be more than happy to buy a t-shirt featuring the logo of the act she has just seen, sometimes regardless of price. Fans also have knowledge that artists depend on merch sales to fund touring (although this may be a myth as discussed here) and that they are helping their heroes when they buy a t-shirt from the artist. Offering payment options – cash, credit card, Apple Pay – will increase the chance a fan will buy a t-shirt, again regardless of price.

OTHER MERCHANDISE ITEMS

Artists are not limited to selling t-shirts at their concerts. Other apparel including hooded tops ("hoodies"), hats, ponchos, and underwear can all be printed with the name and logo of a popular baby act and will sell.

Non-apparel merch is also popular. Posters, stickers, buttons (badges), neoprene waistbands, shot glasses, postcards, and cigarette lights are all familiar sights on merch stands. Trending items, such as fidget spinners in 2018,[3] are ripe for incorporating into an emerging artist's product line and the artist must ensure they do not order too many of any item based on a fad.

SOPHOMORE AND SUPERSTAR ARTISTS

The artist moving into the sophomore or superstar stage of their career will be able to reach more people at each concert and potentially sell more merch as a result. Designing, printing, distributing, selling, and accounting for merch sales at 5,000– 20,000 capacity venues is an operation in itself. Selling any product at this scale requires planning and an appreciation of the market gained from experience. Artists going into their sophomore stage will not have the experience necessary; at the same time, revenue at this scale can be significant. Artists will therefore entrust their merchandise operations to a third-party, specialised music merchandise company to ensure supply and demand are met.

Merch companies enter into agreements with their clients that are similar to a record deal. The artist's merch selling potential will be measured on their "per cap" – a metric used to measure merch sales. Per cap is the monetary amount of merch sold at a show, divided by the number of the audience at that show (usually based on the venue capacity).

An example would be:

Merch sales of $200.00
Venue capacity is 100
200/100 = $2.
The per cap for this artist at this show is therefore $2.

A merchandising company will look at historical per cap figures (hopefully the artist's team has kept a record) and will determine an average per cap for the artist. The company can then present a deal based on the per cap and the artist's projected concert calendar.

The deal will include an advance (similar to a record company advance) which is 100% recoupable regardless of any other consideration. Record companies' advances are written off by the label if they drop the artist. The artist does not have to pay back the advance if un-recouped and they no longer own the copyright the recordings of their songs, which may be more lucrative to the record company down the line anyway. A tour merchandising company will expect to see the advance repaid, even if the artist misjudges demand and sells no t-shirts.

The deal will see the merchandise company undertake the design (in some cases), printing, and distribution of the resulting merch. The company will provide touring merch managers and liaise with venues and festival organisers to ensure adequate stock is available at each concert date and that all revenue is collected, taxes are paid, and monies paid to the artist.

SPONSORSHIP AND ENDORSEMENTS

Sponsorship and endorsements are not usually a direct revenue stream – no cash flows to the artist – but these activities can offset the cost of touring.

SPONSORSHIP

Direct sponsorship of an artist only occurs for artists beyond the superstar stage – Pepsi's association with Michael Jackson, a superstar singer/dancer/actor and self-proclaimed "king of pop", is a case study in how the type of appeal a brand or other entity is looking for when considering sponsoring a music artist. The brand's objectives are to increase the market share and audience awareness, locally, nationally, or globally. Any artist they choose to partner with must be capable of providing and sustaining the influence the brand needs to meet those objectives – there are very few artists who are capable of appeal at scale.

Sponsorship is more likely to be offered for festivals and other large-scale, annual events where the brand can be part of growing the event into a brand of its own.

Sponsorship deals occur after both sides have considered their objectives. Indeed, any sponsorship proposal from artist to brand must set out exactly how the partnership will benefit the brand – the sponsoring company needs a clear return on investment, and this will be non-financial.

ENDORSEMENTS

Endorsements are also non-cash agreements and can offset the cost of touring. Endorsements see artists enter an official programme to "endorse" a particular product or brand. The endorsement deal will see the artist appearing in marketing materials, including advertisements, where they talk about the product and why it is good, why they use it, or similar positive statements.

Endorsements in the live music business are usually of equipment. Musical instruments and accessories (amplifiers for instance) and microphones are the common items for endorsement. The equipment manufacturer will provide the "endorser" (the artist) with equipment at a heavily discounted rate, and the artist agrees to appear in adverts and press releases for the product.

The major music equipment brands such as Fender (guitars, basses, and amplifiers), Roland (keyboards, electronic drum kits), and Sennheiser (stage microphone and in-ear monitoring systems) have dedicated artist relationship departments who are on the lookout for new and popular artists who may be already using their equipment. The manufacturers need exposure for their products, and an artist that will be appearing on TV and at the major festivals (Coachella, Glastonbury, etc.) will be considered highly suitable for an endorsement deal. The artist using a Sennheiser microphone at a televised festival appearance is a perfect fit for the artist relationship team at Sennheiser, for instance.[4]

LIVESTREAMING AND RECORDING FOR RESALE

A concert is a synchronous experience – fans go to one place to view the artist, live on stage. It is not usually possible for multiple numbers of the same event to happen at the same time. The recording, packaging, and sale of concerts to enable more people to "attend", or for those who did attend to capture and re-live the experience, has been accepted since the start of the recorded music industry. Technological progress in the form of more powerful, less expensive computing power and broadband Internet now means the two – a synchronous event taking place beyond the concert hall, captured for posterity and re-sold – is commonplace.

The Rolling Stones (a British rock band) attempted a livestream of a concert in 1994 and there is no doubt the activity required many people with specialised skills, along with tens of thousands of dollars, to be able to achieve a rudimentary internet broadcast. Artists today can use social media or dedicated livestreaming services to capture concerts, backstage shenanigans, intimate acoustic sessions, and even rehearsals and broadcast it to anyone who is interested. Using social media does not necessarily mean the content is free to watch; there are many ways a concert stream can be monetised.

Recording the audio of concerts for re-sale is standard practice – the "live" album which appears somewhere in most heritage artists back catalogue is proof of this. Whether music buyers today still embrace the concept of the album is in some doubt, monetising concert recordings through streaming services is common practice – Spotify have their "Spotify Sessions" which feature concert recordings, for instance.

REVENUE – MULTI-RIGHTS DEALS

The multi-rights deal (the "360 deal") is a type of recording deal. The deal is not a revenue stream for artists but does highlight the significance of the live performance as a revenue stream for the superstar artist.

A standard, exclusive, royalty-based, recording deal sees the record company acquiring the right to record and distribute songs by an artist. The record company makes an initial investment to sign and record the artist and make their return from the resulting sales of recorded music – streams, downloads, and physical copies.

A multi-rights deal (MRD) sees the record company (or other entity) obtain the rights, not only to an artist's sound recordings in the same way as the exclusive, royalty-based deal above, but also to income from some or all of the artist's other income streams – publishing, synchronisation rights ("syncs"), merchandise, and live performances (the "360" refers to the full scope of the artists' revenue streams as degrees in a circle. A MRD involving recorded, merch, and live would be a 270 deal for instance).

MRDs involving live performance and, to some extent, merch are noteworthy in highlighting the importance of these income streams. Any record company insisting to a new artist that they have a stake in the live performance revenue will be invested in that activity and more likely to provide tour support for that artist (see *Part Two: Live Music Production* for an explanation of tour support).

PERFORMING RIGHTS

The composers and writers of songs and lyrics have rights attached to their works (the songs and lyrics themselves). One of those rights is the performance right. Copyright law in most countries states that the songwriter has the right to perform the work in public. The laws also state they should be paid for the performance of their works, and this payment is aside from any performance fee they receive from hard-ticket sales. Songwriters register their works with a performing rights organisation (PRO). Concert promoters and club owners must pay a licence fee to the PROs for the right to have works performed at their event (see *"Promoters' costs"* earlier in this part). The songwriters then receive a share of the licence fees when their works are performed in public.

Income from performance rights is not paid on a concert-by-concert basis. PROs pay their members at set times in the year, and the composer of songs performed every night on a tour can look forward to significant payments at those times.

Songwriters must ensure that their PRO is notified when works are performed live. Accepted practice is for the promoter to collect this information after each concert, as it is they who are paying for the licence. The collected information is sent to the PRO in the form of the setlist of the concert, with indications as to the songwriter and publisher of each song on the list. PROs also send representatives to concerts and festivals to ensure that performances are reported so that royalties can be distributed to songwriters, composers, and publishers (Figure 8.1).

PERFORMING RIGHTS FOR ELECTRONIC MUSIC PRODUCERS

The collection of setlists and the identification of the composers is straightforward for most concert situations. No set by an artist lasts more than 90 minutes or feature more than 20 songs. The setlist is agreed before the performance and is written down (even if by hand) to be placed as a physical document on stage. The composer of each work performed is often the artist themselves, so the necessary information required by the PRO is on hand. The artist may be performing a cover version of another artist's song, not written by themselves, and so should have sought permission from the original rights holder in the first place. In this case, the composer's information should also then be at hand. The entering of the title, composer, and publishing company of each song performed in a 90-minute set may be tedious but is not a huge amount of work for the promoter. The result is rights-holders being compensated for their work.

Figure 8.1 Whether it's reporting a gig, classical concert, DJ set, or festival, PRS for Music members are able to upload setlists from performances to ensure they receive the relevant royalty payment

The collection of setlists and composer's information in nightclubs and at electronic music festivals is not as straightforward, and the composers of club tracks are missing out on performance royalties. In theory, the composers/producers of dance music tracks should be registered with a PRO and many are not, releasing their music in digital format straight to "direct to fan" (D2F) services, such as Bandcamp. DJs should be completing setlists of the tracks they play out, and club owners and promoters should be submitting those setlists to PROs. In practice, this is not happening. DJs do not plan sets in advance and pick tracks in real time to respond to the mood of the crowd. DJ sets can last three or four hours, with the DJ situated in a dark, cramped booth. Taking time to write down the name and composer of each track does not really go with the DJs supposed job of vibing with the crowd and creating a great party atmosphere. Rekordbox, the software that many DJs use when performing, does allow the DJ to download a setlist after each performance, but, unfortunately, very few make use of this feature. The result is that millions of tracks are played out in clubs and festivals every year, and little performance income is being passed back to the rights-holders (producers and composers) of that music (see *Track recognition systems*).

TRACK RECOGNITION SYSTEMS

PRS for Music in the UK, along with DJ Monitor (a supplier of recording, analysing, and reporting services to the music business), have employed music recognition technology (MRT) in clubs and at music festivals to better track what music is played out by DJs.[5] Initial trials in 2019 resulted in the MRT recognising nearly 7,000 pieces of music from DJ sets at Creamfields, SW4, We Are FSTVL, Mint Festival, and Bestival (all UK). The copyright holders of that music will then receive payment for the performance of their work – if they have registered with a performing rights organisation.

DIRECT LICENSING

Direct licensing is an attempt for rights holders to receive performance royalties directly from the promoter of concerts in any foreign country where a work is performed – and not rely on the composer's home PRO to collect that income.

A songwriter will register with the PRO of their own country – a UK songwriter with PRS for Music, a French songwriter with SACEM, for instance. The PRO will collect performance licence income for performances of works in their jurisdiction – the UK in the case of PRS for Music, for example. Performance royalty for performance of works outside of the jurisdiction is complicated, time-consuming, and costly for the rights holder. The administrative fees levied by the PROs are multiplied with the collection of foreign performance royalties, with two or more PROs taking their cut as the royalty amount moves from the foreign country back to the home PRO.

Performance rights can be a major source of income for the songwriters in superstar and heritage acts, and the deduction of multiple fees can be galling. Artists have taken to direct licensing to mitigate these deductions, with varying degrees of success.

Effective direct licensing requires the artist to inform their PRO that jurisdiction does not apply to certain territories and performances. The artist then directly licences their works to the relevant promoters. The promoter of the foreign concerts reallocates the money normally paid to the PRO as part of their licensing agreement straight to the composing artist.

Direct licensing is ideal for a solo, song-writing performer who undertakes a concert tour of another country that is organised by one national promoter. Direct licensing becomes problematic when there are multiple composers in the band, multiple promoters on the tour, if cover versions are being performed, and when the artist appears as part of a festival bill. Indeed, administrating requests for direct licensing from a handful of artists appearing at a multi-day, multi-act festival is a level of bureaucracy that festival organisers are unwilling to entertain.

TICKET AND ALBUM BUNDLES

Artists may see an uptick in sales or streams of their recorded music by offering that music included in the price of concert tickets.[6] This bundling was first embraced by Warners Music Group (one of the three "major" record companies) and helps artists market new albums to fans. The artist does not see extra revenue from tickets, but increasing streaming numbers will add something to the bottom line.

Negotiating the arrangement of a ticket/album bundle can be complex, and specialised companies and divisions of record companies help the record company, artist, concert promoters, and ticketing company with fair terms. Not all concert promoters are fans of the concept.[7] Tickets in bundles must "go up" (go on sale) a lot earlier than some concert promoters would prefer, depending on the album release date. This leads to tickets being in the marketplace for too long, which is expensive for the concert promoter and dilutes the impact of scarcity. Concert promoters also don't see any of the proceeds from the recorded music sales, despite having their tickets used as a marketing tool.[8]

NOTES

1 Live Nation Entertainment, Inc., (2020). *Live Nation Entertainment Annual Report 2019.* Beverly Hills. Live Nation Entertainment, Inc

2 Iyengar, S., and Lepper, M., 2000. *When Choice Is Demotivating: Can One Desire Too Much of a Good Thing?* Washington. American Psychological Association.

3 See this graph here for internet searches for 'fidget spinners': https://trends.google.com/trends/explore?date=all&geo=US&q=fidget%20spinners

4 https://en-us.sennheiser.com/artists

5 "Get played, get paid: Music recognition technology", [WWW Document], n.d. URL https://www.prsformusic.com/m-magazine/features/get-played-get-paid-music-recognition-technology/ (accessed 1.22.21).

6 "As ticket bundles become a go-to chart boost, not everyone is celebrating", [WWW Document], n.d. *Billboard.* URL https://www.billboard.com/articles/business/8030253/concert-ticket-bundles-chart-boost-metallica-taylor-swift-kenny-chesney (accessed 2.2.21).

7 Ibid.

8 Ingham, T., 2018. "Steve Homer and Toby Leighton-Pope", *Music Business Worldwide,* 102.

9

CHAPTER 9
REVENUE STREAMS FROM LIVE MUSIC – PROMOTERS AND ORGANISERS

CHAPTER OUTLINE

A concert promoter may be "in it for the music", implying that the reward is the enjoyment of the concerts and not the money, and sooner than later bills need to be paid. A successful concert promoter will therefore explore all revenue streams.

TICKETS

Money from ticket sales is the primary revenue source for concert promoters, just as it is for performing artists. Hard-ticket shows offer a simple proposition – fans exchange cash for the opportunity to see a concert featuring their favourite artist. The promoter of the concert will make a profit if enough tickets are sold to cover costs and pay the performer. The price of the ticket could be a safety net for the promoter – they will need to sell less expensive tickets to cover their costs.

The pricing of concert tickets has often come under scrutiny. This scrutiny comes usually as a result of upsets involving secondary ticketing and also when concert promoters question the value they are providing in relation to the amount they are charging.[1] Concert tickets could be seen as being under-valued; fans will buy tickets on resale sites for a price many times over the face value. Music lovers also pay far more for live music on a cost-per-minute basis. Research has found that fans paid on average $2.29 per minute to see Adele (a singer from the UK) at the Royal Albert Hall (5272-cap) in 2011.[2] By contrast her fans would pay just $0.24 per listening minute to purchase and listen to her entire recorded output at that time.

DOI: 10.4324/9781003019503-10

The situation is confused when soft-ticket events, such as open-air festivals and college shows, are considered. Here there is no direct correlation between the appeal of the artist and the number of tickets sold. Convention dictates that a strong headliner will help to sell more tickets for a festival for instance, and no data exists to support that idea. Indeed, festivals such as Glastonbury (UK) do not publish the proposed artist line-up when they put tickets on sale.

FOOD, BEVERAGE, AND OTHER CONCESSIONS

This book assumes that sales from food and beverage (FNB), and other concert-related activities such as car parking, are not included in the calculations for gross potential and guaranteed fees. Likewise, the running costs of the venue and employment of day-to-day staff (managers, bar staff, chefs, etc.) are not factored into concert deals. The scope of the deal is for tickets sold and direct costs associated with selling those tickets.

Owner/operators of <500-capacity venues will be looking at FNB as part of the financial picture of their business. Individual deal memos will discount FNB as an income, and the promoter's decision to stage a particular concert may well be swayed by the knowledge that the artist concerned will bring in fans who drink lots of beer. It may also be true that the artist's booking agent has held the owner/operator to a deal with a large guarantee that requires the promoter to sell all the tickets to make even the smallest of profit. Knowing there will be additional FNB income will be comforting.

CONCESSIONS

Venues and festivals operate – spaces or services run by third parties that pay a fee to the venue or festival in exchange for the right to operate there. Car-parking at arenas (5,000 – 20,000 capacity) is an example. Live Nation, an owner/operator of arenas, does not necessarily have or need the expertise and equipment to deal with car parking. Live Nation will instead grant a concession to a third-party car parking company who will operate car-parking facilities at Live Nation's venues and pay a concession fee back to Live Nation.

Festival organisers also count significant revenue from concession holders. Open-air festivals in the UK offer "pitches" (set areas) to FNB vendors in exchange for a flat fee. A concession of this type is typically £2500 for a pitch at a major, weekend, festival such as Latitude (35,000-cap). The income from multiple pitches over the three days will make a significant contribution to the festival bottom line.

MERCHANDISE

Promoters and organisers can mitigate some of their losses by producing and selling merchandise (t-shirts, hoodies, hats, etc.). This merchandise may take the form of branded t-shirts in the case of venues (the legendary New York venue CBGB sold t-shirts to concert goers and tourists during the 80s and 90s) or event-specific apparel in the case of festivals. Offering general event merch (as opposed to specific artist merch) is a good move – reports suggest festival-branded merch brings in 60% of total merch sales for certain organisers. Large-scale festivals such as Reading and Leeds (UK) now have slick ecommerce operations to help sell their merch.[3] Reading and Leeds are operated by Festival Republic, which in turn is part of Live Nation Entertainment. Having the concert giant's expertise in advertising and sponsorship in the background cannot harm the festival's merch marketing efforts.

Fans wearing branded apparel also assist with marketing efforts – merch is not free advertising for a festival or venue but is incremental marketing that rewards promoters with ticket sales in the future.

VIP PACKAGES

The VIP package has gained popularity in the last five years,[4] and involves selling additional activities or physical products, along with the concert ticket, at a higher price. VIP packages can be organised by the artist themselves, cutting in the promoter for a small percentage of additional profits, or by the promoters themselves. Both Live Nation Entertainment and AEG Presents have divisions that plan and execute VIP offerings for their touring artists (VIP Nation and AXS Premium respectively).

VIP packages can offer the following activities to the fan:

- meet and greet with the artist
- attending sound checks
- exclusive merchandise including laminates and programmes
- seating with excellent proximity to the performance area, or access to special standing areas also near the performance area
- backstage tours
- Q&A with the artist or road crew
- complimentary food and beverage
- hotel or accommodation discounts or inclusion in package price
- discounts on food, beverage and merchandise

VIP packages are often seen as the preserve of artists touring at >5,000-cap venues, and this is the case if VIP nation or AXS Premium are involved. Artist's touring in <5,000-cap venues can also offer VIP experiences, and these capitalise on the great deal of time the artist and crew are not working. The amount of time after sound check and before the performance is four hours or more, and that time can be utilised to meet fans, sign merchandise, perform intimate dressing room concerts, or generally hang out with fans – who pay for the privilege.

An artist and her team should be mindful of the fans expectation when organising VIP events either at superstar level, or on a tour of small clubs. Charging for some activities could be seen as mere exploitation – attending a sound check with no permission to meet the artist, or pose for selfies, could be viewed as exploitation of "super fans", for instance.[5]

LIVE STREAMING

Livestreaming of concerts and club nights took place well before the pandemic. YouTube streamed a concert by U2 (a rock band from Ireland) live, and for free to the viewer, in 2009.[6] Industry and public awareness of the format increased during the various lockdowns of 2020-21. Trade magazines and the public media reported, often in excited tones, on how livestreaming was going to enable the live music business to offer an alternative to full-capacity, in-person events, thus keeping concert-related businesses open as well as providing artists with alternative revenue.

Sadly, this has not proved the case. The livestreaming landscape now mirrors that of in-person concerts and festivals: the premier "pay-per-view" experiences offered by well known-artists can attract thousands of ticket buyers, just as superstar artists sell out 20,000-cap arenas and command fees of $1,000,000 + for festival appearances in real life. As with pub, club, and bar concerts, the majority of artists offering poor, "shot on a phone" -type livestreams, did not make any money. The latter approach was obviously a last-ditch effort for many artists to replace lost income and was contrary to knowledge gained about consumer habits. Data gleaned from a previous decade of live streams enables the established platforms to advise artist teams on what content works well for virtual concerts, and how best to monetise that content.[7]

TICKETING FOR LIVESTREAMS

The live music business could be accused of not capitalising on digital innovation[8] and this is true of charging for livestreams before the pandemic. The concert by U2 at the Rose Bowl in 2009 (see earlier) was free to watch on YouTube (although consequently packaged and sold as a DVD). Livestreams were traditionally offered as marketing or PR activities, made free-to-watch for the viewer. One explanation for this, other than experimentation, is the inexperience of concert promoters in charging for online events. Established TV networks (such as ESPN, a sports broadcaster) have experience and the technology to be able to offer "pay-per-view", as do online providers such as Amazon. Concert promoters, until recently, had little experience in online events and lacked the operational infrastructure to offer robust ticketing solutions. That situation has changed, and the revenue-depleting problems of fans being able to share log-in information, or watch on multiple devices, have been solved.

Livestreaming has not replaced in-person concerts and will be an important additional revenue stream for promoters going forward. This is especially true for multi-act festivals. Roskilde (DK), Lowlands (NL), Coachella and Stagecoach (both US), and Montreux Jazz Festival (CH) have all offered livestreaming in the past, and will offer behind-the scenes footage and acoustic session, as well as main stage broadcasts, in pay-per-view livestreams when they return to full-capacity formats in 2022.

COPYRIGHT

Not revenue-related, but of concern to concert promoters, is the issue of copyright. Livestreaming of a concert is a performance and the promoter must ensure that relevant licences and permissions are sought before any broadcast takes place. Adhering to the licensing stipulations is not difficult for "add-on" livestreams of an in-person concert – the promoter will have registered with the relevant performing rights organisation (PRO) and paid the fees necessary to ensure the copyright holders receive their performance royalties. However, these protocols may be overlooked, especially for a socially distanced livestream. The promoter or producer may not be operating in "concert" frame of mind, or simply be ignorant of the need for licensing and permissions. Ideally the artist(s) must give their permission, as well as the artist's publisher, and in some cases, the record company. Livestreams of DJ mixes are problematic. A DJ livestream is broadcasting sound recordings, lots of them, over the two to three hours the DJ is online. Seeking permission from each copyright holder is a monumental task. No one does it, and DJ livestreams often fall foul of copyright detection systems.[9]

THE PROGRESSION FOR LIVESTREAMS

Many livestreams were free to view at the start of the pandemic in 2020. That situation changed over the course of that year, with professionally produced, ticketed events accounting for 40% of concert listings.[10] Even so, live streaming and virtual concerts did not attract anywhere near the numbers of the in-person concert business before the pandemic – just nine percent of consumers "attended" a virtual concert.[11] Having said that, estimates show ticketing revenue from virtual concerts was $0.6 billion in 2020.[12]

Going forward, it is recognised that virtual concerts will contribute to artist and promoter income streams. Tickets can be sold to fans who are not able to attend a concert in person; those fans can view a simultaneous "broadcast". This broadcast may be to the fan's own internet-enabled device, as per the majority of livestreams during the pandemic, or in a "windowing" format where the livestream is shown on a large screen in a public space, such as a cinema or specially constructed marquee. This type of event is common with sports events, such as boxing, and concert promoters could replicate this activity with music artists.

Emerging and new artists should also look to virtual concerts to circumvent the issues in trying to host concerts when at the stage where they have no sizeable audience. Promoters are often unwilling to organise concerts for an artist with no history of selling tickets, for obvious reasons. However, new artists desperately need to capitalise on the interest they are getting from tastemakers and early adopters, and virtual concerts are a low-risk way to do that. Undertaking a weekly livestream is less risky than hiring a venue, paying for transport, accommodation, technical crew, marketing, and trying to sell hard tickets, for instance.

VENTURE CAPITAL AND PRIVATE EQUITY INVESTMENT

A by-product of a buoyant live music business is an increase in investment and funding by venture capital (VC) and private–equity (PE)firms. Live music was seen to be growing faster than the economy as a whole before the pandemic,[13] and canny VCs were able to attract investors looking for better than the average 10% return on their money. Promoters who own venues, and the promoter/organisers of successful festivals were the main recipients, and VCs/PE firms also invested in associated music business tech companies.

Consolidation of companies and services is seen as one of the benefits of investment and acquisition by PE companies. Private-equity management firms will invest and control companies and brands like those of an initial investment in a market. This helps synchronise their investments and creates a portfolio of offerings. Waterland Private Equity (a PE firm based in the Netherlands) demonstrated this in 2018, when they bought up Scandinavian concert promoters and booking agents to create All Things Live, an entertainment company.[14] Artists interfacing with any one aspect of the All Things Live (appearing for one of the company's concert promoters, for instance) can be then offered across the various concert halls and festivals that comprise the All Things Live group.

What benefits promoters may impact upon music fans – ticket prices rise to ensure the necessary return on investment for the investors.

NOTES

1 Bary, E., 2019. "Are concert tickets too cheap? Ticketmaster thinks so", [WWW Document], *MarketWatch*. URL https://www.marketwatch.com/story/are-concert-tickets-too-cheap-ticket master-thinks-so-2019-12-26 (accessed 2.4.21).
2 Mulligan, M., 2015. *Awakening. The Music Industry in the Digital Age*. MIDiA Research, London.
3 You can get your on-point R&L merch at: https://shop.readingandleedsfestival.com/
4 Workshop: VIP and premium ticketing [WWW Document], n.d. URL http://29.ilmc.com/r eport/wednesday/276-workshop-vip-and-premium-ticketing (accessed 2.2.21).
5 This document lists the restrictions put in place for VIP package holders attending a soundcheck as part of their "experience": http://static.ticketmaster.fr/static/html/fr/package/5-sos-soundc heck-special-conditions-europe.pdf
6 *U2360° at the Rose Bowl*, 2021. Wikipedia.
7 Forde, E., 2017. "Sweet streams (are made of this)", *IQ Magazine*, 27.
8 Mulligan, M., 2015. *Awakening. The Music Industry in the Digital Age*. MIDiA Research, London.
9 Hinton, P., 2020. "Twitch has started cracking down on DJ live streams", [WWW Document], n.d. *Mixmag*. URL https://mixmag.net/read/twitch-dj-live-streams-copyright-news (accessed 2.2.21).
10 Mulligan, M., 2020. *Virtual Concerts: A New Video Format*. MIDiA Research Ltd, London.
11 Ibid.
12 Ibid.
13 Grace, A., 2019. "Cashing in on live music", *IQ Magazine,* 50.
14 Ibid.

CHAPTER 10
MARKETING AND PROMOTION

CHAPTER OUTLINE

Marketing and promotion is a cost to the concert promoter in most concert deals, and this chapter follows that convention.

Concert promoters would seem to have a simple job when it comes to marketing and promotion. Only fans of a particular artist will be interested in buying tickets to see that artist perform. The promoter can also only sell a certain number of tickets (as dictated by the licensed capacity of the venue). Finally, the promoter only needs to market the event for a certain amount of time – from announcing the show to the conclusion of the performance. Therefore, the promoter needs to send messages, via marketing and advertising, to fans of that artist to inform them of upcoming concert dates and so are in an enviable position in terms of marketing – they have a defined and engaged market (the fans of a particular artist) and a set time to execute the marketing activities. Marketing and promoting concerts should be inexpensive and effective. Unfortunately, this is not the case. A music fan will rarely make a "like-for-like" choice when it comes to purchasing concert tickets. She will want to see her favourite artist in concert – if she is made aware that the artist is performing in a venue nearby. She probably will not want to see a "substitute" artist. She will not attend another artists' show because tickets are not available for her chosen artist, or if she misses the original concert date. She may, however, elect not to buy a concert ticket to see her favourite artist, due to factors that shape consumer buying behaviour.

CONSUMER BUYING BEHAVIOUR APPLIED TO CONCERT TICKETS

Kotler et al (2020) propose a model of consumer buying behaviour.[1] Central to the model is the idea of the "black box" of the consumer's mind.[2] A concert promoter can influence the environmental variables surrounding the purchase of a concert ticket – the marketing stimuli (the 4 Ps – see later) and economic, technological, social, and cultural influences.

DOI: 10.4324/9781003019503-11

The promoter also knows the "buyer response" they want – a person to buy concert tickets and perhaps to share news about the concert with friends and family. The concert promoter must influence the black box by correctly setting the variables. Even then the buyer's characteristics and decision process may lead them to not buy a ticket.

THE "ENVIRONMENT" VARIABLE

The marketing stimuli are the 4 Ps of marketing – product, price, place, and promotion. Table 10.1 shows these applied to the promotion of concerts.

Table 10.1 The 4 Ps applied to concert promotion

PRODUCT	Differentiation between "products" (artists performing live) is high. Alt-country fans will probably not want to buy tickets for hip-hop performers when choosing between entertainment options. Differentiation is vital for music festivals. Similarity of location, time of year, amenities, and ticket price, between competing events is only differentiated by the artist line-up.
PRICE	A concert promoter may decide to compete on price, offering inexpensive tickets, but this is rare. Price-cutting also limits the potential profit for both promoter and artist. Concert promoters have experimented with "elastic", or "variable" pricing, where the price of tickets for an event fluctuates based on demand or is less expensive for a concert on a Tuesday as opposed to a Saturday. The prices achieved on the secondary market is evidence that concert tickets are under-valued.
PLACE	The choice of venue is a form of positioning. Fans of a platinum-selling heritage act would not expect to see the artist perform in a warehouse-type venue. The team trying to break a new grime artist might explore a concert in that same warehouse venue, as the venue would support expectations of being "edgy" or have counter-culture appeal. Positioning applies to festivals; a festival may position itself by appealing to fans of a genre, for instance. Place also refers to the "place" occupied by the purchasing decision in the mind of the buyer – see below.
PROMOTION	Experts in marketing refer to the "promotional mix" – the variety of advertising and public relations activities used to promote a product or service. The promotional mix for the concert promotion business favours advertising. Social media marketing and public relations can be utilised and this is true for arena, stadium, and green-field, open-air events. Differentiation (again) – many venues advertise frequently in print magazine and newspapers, utilising the same display design each time. Each new edition of the advert simply features the new artist added to the forthcoming attractions. There is no differentiation – is the name of an act in a new advert enough to create demand? Concert tours by artists may feature in local newspapers or online blogs.

Table 10.2 Other environmental influences on buyer behaviour

ECONOMIC	Changes in the economy (for better or for worse) will influence buyer behaviour. Investment in concert-related businesses by private-equity groups creates higher ticket prices, for instance. The buyer's current employment situation may curtail spending on entertainment.
TECHNOLOGICAL	The pandemic allowed artists and promoters to introduce livestreams to a wider audience. Improvements in audio and video screen technology enable audience members to see and hear performers on stage at increasing distances. Concert promoters can offer a satisfying concert experience in larger venues.
SOCIAL	The buyer is part of social groups, networks, and adopts social roles. At a simple level word-of-mouth may spread news about a concert. Social influence may create "fear of missing out" (FOMO) within groups or amongst individuals, thus creating demand.
CULTURAL	Music serves as a cultural identifier. Subcultures are reflected in genres. "Metal", as a genre, could include heavy metal, heavy rock, nu-metal, thrash metal, stoner rock, black metal, djent, progressive metal, and others, depending on the cultural outlook of the buyer. Cultural shifts can create demand, or suddenly dictate that something no longer has appeal to a particular cultural group – "that ain't cool no more".

As noted in Table 10.1, the concept of "place" does not just refer to the physical location of a product or service. The idea of place ties into the second column of box A. The buyer's purchasing environment is affected by economic, technological, social, and cultural influences.[3] (Table 10.2) These influences act upon the buyer's behaviour and create the "place" in the buyer's mind on which she will base her decisions.

Economic – changes in the economy (for better or for worse) will influence buyer behaviour. Investment in concert-related businesses by private-equity groups creates higher ticket prices, for instance. The buyer's current employment situation may curtail spending on entertainment.

Technological – the pandemic allowed artists and promoters to introduce livestreams to a wider audience. Improvements in audio and video screen technology enable audience members to see and hear performers on stage at increasing distances. Concert promoters can offer a satisfying concert experience in larger venues.

Social – the buyer is part of social groups and networks and adopts social roles. At a simple level, word-of-mouth may spread news about a concert. Social influence may create "fear of missing out" (FOMO) within groups or amongst individuals, thus creating demand.

Cultural – music serves as a cultural identifier. Subcultures are reflected in genres. "Metal", as a genre, could include heavy metal, heavy rock, nu-metal, thrash metal, stoner rock, black metal, djent, progressive metal, and others, depending on the cultural outlook of the buyer. Cultural shifts can create demand or suddenly dictate that something no longer has appeal to a particular cultural group – "that isn't cool no more".

The influences of Table 10.2 may be out of the control of the concert promoter. A marketing strategy is meant to affect the buyer with as many of the stimuli as possible. Advertising is one way to do this.

ADVERTISING AND MEDIA BUYING

The live music business uses advertising as a primary part of the promotion mix. Costs are low for advertising (depending on the chosen media) and are in proportion to the scale of the event. A dedicated two-month PR campaign with (paid-for) celebrity endorsement is not appropriate for a single concert in a 5000-capacity venue, for instance. Informative advertising[4] – telling the consumer about concert tickets for a new event – is appropriate.

The concert promoter will want to balance initial outlay for informative advertising against the reach and cost-effectiveness of the resulting adverts. Budgeting for advertising at 3–5% of the gross potential of the concert is normal.

Advertising effectiveness is calculated as a cost per 1000 views (or impressions for online ads). For example, a genre-specific national monthly music magazine may have a circulation of 50,000 people and offer a half page advert for $2000.00 per month. The cost to reach each set of 1000 music fans is $40. By comparison, a national daily newspaper may have a circulation of 9,000,000 and offer a half page ad on Monday to Wednesday for $35,000. The cost per 1000 is $38 to advertise in the national newspaper, which is cheaper per 1000 than the music magazine. The advert in the newspaper may be seen by considerably more people, but only for three days, and the people that do see the ad may not be interested in music, let alone buying concert tickets. The concert promoter would probably elect to advertise in the monthly magazine, despite the higher cost per 1000.

The process of choosing where to advertise, and how much to pay, is part of "media buying". A concert promoter can choose to advertise by buying media such as:

posters and flyers
local and national print adverts
radio and TV adverts
social media adverts

POSTERS AND FLYERS

Traditional media buying includes distributed print media, such as flyers (small A5-size adverts given out by hand), posters, and billboards (both larger size adverts affixed to walls, transport stops, and inside public spaces). Flyers and posters are relatively cheap to produce and can catch the attention of the target market segment. They must be strategically placed where they will be noticed, and the message and visuals must be targeted at that audience.[5] It may be seen as old-fashioned to print posters and flyers in this age of social media and online marketing. However, the concert promotion business still firmly believes in the effectiveness of distributed print media. Local and regional promoters are especially keen – concert-goers will be familiar with the ritual of having a myriad of flyers (often advertising concerts and events by rival promoters) thrust at them as they leave a concert or club. The situation is such that many venues now ban "flyering" by third parties in the immediate vicinity of a concert.

LOCAL AND NATIONAL PRINT ADVERTS

You looked at the case of choosing to advertise in a particular newspaper or magazine earlier, based on cost per 1000 people. Even though an advert is for a particular artist in concert, the expense for insertion and printing of adverts is borne by the promoter, and the artist simply reaps the benefit of this expenditure when they (hopefully) sell more tickets.

The concert date may be part of a tour by the artist. Media-buying costs will be shared by the various regional promoters to produce promotional materials that cover the territory of the tour dates. These posters and print ads will be paid for in part by each regional or national promoter involved. The tour is promoted by X, Y, and Z, and they would agree to contribute to the cost of such as national poster and magazine ad campaigns. This expense shows as "national ads" in the promoters show costs. (Table 10.3)

Table 10.3 The advertising section in the settlement for a concert tour. The table shows the amount spent by the promoter on national ads, posters, and leaflets ("flyers")

An artist – August 2021				
Marketing spend @ 20.08.		**Manchester**	**Birmingham**	**London**
	Saleable Cap	260	350	250
National Advertising	**£874.20**	£291.40	£291.40	£291.40
Local advertising	**£24.09**	£24.09	£0.00	£0.00
Advertising production	**£92.50**	£30.83	£30.83	£30.84
Leaflets	**£160.09**	£124.09	£0.00	£36.00
Posters	**£106.00**	£30.00	£38.00	£38.00
	£1,256.88	£500.41	£360.23	£396.24

RADIO AND TELEVISION ADVERTS

Advertising concerts on TV is not cost-effective for concert promoters. The average cost for 30 seconds of advertising time in the US is $112,100.[6] The cost of air time is dictated by the day of the week and the time of the ad placement. An ad aired on a weeknight (early morning) slot could fall to as little as £5000 per airing – and so would the number of people who saw the ad. Viewers have a great deal of choice now, and technology provides ways to avoid seeing adverts on TV.

Advertising on radio should make more sense to concert promoters. Music is played on the radio, and many genre-specific commercial music stations exist. Radio has strong local acceptance which is useful in advertising select tour dates for instance. Advertising on the radio is a lot less expensive than on the TV and can be targeted to reach the desired audience easily. However, radio advertising is often "tuned out" by the listener – radio is known as the "half-heard medium".[7]

SOCIAL MEDIA ADVERTS

Advertising on social media may be less expensive per 1000 views than the equivalent newspaper and magazine advertising. For example, the average cost per 1000 impressions (called CPM, or cost-per-mille) on Facebook is $2.50. The CPM is variable depending on the advert type and the country in which it is shown; you can see the cost is low compared with print or TV.

An effective social media campaign ideally employs a dedicated team to create content and track engagement of both paid-for, and "organic" (free) content. A concert promoter may do this work in-house or hire a social media marketing company to run the campaigns. This is an added cost, either way.

NOTES

1 Kotler, P.T., Armstrong, G., Harris, L.C., and He, H., 2020. *Principles of Marketing*, Eighth European ed. Pearson Education Limited, Harlow.
2 Ibid.
3 Ibid.
4 Ibid.
5 Kolb, B.M., 2015. *Entrepreneurship for the Creative and Cultural Industries*. Routledge, London.
6 Kotler, P.T., Armstrong, G., Harris, L.C., and He, H., 2020. *Principles of Marketing*, Eighth European. ed. Pearson Education Limited, Harlow.
7 Ibid.

CHAPTER 11
FESTIVALS

CHAPTER OUTLINE

DOI: 10.4324/9781003019503-12

Open-air, green-field, music festivals have become a live music activity in their own right, and so deserve distinct examination.

Artists rely on festivals as an income stream and as a marketing opportunity. So much planning of an emerging artist's career revolves around festival performances, judging each festival appearance as a stepping stone to the next level of audience engagement.

At the same time, there are an ever-increasing number of new music festivals. Accusations that the festival market is over-saturated do not deter new entrants, and there is certainly enough artist talent to fill all the time slots at these new festivals.

REASONS FOR THE IMPORTANCE OF MUSIC FESTIVALS

Music festivals are no longer the pleasant distractions for the music industry during the summer months they were 30 years ago. Festivals such as Coachella (US 125,000-cap), Boomtown (UK 76,999-cap), Wacken Open Air (DE 80,000-cap), Pukkepop (DK 13,000-cap), and Rock en Seine (FR 40,000-cap), epitomise the modern festival experience – each a "tent-pole event"[1] for artists and audiences alike. The popularity and importance of festivals (and festival "season") has created a separate business, within that of live music, that deals exclusively with festivals (Figure 11.1).

Figure 11.1 One of the stages making up Rock en Seine festival (40,000-cap), which takes place alongside the River Seine in Paris. Image courtesy of the author

The importance of festivals can be attributed to these factors[2]:

COMMUNITY

Music festivals were started to bring people together. There was an effort to create a community, or sense or community, sharing ideas and thought surrounding issues of the day (Woodstock, Glastonbury, et al). The organisers of those first community-driven events were not concert promoters and had little motive to create profit. Historical accounts document the shambolic, and financially ruinous, nature of early music festivals. Community is hard to establish when the resulting organisation is poor, conditions are inhospitable, and money is being squandered or lost. The reputation of music festivals suffers when these conditions apply.

Compare that reputation with that of modern music festivals. These events are run by experienced concert promoters who can monetise all aspects of an event, run them in a professional and safe manner, and still turn a profit. A sense of community can be achieved; children and parents are attending the same concert events – "and it's not embarrassing".[3]

CONSUMPTION OF MUSIC

The consumption of music has changed. Consumers now "drive the business through new technology and digital platforms".[4] Fans have a subscription to streaming platforms and view music as "free" (subscription costs are so low as to be forgotten). Music fans have discretionary spending power for other music-related items, such as concert tickets and music merch. Often quoted research points to consumer spending favouring experiences over possessions.[5] Music festivals offer experiences, and these experiences can be shared, creating a sense of community.

THE ARTIST'S FINANCIAL EXPECTATIONS

You shall look at the amounts offered by festivals as fees in "*Festivals – the deals*" later in this part, and it is generally assumed artist fees are high for festival performances. It is true, and the fees demanded by agents have grown in the last decade as well. The expectation of high earnings has led to the view of the festival as a "cash-cow" with artists (and agents) then pinning expectations on the season. Festival organisers may have contributed to this expectation by paying higher fees to secure exclusive performances.[6] High fees for one or two performances may dissuade artists from organising their own hard-ticket tour, which may compete with the festival for ticket buyers.

PROFESSIONAL PROMOTERS

Music festivals are often run (and owned) by professional concert promoters such as Live Nation Entertainment and AEG. AEG's profit from its festivals was 10% of its total in 2010; festivals now contribute over one-third.[7]

Profit is the key word here. A concert promoter's ability to make money from performances in concert halls, even stadiums, is dwarfed by the potential of income from a music festival. Hard-ticket shows quite rightly favour the artist; income from festival activities, such as food and beverage, VIP packages, and broadcast rights, are largely controlled by the promoter.

The potential of steady, yearly income, from established festivals may explain the proliferation of events throughout the summer and beyond. Although there has been much speculation about the festival market being saturated,[8] new entrants are being announced, even in this time of pandemic.[9] New festivals mean new talent buyers who need artists to populate, and headline, their events.

THE RISE OF THE FESTIVAL MARKET IN THE US

The US popularised the concept of the large-scale, open-air music festival when John Roberts, Joel Rosenman, Artie Kornfeld, and Michael Lang, organised the Woodstock music festival in 1969. Other festivals, such as Newport Jazz and Monterey, helped to establish the format. European music festivals began in the seventies, either aping their US counterparts or responding to the wishes of US artists wanting to perform at something similar abroad. The UK and European festival market has grown ever since, with some 130 music festivals taking place each year between May and September.[10]

The US market did not grow in the same way as over in Europe. US music fans have been able to attend concerts in semi-outdoor auditorium ("sheds") which offer a similar combination of sunshine and music to that of an open-air music festival. American consumers were also not that enamoured of the conditions found at a typical multi-day music festival – sleeping in tents, poor sanitation conditions, and over-priced food and beverages.[11]

Saturation in the building of sheds and arenas, and the lack of naming rights opportunities for those venues, saw investors and developers looking to other music-related opportunities.[12] Existing festivals had an image problem, and companies such as Live Nation helped to re-energise the market by applying lessons learnt from general concert attendance. Many festivals now take place in or nearer to urban areas than previously, recognising that US concert goers are uncomfortable venturing far or staying overnight. 2014 saw the peak of US festival success, with 58 festivals making it onto the Pollstar charts (including the Top 200 North American Concert Grosses chart) for that year.[13]

SPONSORSHIP

The potential for festivals to attract sponsorship has contributed to the growing number of festivals starting each year. Sponsorship by brands, products, and service companies may not result in a direct cash injection for the festival organisers (other than the rental of ground space for the brand activity), but the reach created by a strong sponsorship partnership will benefit both the sponsor and the festival itself.

Sponsors enter into partnerships with the festival and supply relevant activities or "touchpoints" such as themed transport, phone charging points, wellness centres, branded luxury camping, and so on. Festivals have a captive audience they can offer brands[14] in return, and the major promoters such as AEG and Live Nation are "media owners" with access to consumer insights, databases, social communities, and reach.[15] Brands are willing to pay for this access, with sponsorship of music events, including festivals, totalling an estimated $1.61 billion in 2018.[16] The exposure for brands is not limited to the three or four days of the event – festivals are marketing themselves online 365 days a year, and a sponsoring brand can be involved in that "story" year-long.[17]

FESTIVAL FORMATS

The term "music festival" is often associated with the open-air, green-field, multi-day festival as epitomised by the likes of Glastonbury (UK), Coachella (US), and Roskilde (DK). Music festivals can be presented in several formats. Table 11.1 shows a table of festival formats, with examples.

CAMPING, MULTI-ACT, MULTI-DAY, OPEN-AIR (CMAMDOA)

This format is most associated with the term "music festival". The success and size of festivals such as Glastonbury and Coachella have meant their impact has spread beyond the music fan – for instance, former US president Barack Obama referenced Coachella in speeches made to encourage young people to vote.[18] At the same time, mud, rain, lost wellington boots, and disgusting toilets have become the common reference points for any discussion of a music festival. Festival organisers may downplay these associations and now offer a superior festival-going experience to that of the 70s and 80s.

CMAMDOA festivals (also referred to as "green-field" festivals) will typically offer several stages, or arenas, where live music is presented. A main stage will act as the

Table 11.1 Festival formats with examples

FESTIVAL TYPE	EXAMPLE
Camping, multi-act, multi-day, open-air	Coachella (US), Roskilde (DK), Download (UK)
Non-camping, multi-act, multi-day, open-air	Wireless (UK), Primavera Sound Los Angeles (US)
Headline act curated, open-air	Camp Flog Gnaw (Tyler, the Creator), Roots Picnic (The Roots)
Multi-act, multi-day, multi-venue	The Great Escape (UK), SXSW (USA), Montreux Jazz Festival (Switzerland)
State fair	Illinois State Fair (US)

centrepiece, and this is where the headline acts will perform. Other stages will offer a smaller viewing area (1000 people compared with 10,000 people in front of a main stage for instance), and the acts on these other stages will be upcoming in popularity, or of interest to a niche audience. Stages may also be "themed" or programmed in such a way as to present only music in a certain genre. An example of this would be genre-specific stages (usually indoor areas) at dance music festivals – "the drum and bass tent" is a common stage at festivals such as Nocturnal Wonderland (US 50,000-cap), for instance.

The largest festivals of this type may also offer non-music live entertainment, such as comedy, spoken word events, workshops, and children's activities.

Multi-day festivals are situated in open spaces such as farmers' fields (Glastonbury), park land (Latitude – UK 35,000-cap), or even forests (Future Forest US 2,000-cap). The secluded nature of the sites, their distance from the nearest town, and the size of the site itself, dictates that accommodation for the audience must be on-site. CMAMDOA festivals therefore include camping areas, with spaces offered as part of the ticket price. Fans can either bring their own tents and sleeping bags, and pitch in one of the designated camping areas, or rent pre-built tents, yurts, cabins, or trailer/caravans, that are supplied as part of VIP or "glamping" (glamorous camping) packages. Glamping has become popular with festival goers, and CMAMDOA festivals of all sizes now offer some kind of "VIP" package to their audience (Figure 11.2).

Figure 11.2 "Glamping" at a music festival. Luxury accommodation is pre-built for the camping music fan. Image courtesy of the author

NON-CAMPING, MULTI-ACT, MULTI-DAY, OPEN-AIR (NCMAMDOA)

The non-camping version of the multi-act festival is situated in a city, or area close enough to an urban area that on-site accommodation for the audience is not necessary. Examples include Lollapalooza (Chicago, US 100,000–cap), and Wireless (London, UK – 49,000), both of which take place in parks in their respective city centres. Ticketholders live close enough to the site to be able to drive, or take public transport, home after each day of the festival.

Non-camping festivals have a main stage/other stages format in the same way as a green-field festival. Space may not permit such a diverse number of stages, or number of artists performing as the green-field equivalent, and the festival may be branded as a "headliner-curated" event to differentiate the event. Examples would be Camp Flog Gnaw, curated by Tyler, the Creator, and the Roots Picnic, which is headlined and curated by The Roots.

MULTI-ACT, MULTI-DAY, MULTI-VENUE (MAMDMV)

Not all music festivals take place in fields – muddy or otherwise. Multi-venue festivals, such as Montreux Jazz Festival (CH 250,000 attendees), occupy several indoor and outdoor venues in a city or district, with two or three different artists performing in each venue. Montreux Jazz Festival takes place over two weeks each year, and the music element of South by South West (SXSW) is part of a three-week art, film, and music meeting.

Music related multi-venue festivals often have an industry conference and networking element to them. The Great Escape (UK) is a week-long festival with a conference that attracts some 3000 delegates each year.[19] Artist managers, booking agents, other concert promoters, and other industry professionals, have the chance to attend seminars, workshops, and keynote speeches in the day and see new, up-coming artists showcased in one of the many venues around Brighton, where the festival is held.

GENRE

Festivals are increasingly genre-specific, appealing to niche music tastes. Four Chord Music festival (US 5,000–cap) presents pop-punk, guitar-based bands to the audience, and Copenhell (DK) and Hellfest (F 55,000–cap) cater to an ever-loyal audience of metal and hard rock fans.

THE APPEAL TO ARTISTS

Relatively high performance fees may be part of the appeal for performing at festivals, but that is not the only appeal for artists. A newly successful or emerging artist from the US may lose money when performing at a festival in Europe for instance – the cost of transport and accommodation will most likely be greater than the performance fee.

Other factors contribute to most artists' interest in performing at music festivals:

RITE OF PASSAGE

A consideration for the appeal to artist is that of emulation. The popular artist of today probably attended music festivals when they were younger and now wish to emulate their heroes by performing on those same stages. For instance, the United Kingdom has held contemporary music festivals for the last 50 years. Some of these events are now well-known – Glastonbury Festival, Reading and Leeds festivals, and the Isle of Wight Festival are examples of events that are recognised by the wider public. The parents of a musician appearing at one of these events will be appreciative of their daughter's achievement – perhaps more so than other music business milestones.

NEW AUDIENCES, NEW MARKETS, AND CEMENTING APPEAL

Performing at festivals should be part of the strategy for artists at all stages of their career. There is an assumption that festival shows can help break a baby band, and that may be true. Equally, an act that has "broken" (become popular or achieved some level of success) in their home country may use festival appearances abroad to reach new fans in that market. Artists that are popular in multiple territories may appear at summer festivals merely to keep themselves in the minds of the public, especially if they have not released any new music for a while. Finally, superstar artists will headline festivals to cement their place as world-class acts.

LOW PRODUCTION COSTS

Artists incur costs when they perform live, and you will examine these in *Part Two: Live Music Production*. For now, you only need to know that an artist performing in >1000-cap venues may have certain production costs for audio, lighting, and other elements.

A benefit of performing at a festival is the supply of world-class sound and lighting equipment (plus the crew necessary to operate), all supplied at no cost to the artist. Artists capable of touring at the 1000–5000-cap level need not pay for equipment rental and associated transportation for their festival shows; a summer-long campaign of festivals will also see the artist potentially reach more fans.

MARKETING REACH

A festival must spend a great deal of money to ensure music fans will buy tickets and not tickets for a competing event. Festival organisers can do this by booking high-profile headline acts (which will cost them dearly) and then spend more money on marketing and advertising activities. Artists booked to appear at the festival will benefit from this marketing reach – the artist's name will feature on line-up announcements, exclusive interviews on the festival website, mentions, and announcements on social media (to name a few activities) – all at no cost to the artist.

Marketing and reach is all well and good, and the music industry trade press continually report on the sales and stream surges for artists who have appeared at one of the summer's bigger festivals. Performances at festivals that re-televised, such as Glastonbury

Festival and Reading & Leeds festivals in the UK, also see a strong increase in streams, sales, and renewed interest in those performers.[20]

DRAWBACKS OF FESTIVAL APPEARANCES

Despite the appeal to artists, festival appearances are often not an ideal situation. There are disadvantages in accepting an offer to perform at a festival, and the artist and her team should weigh up the pros and cons.

THE POTENTIAL EFFECT ON HARD-TICKET CONCERTS

A primary concern must be the potential effect festival appearances have on plans for hard-ticket shows by the artist in the immediate future. The rhetorical question is "will a fan pay to see the artist at a venue in the fall after seeing the artist perform at a festival that summer?" There is no definitive answer to that question, and the artist's team must weigh up the possibility of diluting hard-ticket sales. The scenario is prevalent for "lower tier" touring acts – those artists who could sell-out 2,500–5000-cap theatres and large clubs. Ticket sales for performances at that level can be affected by the artist undertaking a summer of energetic festival shows.

THE POTENTIAL EFFECT ON MERCH SALES

Festivals offer artists the opportunity to sell their own merchandise. The merch is offered for sale from booths situated around the festival arena. The festival will charge a commission on any sales, and the artist must usually adhere to a set pricing structure – all t-shirts are for sale at the same price, regardless of the stature of the act.

The festival itself may do considerable business with its own apparel over the weekend, and many fans earmark some of their proposed spending towards the purchase of "the festival t-shirt". Artists, on the other hand, do not sell significant numbers of merchandise at open-air, green-field festivals.[21] A per cap in the range of cents, rather than full dollars at hard-ticket shows is the norm for artist festival merch sales. An artist with a high-per cap at their own concerts will be losing out on merch sales in a summer of festival appearances. A decision must be made regarding the potential increase in fees for the festival appearances, versus the potential loss in merchandising income.

PRODUCTION LIMITATIONS

There are numerous production limitations associated with festival performances. Open-air, green-field festivals are temporary affairs – the stages and any sound, lighting, and video elements are put in place for the time of the event only. It is true that large theatre and arena-scale touring sees production being brought into the venue just for that sole concert, and theatres and arenas are permanent structures with the necessary infrastructure in place. Concert and arena shows also only have to cater for a handful of acts each night (the headliner and any opening acts). Festivals, on the other hand, must cater for hundreds of acts over the performance days, and every part of the production, including the stages themselves, must be brought to the site, assembled, and broken down again after the festival finishes.

NO SOUNDCHECK

The biggest drawback of a festival performance is the lack of any soundcheck time for the artists. You will learn more about the logistic of multi-act festival production in *Part Two: Live Music Production*; for now, you should know there is no possible time for artists to assemble their equipment and test the sound sources as they would do in a conventional concert setting. The lack of soundcheck and preparation time is accepted by most artists and may be an issue for a "baby band" or an artist with little experience of performing on open-air festival stages. Emerging artists with overly complicated instrument setups, or those that rely on darkness and volume for impact, will suffer in the average open-air festival setting.

SUPPLIED EQUIPMENT

Performing artists must make do with whatever sound, lights, video, and stage size is provided for them. An artist may have a certain stage set, lighting design, or video content that they usually use for their performance. The artist may find she cannot use these production assets for her festival appearances. The "bringing in" of production is usually reserved for the headliners of each stage per day, and artists further down the bill may have to work with hanging a simple backdrop for the duration of their performance(Figure 11.3).

SOUND PRESSURE LEVEL LIMITS

Many open-air festivals operate with sound pressure level (SPL, or volume) limitations. These limits are imposed as either a condition of obtaining the licence necessary to hold the festival or because national law has set SPL limits for concerts – or a mixture of

They will both be located backstage during the weekend.

WESTON PARK STAFFORDSHIRE

BACKDROPS

Please note that there is limited use of backdrops on the "V" stage and 4 Music stage (normally headline act only on the 4 Music stage) so let us know if you want to use one and we can work out if it will be feasible. **There is no facility for the use of backdrops in The Arena or Undercover by Virgin Media, so please do not bring them with you.**

PRODUCTION SUPPLIERS

Sound

Figure 11.3 Information supplied to artists regarding the hanging of backdrops on various performance stages. This excerpt is from the now-defunct V Festival which took place in the UK

both. The artist and their engineers must comply with these regulations, for the duration of their performances, or face heavy fines and termination of their set.

The impact for audiences of these SPL limits is questionable – every artist on every stage works within the same guidelines, so the audiences are exposed to a uniform sound volume throughout the day. The limits are usually set to help mitigate "nuisance" sound off-site – people in the house near the festival site might not want to hear the music that others have paid to enjoy. There is no doubt that music that relies on the low frequencies (electronic club music and hip-hop for instance) do suffer from volume limits – the sub-bass frequencies are the most troublesome to those nearby residents; those sub-bass frequencies are monitored closely, making it almost impossible for artists to "pump up the volume" (Figures 11.4 and 11.5).

Figure 11.4 Handheld noise measuring equipment. This type of device would be used to measure SPL at boundary locations. Image courtesy of the author

Figure 11.5 SPL measurement system in place at the FOH audio control position at a festival. The display on the laptop shows the audio levels are within the agreed levels. Image courtesy of the author

THE HEADLINER'S PRODUCTION

A by-product of the popularity of festivals is the "arms race" of artists commissioning increasingly ambitious stage sets and production elements for their headline appearances. Recent festival appearances by Beyonce (a US singer) at Coachella, in 2018, and Stormzy (a UK rapper) at Glastonbury Festival in 2019 featured large set pieces, video content, and numerous dancers, choir singers, and acrobats. These stage sets, and associated video panels, must be built directly onto the performance area during the "changeover" – the period of time between two performances (you will examine festival changeovers in detail in *Part two: Live Music Production*). These pieces must be stored somewhere before the changeover, and as the stages are temporary structures, storage space is usually at a premium. Set pieces and extra lighting equipment for headliners must be stored in every available nook and cranny in the stage and wings, creating a logistical nightmare for stage managers, as well as decreasing available working space for other acts. There has been a worrying trend of headliners' set pieces and lighting equipment taking over the backstage of even the largest festival production areas in recent years, as organisers encourage headliners to create bigger and more audacious "looks".

DAY LIGHT

Rock 'n' roll does not work in daylight! (Or in the rain).

COMPETITION

Festivals, by their very nature, offer a variety of entertainment to attendees. Organisers may want to offer the most value for the ticket price and create scheduling clashes by doing so. Figure 11.6 shows a screenshot of Clashfinder, an online tool that sets out the

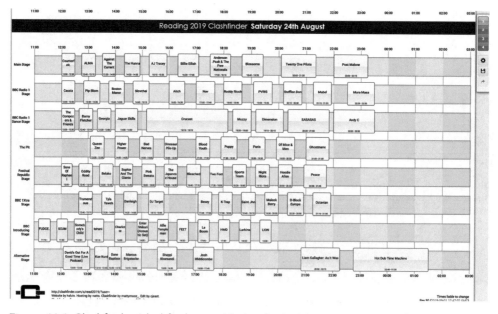

Figure 11.6 Clashfinder (clashfinder.com) helps festival goers to organise their music viewing. But why should they need to?

running orders for popular music festivals. The idea is that the fan can see, at a glance, which acts are on which stage, at what time, and where those schedules clash.

Performance schedule clashes are unavoidable with multi-act, multi-stage events unless organisers build in longer changeover times between acts on each stage. Artists performing on smaller-capacity stages, or lower down the bill on the larger stages, may then find themselves performing at the same time as another, perhaps more popular, artist. The second artist may draw fans away from the first stage – which negates the whole point of the first artists festival appearance!

WORK SCHEDULE

Most European festivals take place at weekends in summer, typically Friday – Sunday from late-May to the end of August. There are then four days of the week with little work for touring artists. European and UK DJs and bands can travel back home after each weekend of festival appearances. US artists (unless in the superstar category) cannot afford to travel back to the US every week and so face increased accommodation costs.

The artist's own crew also suffer from the irregularity of the summer festival schedule. An artist may be booked to appear at one or two festivals every weekend in July and August for example, and that schedule amounts to 16 days of work, spread over two months. The crew person's average weekly wage plummets during festival season compared with during regular hard-ticket touring (Table 11.2).

UNINTENDED EXPOSURE

The combination of production limitations such as volume limits, no opportunity for soundcheck, daylight, rented instruments, and national TV coverage may be too much for some artists, and their appearance on the festival stage may be less than stellar. These artists are just not suited for performing with some or all of the limitations mentioned above – unfortunately, anyone witnessing the resulting poor show will form an opinion about that artist, which may be indelible.

FESTIVALS – THE DEALS

The deals and contract terms for festival performances differ from that of a hard-ticket show.

THE FINANCIAL DEAL – HEADLINERS

The festivals fees ("guarantees") offered to artists are not based on the gross potential of the venue. An artist does not have to sell a certain number of tickets as with a hard-ticket show. Festival deals are offered at a flat fee, and it is up to the promoter and the artist's booking agents to negotiate that fee. You should refer to Figure 8.1 for the range of fees offered to artists.

Table 11.2 Festival work is mainly at weekends, with numerous travel and days off. Neither of which earn the act any money

	AUGUST
Saturday	1
Sunday	2
Monday	3
Tuesday	4
Wednesday	5
Thursday	6
Friday	7
Saturday	8
Sunday	9
Monday	10
Tuesday	11
Wednesday	12
Thursday	13
Friday	14
Saturday	15
Sunday	16
Monday	17
Tuesday	18
Wednesday	19
Thursday	20
Friday	21
Saturday	22
Sunday	23
Monday	24
Tuesday	25
Wednesday	26
Thursday	27
Friday	28
Saturday	29
Sunday	30
Monday	31

An assumption is that festival organisers need to announce successful and popular artists to top the bill ("headliners"). The thinking is that the inclusion of superstar artists on a festival bill helps sell more tickets. Not all festivals announce their proposed line-ups when announcing tickets going on sale (Glastonbury being an example); however, many organisers will need at least one main artist attraction to help sell tickets. Organisers will therefore have to offer the right fee (and other inducements) to their proposed headliners to secure their services. Festival promoter/organisers may then find themselves in a "bidding war" over certain acts – for instance, the booking agent of a newly popular act can afford to play off promoters against each other in order to secure the best deal for her artist. In any case, a festival promoter will want exclusivity when securing a headliner (perhaps by insisting on radius and time-period restrictions) which will drive up the price being sought by the booking agent. An artist who accepts a deal with an attached radius clause is limiting their earning potential in that territory or time frame and will want adequate financial compensation in return.

THE FINANCIAL DEAL – THE REST OF THE BILL

If arranging headliners for a festival is a seller's market (the potential headliners have the upper hand in the power equation between promoter and agent), then a buyer's market exists for the other time slots on many festival line-ups.

We can look at Reading festival (UK 105,000-cap) as an example of this buyer's market. Reading is a popular festival, taking place over a public holiday weekend in the UK. The festival runs over three days and had eight stages and performance areas in 2019. Each stage had an average of ten performance slots available, meaning perhaps 80 slots to be offered to artists that year. That number of slots cannot possibly meet the demand for every suitable artist wanting to perform at the festival. The booking team behind Reading festival are in a strong position when dealing with requests from booking agents trying to secure their act onto the bill, especially for the early timeslots on each day. The agents need to get their acts onto the line-ups of popular festivals, such as Reading, and they will be amongst numerous agents, all pitching their various acts.

Other festivals may not be in such a strong position as Reading – either they are a new entrant to the market or have limited geographic appeal. The power equation may be equal in these cases – promoter and the booking agent both need to make the deals, and neither has the upper hand.

NON-FINANCIAL DEAL POINTS

The contract for a hard-ticket show will usually include various "plus" points – the guarantee/fee plus sound, plus lights, plus catering, etc. Festival deals may also include these plus points. As well as sound, lights, and catering, these may include:

- accommodation
- flights
- ground transportation (aka "grounds")
- extra production – the promoter contributes to, or pays for, the cost of extra sound, lighting, video, and stage elements brought in for the artist's sole use.

The plus points will be individually negotiated and will be based on the artist's contract rider. However, riders are not usually acknowledged for festival performances. Any rider attached to a contract for a festival show will be marked "festival conditions apply",

Table 11.3 A sample of the many site and infrastructure costs for an open-air, green-field music festival

WAGES	Stewards
	Security
	Refuse pickers
	Freelance specialists for site planning, licence application, security liaison, noise management, etc.
	Festival admin staff
TRANSPORT	Trackway and temporary roads
	Signage
	Road diversions
	Shuttle buses
	Car parking space and management
	Buggies and carts
	Charging points
	Plant hire, operation, and storage
	Fuel bunkers
ACCOMMODATION	On-site and off-site workers accommodation
	Production cabins
	Site offices
	Secure storage containers
	Field EMT stations
SITE	Site preparation – tree safety, long grass removal, damming or diversion of streams and rivers.
	Power – supply of temporary event power generation and distribution of local mains supply.
	Fencing
	Lighting
	Toilets – site, camping areas, car parks
	Showers – camping areas and crew accommodation
	Potable water supply and management
	Waste management and removal
	Recycling management and removal
	Grey water management
	Turnstiles
	Metal detectors – walk-through and wands
	Communications – phones, Internet, radio handsets("walkie-talkies")
	Repair of site ready for handover from festival organisers
WELLBEING	EMT – staff, vehicles, operation control structures
	Police – observation towers and operation control points structures
	Catering – festival staff. Kitchens, storage, etc. Creation of rotas and menus
	Catering – public. Bars and kitchen vendor liaison,
	Provision of assistance with "Lost and Found"
	Drone management

(Continued)

Table 11.3 (Continued)

FESTIVAL	Ticketing
	Point of sale machines
	Technology and operation for cashless transactions
	Wristbands
	RFID readers
	Production of documentation – site plans, event management, etc.
	Project management software
	Social media team – marketing and day-to-day
	Festival radio station, documentary maker, and other asset collection
	Camping – organisation and management
	Pre-event site visits, meetings, tender documents, ariel photography
	Sponsorship and brand liaison
	"VIP" areas (not backstage)

or "standard festival rider supplied" by the promoter when signing and returning the contract. Supplying individual sound, lighting, and catering requirements for each artist would be expensive and impractical. Festival organisers therefore supply each artist with standard food and drink packages, and rider requirements for dressing rooms, sound equipment, humidity, stagehands (as examples) are ignored.

Potential headliners may not be suited to performing in the common multi-act, multi-day, open-air setting and may require the promoter to supply additional inducements to close the deal. Artists in club-based genres (hip-hop or electronic dance for instance) will find it hard to reproduce the intimate atmosphere needed to appreciate their music when performing in a large, muddy field and so will plan extra production elements (video, stage set pieces, relaxation of sound pressure limits, etc.) to enhance their performance. The booking agent will do her best to make sure the promoter pays for these extras as part of the deal or, at least, makes a financial contribution to the resulting extra costs.

THE FESTIVAL PROMOTER'S COSTS

The festival promoter or organiser will have the same cost categories as the promoter of a hard-ticket show in a club, theatre, or arena (see *Creating the Deals* earlier in this part). Traditional music venues will have the necessary infrastructure in place for a concert to take place.

The promoter for an open-air, green-field festival will be starting with limited, or non-exist-ent, infrastructure at their venue. The festival may be planned to take place on farmland, in a national park, or even on mountains at a ski resort,[22] for instance. The promoter must plan, and pay for, every element necessary for a satisfying and safe festival.

Costs for open-air festivals can be divided into two categories: site and infrastructure costs and talent and production costs.

SITE AND INFRASTRUCTURE COSTS

The creation of a temporary city necessitates installing a complete infrastructure for the duration of the event. Table 11.3 shows some of the many aspects of site infrastructure that need to be planned, and paid for, by the promoter of an open-air festival.

TALENT AND PRODUCTION COSTS

The provision of the infrastructure required for artist performances is separate from that of the site setup and is used by the artists and their own crew only and is directed by those familiar with concert touring. Table 11.4 shows some of the aspects that have to be planned and paid for as part of the festival production.

Table 11.4 A sample of the many talent and production costs for an open-air, green-field music festival

TALENT BILL	Fee for each performer
WAGES	Production management and associated staff
	Artist liaison staff
	Stage managers
	Stagehands
	Artist catering – chefs and prep staff
TRANSPORT	Parking for artist vehicles
	Production shuttle buses and carts
ACCOMMODATION	Dressing rooms and production offices
	Backline storage
	Dressing room supply storage
	Structures for associated activities – broadcast operation centres, etc.
	Production staff accommodation – on site or off site
PRODUCTION	Power – temporary event power for each arena. Supply of artist ("guest") temporary event power
	Stages and arenas – multi-pole tents, open-air stage structures, decking, and risers
	Sound for each stage or arena to headline artist's specifications
	Stage lighting for each stage or arena to headline artist's specifications
	Video for each stage or arena to headline artist's specifications
	Backline in stock as an emergency precaution or as a standard for smaller capacity/local band stages
	Sound level measurement – organisation and management
	Broadcast – liaison and supply of necessary infrastructure
	Dedicated production communications – Internet, radio handsets, phone lines, etc.
	Artist catering and leisure facilities

NOTES

1 A "tent-pole" event is one where a metric, such as internet searches, social media mentions, or ticket sales, are viewed as a graph over time. The resulting graph of a popular event will grow to a peak that coincides with the time period of the event itself. The display of internet searches or social media mentions will then decrease in time after the event has taken place. The resulting graph looks like a tent being held up by one pole − − hence the name.

2 Gajanan, M., 2019. "How music festivals became a massive business in the 50 years since Woodstock", [WWW Document], *Time*. URL https://time.com/5651255/business-of-music-fe stivals/ (accessed 12.23.20).

3 Shah, N., 2015. "Music festivals: Peace, love and a business battle", [WWW Document], *Wall Street Journal*. URL http://www.wsj.com/articles/music-festivals-peace-love-and-a-business-battl e-1438296207 (accessed 9.6.16).

4 Gensler, A., 2019. "Q's with...Marc Geiger WME partner & head of music on the decade and what lies ahead", *Pollstar*, 39, 15–16.

5 Bacon, J., 2015. "Millennials look for experiences over possessions", *Marketing Week*. URL https ://www.marketingweek.com/millennials-look-for-experiences-over-possessions/ (accessed 12.23.20).

6 Gajanan, M.(2019) "How music festivals became a massive business in the 50 years since Woodstock", [WWW Document], n.d. *Time*. URL https://time.com/5651255/business-of-music -festivals/ (accessed 12.23.20).

7 Shah, N., 2015. "Music festivals: Peace, love and a business battle", [WWW Document], *Wall Street Journal*. URL http://www.wsj.com/articles/music-festivals-peace-love-and-a-business-battl e-1438296207 (accessed 9.6.16).

8 The UK festival market has been pronounced saturated in various trade magazines since 2016.

9 IQ (2020) "Festival frenzy: New events scheduled for 2021",. *IQ Magazine*. URL https://www .iq-mag.net/2020/12/festival-frenzy-new-events-2021/ (accessed 12.23.20).

10 IQ (2019) "European festival report 2018". *IQ Magazine*. URL https://www.iq-mag.net/2019/02/ european-festival-report-2018/ (accessed 12.21.20).

11 Rendon, F. (2018) "Looking at the growth of festivals through Pollstar's charts", [WWW Document], n.d. URL https://www.pollstar.com/News/looking-at-the-growth-of-festivals- through-pollstars-charts-134941 (accessed 12.21.20).

12 ILMC 2016.

13 Rendon, F. (2018) "Looking at the growth of festivals through Pollstar's charts", [WWW Document], n.d. URL https://www.pollstar.com/News/looking-at-the-growth-of-festivals- through-pollstars-charts-134941 (accessed 12.21.20).

14 Eventbrite (2019)"The new era of concert & music festival sponsorships − − Eventbrite", [WWW Document], n.d. *Eventbrite US Blog*. URL https://www.eventbrite.com/blog/academy/concert -music-festival-sponsorships/ (accessed 1.6.21).

15 McCormack, G. (2015) "Unpredictable brands are the headline act for festival sponsorship", [WWW Document], n.d. URL https://www.campaignlive.co.uk/article/unpredictable-brands- headline-act-festival-sponsorship/1329801?utm_source=website&utm_medium=social (accessed 1.22.21).

16 IEG (2018)"Music sponsorship 2018: $1.61 billion", [WWW Document], n.d. URL http://www .sponsorship.com/Latest-Thinking/Sponsorship-Infographics/Music-Sponsorship-2018--$1-61 -Billion--2-.aspx (accessed 1.22.21).

17 Ibid.

18 "Barack Obama urges young people to vote, says 'More People Go to Coachella' than decided presidential election", [WWW Document], n.d. *Billboard*. URL https://www.billboard.com/arti cles/news/politics/8480450/barack-obama-urges-young-people-vote-video-coachella (accessed 12.22.20).

19 *The Great Escape Festival*, 2020. Wikipedia.

20 Paine, A (2019)"Pyramid scheme: Glastonbury delivers big sales boost for headliners", [WWW Document], n.d. URL https://www.musicweek.com/media/read/pyramid-scheme-glastonbury -delivers-big-sales-boost-for-headliners/076716 (accessed 1.22.21).

21 This observation is based on the authors experience.

22 See www.snowbombing.com.

12

CHAPTER 12
STRATEGY

CHAPTER OUTLINE

Practitioners in the live music business have two expectations:

● live performance will help market the artist
● there will be a strategy to put this in place

The expectation of a strategy is based on the assumptions listed in Table 12.1. The strategic vision will acknowledge these assumptions and form the plan for the artist going forward.

Taking the first entry, the artist and her team must be aware that performing live is expensive. You will study the costs associated with touring and performing at festivals in *Part Two: Live Music Production*. For now, you need to know that an artist without a strategy for live performance work will encounter cash-flow problems. Not every concert will earn a profit for the artist, and those money-losing shows must be supported by other, profit-making activities elsewhere.

Our strategy must also consider the commitment of time necessary to undertake live performances. A one-off headline concert is technically an activity taking place one evening between 21:00 and 23:00. However, as you shall see in Part Two, the time commitment necessary to deliver a successful show may require days, even weeks, of planning, rehearsing, approving, and so on.

Touring (performing concert after concert in a different city each evening) is obviously a commitment, and one where other activities are difficult to complete successfully. Creative time for song-writing is affected by constant travel, for instance. Activities involving collaboration with other music artists or creators, such as photographers and

DOI: 10.4324/9781003019503-13

Table 12.1 The team will have these assumptions when planning the live performance career for the artist. The team must allow for the reality of outcomes based on these assumptions – is touring expensive for a DJ or a singer-songwriter and her acoustic guitar, for instance?

ASSUMPTION	CONDITIONS
Performing live is expensive for the artist	Transport and accommodation are required at any level of touring. Both cost money.
Performing live is time-consuming to organise and undertake	Lead-times for organising a tour can be 3–9 months. Touring requires a time commitment from the artist. Other activities are difficult to complete while on the road.
There are barriers to entry for new artists	Lack of credibility or commercial success may deter concert promoters from engaging with a new artist.
There is competition from other events	Sporting events, national holidays, non-music festivals, and the weather itself, are all competing activities.

video directors, is also difficult – schedules need to be synchronised with both parties, hopefully enabling an artist to visit the creator in her home city during a tour date.

The record label must be involved with setting out the strategic vision for the artist as long-term touring commitments will hamper releasing new recordings. An example would be the lack of a new album perhaps creating demand in the future, or the record company deciding to release a "live" album, in the interim, to keep fans engaged with the artist.

Any strategy must consider a new artist's lack of commercial success to date. You know from Chapter 2, *The Booking Agents*, that there is a lack of suitable venues in most major "music" cities. Promoters in those cities have more than enough supply of artists to book into the available venues and will favour those with a history of good ticket sales, or those artists whose demand can be gauged with online metrics. A new and emerging artist will not have historical ticket sales data on which to determine their popularity, as they have rarely, if ever before, performed hard-ticket concerts. The strategy for a new artist must therefore look to including a booking agent in the team as early as possible – if performing live is part of the plan.

Finally, the artist's strategy should consider the assumption of competition. For instance, non-music events, such as football marches in the World Cup tournament, can reduce interest and attendance at concerts in the 100–500-cap market. Concerts at this level have a large "walk-up" appeal – music fans buying a ticket at the venue ("on-the-door") on the evening of the concert, as opposed to buying a ticket in advance. A competing football match will cut those walk-up sales as fans are either at the match or watching the proceedings on television at home or at a bar. In this case a simple strategy would be to offer half-price entry to supporters of the losing team. How the ticket buyer proves their allegiance could also be a marketing stunt in itself!

A LIVE PERFORMANCE PLAN
FOR A NEW ARTIST

Figure 12.1 shows a three-year plan for live performances to help "break" a new artist. The record company and independent publicists are working to get the artist played on the radio as much as possible during the first two years. The strategy is to complement and build on that exposure by being available for live performances during the first three years. Booking concerts in years two and three will not be possible in year one, and the strategy is that artist be will ready and available when those opportunities arise. The plan includes <300-cap club shows, opening slots, and festival appearances for the first year.

YEARS "MINUS ONE"

The artist will have organised her own shows in the winter of year "minus one", and at the start of year one. These concerts will be a mixture of hard-ticket shows in <100-cap bars or pubs, opening slots at larger capacity venues, or showcase performances perhaps at music-industry conferences, such as The Great Escape (UK) and Reeperbahn Festival (Germany). The artist should be developing their strategy at this point with a view to becoming accomplished performers who are able to attract and engage an audience.

The plan in Figure 12.1 assumes the artist is signed to a record company contract or has some other major source of funding and promotion during year "minus one".

BOOKING AGENT

The strategic vision for the artist must be that the artist has the potential to sell hard tickets in the future. Placing the artist into hard-ticket concerts will be difficult initially. The artist has no ticket sales history as they have not previously performed live. Promoters will need evidence of demand, or potential, to risk organising concerts for

Figure 12.1 The 3-year plan to break a new artist using live promotion. The strategy is to complement the work of the record company and PR people who are engaging national radio stations

the artist. The artist and her team must work strategically to include concert promoters and, more immediately, to attract a booking agent. Having a booking agent on board will help to persuade promoters to take the risk on hard ticket shows. You should refer to Chapter 2, *The Booking Agents*, to see the exact work of the agent in the early days of an artist's career; for now you need to know that the agent will work with promoters and owners at <300-cap venues to organise concerts for the artist. These concerts may be headline shows or, more likely, opening slots with other, more established artists. We are assuming these concerts take place in the winter of year "minus one" and at the start of year one.

YEAR ONE

The booking agent will work to get some low-key festival slots for the artist in year one proper. These appearances will expose the artist to new audiences and, more importantly, help the artist develop their stagecraft and appreciation of the unique conditions of concert performance. The festival shows will also showcase the artist to promoters who may then be persuaded to book the artist into <400-cap venues for the autumn/winter of year one and for festivals the following summer. These festival performances might be reserved for the festivals that have a good "look" for the artist and will therefore be able to place them higher up the festival bill next year – and pay the artist more money.

THE "STORY" FOR RADIO

The strategy is to cross-promote the artist with radio play and live performance. Record companies and "pluggers" (publicity specialists who work to secure radio plays) need a "story" to convince radio presenters and their producers to play an artist on their pro-grammes. Announcing tour dates or festival appearances is a good story, even for a new artist. Narratives can be woven around an artist's upcoming first major festival gig, for instance.

FUNDING

The artist team should strategise as to securing concert activities that can help fund other activity. Festival appearances will pay more than hard-ticket shows in the early days of the artist's career, and a summer of festival dates may be enough to underwrite the cost of the autumn/winter headline tour, for instance. The acceptance of festival deals must therefore be viewed in terms of a festival's "look", versus the proposed offer. The booking agent may be able to negotiate performance slots that are less than ideal in terms of the artist's audience (the festival may lean towards a different genre to that of the artist, for instance) but will pay a high fee for the artist. Conversely, a slot at Coachella (US 125,000–cap) is almost universally agreed to be a defining point in establishing an artist, and slots are highly coveted. Importantly, Coachella takes place over two weekends, with artists usually contracted to perform twice, once at either end of the week. Many artists therefore lose money when performing at the festival, as they face high accommodation and travel costs for the week.

The artist team must decide on tactics for festivals – perhaps encouraging the agent to obtain a few high-paying slots with a less than stellar look, only as they will fund future activity.

MERCHANDISE

Concert-specific merch must be considered if an artist's strategy involves live performance. Designing and creating tour merch might not be appropriate. Touring DJs, for instance, do not sell merch – the club environment is not the same as a hard-ticket concert venue and the club-goers' expectations do not include buying a t-shirt after a night out.

Sales from merch will be lucrative, if planned, however. This planning must consider the format of the artist's appearances in years one and two. For instance, artists do not sell significant numbers of t-shirts at festival appearances (indeed, they're unlikely to sell any shirts – see Chapter 11, *Festivals*). There is little point paying for the design and creation of tour merch if the artist is committed to performing a summer season of festival shows and a handful of club dates that first year. Merch would be a consideration for the artist's first headline tour of >500–1000-cap venues in the autumn/winter of year two, and money should be earmarked to produce relevant apparel for that time.

YEAR TWO

The artist will have received solid support from radio throughout the autumn and winter of year one, and promoters will be confident of placing the artist into >500-cap rooms in the spring of year two. At the same time, the booking agent will be working with international festival organisers to secure the artist onto foreign festival bills. The artist will incur high production costs (wages, transport, and accommodation) to perform at the international dates, and it will be necessary to confirm some of the high-paying domestic festivals that were planned during the winter dates of year one.

THE WINTER HEADLINE TOUR

The plan is leading up to the winter domestic headline tour – a milestone in the artist's career. This is the point where the artist can sell out 1000–2000-cap venues. Radio support should still be strong at this point, and the strategy allows for capitalising on new exposure with live performances.

New artists may be tempted by the higher fees offered by festivals, but relying on summer festivals to progress a career is not a good strategy. Selling hard tickets and progressing in venue capacity will ensure the longevity, and earning potential, of the artist.

YEAR THREE

The artist will have been able to write and record new material during the late summer/early winter of year two, and a new album should be ready for release in the second quarter (April–June) of year three. A new album is obviously a great story to take back to radio, and hard-ticket sales will also benefit from announcements about tour dates and new material on the radio.

However, other territories are now clamouring to see the artist live, and consideration must be given to that demand. The artist will have performed at a handful of international festivals in year two, and a winter tour of key countries is plotted out for the winter of year three.

ONE PROMOTER

The artist will have worked with a variety of local, regional, and national promoters so far. A national or international promoter, such as AEG/Goldenvoice, SJM concerts, or Live Nation, may now be interested in promoting a tour for the artist as opposed to one-off shows. The national promoters mentioned above all organise or own festivals and so can offer the artist a mix of festival slots and hard-ticket concerts.[1] This mix of formats will be planned for spring/summer of year three. The festival appearances will help with the marketing of the new album and provide the funding for international touring at the end of year three.

NOTE

1 Renton, F (2018) "Q's with UTA's Ken Fermaglich: Powerhouse rock agent talks clients, industry", [WWW Document], n.d. URL https://www.pollstar.com/News/qs-with-utas-ken-fermaglich-powerhouse-rock-agent-talks-clients-industry-135722 (accessed 3.12.21).

PART TWO
Live Music Production

The production of live music is intrinsically linked to the management of the live music business. The cost and complexity of modern concert touring must be examined, as both influence the successful delivery of concerts, tours, and festival appearances. We will be examining the planning and logistics of live music production from the artist's perspective in this part.

DOI: 10.4324/9781003019503-14

13

CHAPTER 13
PLANNING A TOUR

CHAPTER OUTLINE

A tour, or series of consecutive concert dates, is planned in stages, with some stages overlapping others. Common planning phases would be:

Phase 1: Identification of time for touring
Phase 2: Seeking and accepting offers from promoters
Phase 3: Agreeing contracts and announcing on-sale dates
Phase 4: Marketing
Phase 5: Budgeting, logistics, and planning ("pre-production")
Phase 6: Rehearsals
Final phase: On the road

Figure 13.1 is a chart that shows the approximate time periods necessary for different levels of touring. You have looked at the processes involved in phases 1–3; details about phases 4–6 follow in subsequent chapters.

The structure of planning is a fluid process. Artist teams comprise a few people, so there is no need for a rigid hierarchy. Several phases may be implemented at the same time depending on the level of touring, whether non-production or production venues, and the capacity of the venues. A promoter who makes an offer to stage a concert as part of a tour of stadiums (>30,000-capacity) must ensure the venue is available on the date they propose and that they secure the venue with a deposit. Stadiums have limited availability for concerts, so the promoter should not assume the venue will be available unless it is secured – typically 18 months before the proposed concert date.

PLANNING FOR TOUR SUPPORT

The artist team must ensure the artist can afford to undertake the tour. A budget must be drawn up as soon as the proposed income is received from promoters. You will see more about artist tour budgeting in *Part Two: Live Music Production*; you should know for now that it may be the case a proposed tour or festival appearance is deemed too expensive to undertake without additional revenue.

DOI: 10.4324/9781003019503-15

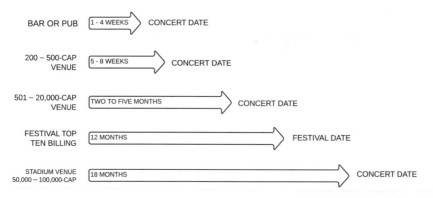

Figure 13.1 The time scales needed to organise concerts at different capacity venues

Artists signed to a record company may have the option of applying for tour support. Tour support is an agreement by the record company to loan (as part of the record deal's advance) the money necessary for the artist to fulfil touring commitments. You will see more about tour support later in this part, but you should know that an application for tour support, and payment made for a successful application, can take three to four months. Tour support is going to be vital in making sure goods and services from suppliers can be paid for. The transportation companies that specialise in music touring will require a significant percentage of the total cost to be paid before the tour starts, for instance. An artist's team that has not factored in the time needed to apply for tour support and receive the funds risks not being able to pay for the very tour services they need. Phase one of the planning process should therefore include the artist's record company so that a realistic time scale for support can be established.

VENUES

The expense required to undertake a tour is dependent on many factors, the two main ones being the distance between dates on the tour and the type of venues. The distances between stops on the tour will influence the mode of transport, and you shall examine that in a subsequent section. The type of each proposed venue – its capacity and whether or not it contains any sound and lighting equipment – will influence the budget. Table 13.1 shows the accepted categories of suitable concert venues.

Live Nation Entertainment also lists Restaurants and Music Halls (1,000–2,000 capacity) as a venue category.[1] The company states that these indoor venues, as personified by its own House of Blues brand, "offer customers an integrated live music, entertainment, and dining experience". They go on to say this type of venue "attracts customers independently from a live music event".

NON-PRODUCTION AND PRODUCTION VENUES

Venues can be sorted by capacity, allowing promoters to choose a suitable venue that caters to the demand for an artist. Venues may also be sorted by whether they have sound, lighting, and staging as permanent fixtures.

Table 13.1 Accepted categories of venues with indicative capacity

VENUE TYPE	INDICATIVE CAPACITY
Small to large clubs, including night clubs	100–2,000 capacity
Ballrooms	800–1,500 capacity
Theatres and performing artist centres (PACs)	1,000–6,500 capacity
Auditoriums	5,000–10,000 capacity
Mid-size arenas	15,000–20,000 capacity
Amphitheatres ("sheds")	5,000–30,000 capacity
Stadiums	15,000–100,000 capacity
One-off, alternative venues	>100,000 capacity

Sound (also called PA), lighting, video, and staging equipment are collectively called "production". An artist that tours with rented PA and lights is said to be "carrying production". An artist need not worry about this in the early stages of her career – she will be performing in <750-capacity venues that have permanent, installed, PA and lights – so called "in-house". Oslo in London (375-capacity) is an example of a venue with in-house PA and lighting production. An artist does not need to rent production to tour in venues at this level – the Lexington is a non-production venue. The non-production venue will also supply sound and lighting technicians to assist the artist and her crew. The cost for these is included in the hire of the venue.

The likelihood of the venue containing permanent in-house sound and lights decreases as the capacity increases – venues with a capacity of >2000 will rarely have in-house sound and lights. There are economic reasons for this. Venues in the >2000-capacity range have fewer concerts per week than the smaller ones. PA and lighting equipment is expensive and a waste of money if not used for days at a time.

The O2 Academy Brixton (4921-capacity), on the other hand, is an example of a production venue. There, the artist will need to have all necessary production (PA, lights, stage risers, etc.) supplied by renting from specialists for the individual concert Figure 13.2). A deal for a concert at the O2 Academy Brixton will see the promoter paying to bring in the PA and lights, this being specified in the contract with the artist (a clause that specifies the guaranteed fee the promoter will pay, plus PA, lights, and catering). The artist may leave it up to the promoter to find a suitable PA company for a one-off show at this venue, for instance, and therefore have no production expenses related to PA hire.

CONTINUITY IN PRODUCTION VENUES

Logistics and costs change significantly for a tour of production venues as opposed to non-production venues. Artists will want continuity of sound, lights, video, etc., for the duration of the tour – this is difficult with different vendors supplying sound and lights in different venues each night. A convention is for the artist to rent one system from one supplier and then transport that system themselves from venue to venue for the duration

Figure 13.2 The O2 Academy Brixton is a 4921-capacity production venue, seen here at the start of a concert day. The building contains no concert sound or lighting equipment, so the promoter must rent in all the necessary equipment. Image courtesy of the author

of the tour. Individual show contracts remain the same, however, with the promoter agreeing to supply PA, lights, and catering at their expense. The artist hires the PA system, for example, and the promoter contributes towards the cost of that PA system rental, and this contribution covers the PA rental costs. The reality is that the artist will specify a PA system far more expensive to rent than covered by the promoter's contribution. The artist ends up paying for audio rental, even though the contract stipulates the promoter pays for that rental.

NOTE

1 Live Nation Entertainment, Inc.,(2020). *Live Nation Entertainment Annual Report 2019.* Beverly Hills. Live Nation Entertainment, Inc.

14

CHAPTER 14
BUDGET

CHAPTER OUTLINE

Performing live is expensive for the artist. Budgeting for the tour or event is therefore a vital part of the planning for the activity. An artist's booking agent and management may agree on a proposed set of dates for a tour, or a run of open-air festival appearances, and someone on the artist team must determine if the artist can afford to undertake the tour or festivals.

The term "budget" is used to describe the list of anticipated income and expenses. The artist manager may draw up a budget or may hire on a concert tour manager (CTM) to look at the logistics of the touring period and then draw up a budget.

Completing a budget serves two purposes: the primary purpose is to indicate to the artist how much profit or loss they will make from the proposed live performance activity (a loss is called the "shortfall"). The artist can then decide whether they are willing to undertake the activity and where to find additional revenue to cover a shortfall.

The second function of a tour budget is to act as a to-do, a checklist of services and activities that must be rented, purchased, or planned for, in order for the tour to go ahead. CTM's will use a tour budget template for this reason. The template is written in a spreadsheet program and has been created and amended based on the CTM's experience of working on concert tours in the past. The CTM will have added services and activities that are necessary as part of the tour planning process; working through the budget not only necessitates enquiring as to the cost of a service or item, the line entry in the budget also reminds the CTM (or whoever) to enquire or plan the service or activity in the first place. An example of a tour budget template can be found in Appendix 5.

Wages for a merch seller on a tour of non-production venues can serve as an example of the budget template used as a memory aid. The cost of producing merch would not be included in a tour budget as the income from sales cannot be guaranteed. A separate budget for the cost of sales for selling t-shirts would also be needed, and this budget may be drawn up by someone other than the CTM. That budget would include the wages for a merch seller. However, the merch seller would need transportation, feeding, and somewhere to sleep along with the rest of the touring cast and crew, and so these costs

DOI: 10.4324/9781003019503-16

must be included in the main touring budget. A line item regarding "merch seller" would remind the CTM of this cost, even if they were not producing the budgeting for the merchandise operation.

TOUR SUPPORT

The tour budget may identify a shortfall. An artist signed to a record company may apply for tour support, a load of money to cover the shortfall in touring income. The tour support is recoupable – it must be paid back from income the artist receives from streaming, downloads, and physical sales.

The record company will want to see a realistic budget to support an application for tour support. Touring may be in the interest of the record company (the traditional activity of touring is to promote a newly recorded release), and the record company will be careful in deciding how much money to provide for support. The company will already have invested significant sums to bring the artist to market and will want a return on their investment. The IFPI, a trade body, suggest that tour support investment to break a new artist would be $100,000.[1]

An application for tour support is usually made to the business affairs department of a record company, accompanied by the budget and support from the artist's A&R team within the company. The application will have not come out of the blue, as the record company will hopefully have been consulted and involved with phase one of the tour planning. The business affairs department may request amendments to the budget to decrease the amount needed to cover the shortfall. The artist will have to look again at proposed expenses and see where cuts can be made. The bill for wages is usually a major expense for any organisation and this is true of touring artists; it may be necessary to reduce salaries or cut a production element (video or stage set, for instance) that requires extra technicians on the road. The ratio of payments varies from deal to deal, with 75% upfront and 25% on completion being common.

Hopefully a compromise will be reached, and the record company will approve the budget and the amount of tour support required. The transfer of funds is not automatic. The artist will have to invoice the record company for the tour support money, and payment of the funds can take up to 90 days. The total amount of the tour support is also not paid in full. Tour support is conventionally paid in two tranches, with an amount eligible for invoicing before the tour starts, and the rest being eligible for invoicing after the finish of the tour and "on receipt of completed tour accounts".

The staggering of payments can cause problems for the artist. Consider why the artist is applying for tour support in the first place – they do not have enough income from the upcoming shows to pay all their suppliers. The tour support money is supposed to alleviate that problem, yet only receiving 50%, for example, of the agreed support money may not help the artist's financial situation. Table 14.1 shows a scenario where the payment of tour support still leaves the artist with a shortfall before the tour.

Table 14.1 An artist receives 75% of the agreed tour support before the first date, and still does not have enough money to pay imminent bills

Shortfall is:	$10,000	
75% of shortfall is payable in advance:	$7,500	
Pre-tour costs		
WAGES		
Payroll for 1st week	$2,000	*2 crew @$200 per day, x 5 days*
Per diems	$300	*$10 x 6 people x 5 days*
TRANSPORT		
Sleeper bus	$5,000	*$10000, $500 a day x 20 days.* **50% deposit up front**
Crew travel	$200	*To rehearsals*
ACCOMMODATION		
PRODUCTION		
Rehearsals	$1,000	*2 days in a room at $200. Crew hotel @$150 x two rooms x 2 nights $600*
Insurance	$1,600	
Carnet	$600	
Tour books, laminates, etc.	$400	
Consumables – strings, sticks, etc.	$300	
Total pre-tour spend:	**$11,400**	*Total spend is more than the tour shortfall.*

BUDGETS FOR PROMOTIONAL ACTIVITY

An application for tour support is applicable for the artist undertaking hard-ticket concerts or festival appearances. The artist earns money from ticket sales – indirectly, in the case of festivals.

The artist will also undertake live performance activity purely for promotional purposes (not for a fee), and the costs of such activity are paid for by the record company. These costs are non-recoupable. The record company views them as a direct marketing cost and picks up the bill accordingly. Common live promotional formats include:

- "sessions" on the radio – the artist performing live for a particular radio presenter
- special guest spots on television shows
- televised awards shows
- in stores - small concerts in music or fashion stores
- album launches – performances in unusual locations as a way of drawing attention to the release of new material by the artist

Live promotional ("promo") activities are organised by the promotional department of the record company. Activities may be concurrent with an artist's touring activity, and the touring transport, crew, and equipment may be used to implement the promotional activity. For instance, the artist may have a concert in Brighton, England as part of a tour. The record company, working with an independent radio "plugger", may secure a session for the artist on 6 Music, part of the BBC, the national broadcaster. The session takes place on the morning of the Brighton show. It therefore makes sense that the tour manager, backline technician, backing singer, instruments, and splitter van that are being used for the tour are used for the session. However, the artist is paying for the crew and from their touring income (probably funded by record company tour support). The use of the van, equipment, and crew for the 6 Music session will be paid directly by the record company. A separate budget is required when planning the promo activity, and separate invoices must be raised for transport and wages costs for that session alone.

INVOICING THE RECORD COMPANY

The artist must invoice the record company for the agreed tour support, and, in the case of promotional activity, all suppliers should also invoice the record company. The latter activity causes much frustration amongst concert production suppliers and crew, and an explanation is warranted.

In the example above, a splitter van rental company will have quoted to supply a van to the artist for the tour. They will invoice the artist directly for the resulting bill. If the artist uses the van for promo activity, as above, then the artist will want the record company to pay directly for the use of the van for that activity. The artist will instruct the van rental company to invoice the record company directly. Now the van rental company is owed money from two separate entities for the same vehicle during the same time! To make matters worse, most record companies, especially the three majors, operate bureaucratic invoicing and payment system for their suppliers. A supplier must first register on a computerised system. Once accepted, the supplier must quote for the proposed work (even if the activity has taken place) and then be given a purchase order number (PO number) if the quote is agreed. Armed with a PO, the supplier can use the system to raise an invoice. To add a further layer of complexity, the record company may stipulate its payment terms as part of the terms and conditions, and those terms may include payment of invoices only after 30, 60, or even 90, days from receipt of invoice. The whole procedure can lead to frustration – the van rental company in the example having to wait three months to be paid for one day's hire!

SCOPE OF LIVE PERFORMANCE EXPENSES

Consider a baby band performing at a bar in a town in the next state. A list of expenses might include:

- renting a rehearsal room for two nights before the show
- buying new guitar strings and drum sticks

- gas and oil for their van
- three rooms in a cheap hotel
- buying breakfast the morning after the show ...

... and so on. Concert touring and performing live at any scale will incur a myriad of expenses in the following four categories:

- wages
- transport
- accommodation
- production

We shall examine the costs in each category in the following chapters.

NOTE

1 IFPI, 2019. *Global Music Report 2019.* International Federation of the Phonographic Industry, London.

15

CHAPTER 15
WAGES

CHAPTER OUTLINE

The wage bill for a touring artist will be the biggest expense for the tour. Expenses are dictated by venue type and distance – for example touring production venues requires additional crew to that of the accepted provision of a "sound guy" for non-production touring.

The budget needs to not only reflect the daily or weekly salary of touring cast and crew members but also pay for work in the period leading up to the tour. A discussion also needs to be had about the pay rates for non-workdays, such as days off while on tour. An example would be putting crew on to 75% of their daily rate for non-show days, and this would have to be proposed and agreed at the budgeting stage.

Wages for touring personnel can be split into two categories:

performers
non-performers

PERFORMERS

Performers are not limited to the members of a "traditional" band. Many artists are individuals who employ other musicians, singers, and dancers to augment the live show. The performers are paid on a show-by-show basis, or may be retained, receiving a monthly salary.

PROFIT SHARE

Members of a band (a group of musicians in the traditional sense) are usually in an unofficial profit share agreement for live performances with the other band members. Profit from touring activity is split between the members and there may be no profit at the start of the band's career. Applications for tour support may include a small salary for each member for the duration of the tour.

DOI: 10.4324/9781003019503-17

Table 15.1 The Top 10 artists of 2020, as reported by Billboard magazine. All ten are solo artists

POSITION	ARTIST
1	Post Malone
2	The Weekend
3	Roddy Ricch
4	DaBaby
5	Drake
6	Juice WRLD
7	Lil Baby
8	Harry Styles
9	Taylor Swift
10	Pop Smoke

The band members will hopefully see a return on their investment of time as they begin to command higher performance fees in venues with larger capacities.

SESSION MUSICIANS

Music production technology and web services enable artists to write, produce, mix, master, release, distribute, and promote their own music without having to sign to a record company. The result of this is the number of successful individuals (so called "solo artists", in contrast to bands/groups, who attract the attention of new fans (Table 15.1).

Launching a solo artist into the world of live performance can result in a large wage bill. The artist will need music to perform on stage, and they can decide to play instruments themselves onstage, perform using playback systems, have other musicians performing the parts live, or a combination of the above. Choosing to have other musicians on stage will mean paying those performers for their work.

There are a couple of scenarios that are common to the solo artist and ancillary musicians. The first sees the artist surrounding herself with friends, who have always performed with her, and that have grown with the artist as she is able to sell-out larger capacity venues. The musicians may have received little, if any payment, for gigs in the past, and will now expect an appropriate daily rate of pay now that the named artist is becoming well-known.

The second scenario is that of the solo artist (or duo) who have never embarked on any live work before and must put a band together to perform at festivals and on radio sessions. The solo artist in question may not know other musicians or wishes to engage with more talented performers. In either case it is likely that session musicians will be hired. Session musicians are professional performers for hire and are adept at learning new material, working together in rehearsal spaces, and acting in a professional manner to help project the talent of the named artist. These qualities also mean that session musicians can charge a significant daily rate for their services – something that will add to the bottom line of the tour budget.

MUSIC DIRECTOR

Hiring session musicians will require the services of a music director.

The MD was traditionally the person who would audition and hire suitable musicians for music touring, TV shows, and other situations requiring the use of session musicians. The MD would also adapt the recorded material for live performance, creating special charts of sheet music for each section in the resulting band of musicians.

The role of the MD is similar today, and a competent MD must now be able to use music production digital audio workstations (DAW) such as Ableton's Live and Avid's Pro Tools. The artist probably created their music in such DAWs in the first place; the MD must be able to take the original parts and decide on how best to incorporate human elements into the resulting live production. The MD has become pivotal in the process of taking an artist from "bedroom to stage" (from initial naive solo recordings to professional stage shows), and good ones are sought-after. Unfortunately, this expertise comes with a high price tag; MDs will not only work with the act on tour, they will also spend considerable (paid) time arranging the material and rehearsing with the artist and other session musicians.

RATES OF PAY AND MUSICIAN UNIONS

Setting a daily rate or salary for MDs and session musicians will be part of the budgeting process. The musician may have a daily rate in mind when being auditioned and it will be up to the artist's team to discuss that rate if the musician is successful in gaining a place in the touring band. The budget will guide the discussion, and pitching a realistic starting rate is difficult. Rates for session musicians are often based on convention and previous practice, but those rates may be unachievable for an emerging solo artist.

Unfortunately for artists, musicians are also members of unions or federations who want to establish pay rates for their members. These organisations have the interests of their members at heart and publish guides of recommended pay rates for session musician activities. Some unions have been able to negotiate and set rates directly with entities who employ session musicians. The Musicians' Union (MU) in the UK has worked with the BBC (a national broadcaster) to set rates for work on TV and radio. These rates have not yet become standard in concert touring, but the MU does publish recommendations of pay rates for this activity (Table 15.2). These guides serve as a useful starting point for any member musician who is approached to work as part of a touring band. The American federation of Musicians in the US (AFM) has similar guidelines, with $275 a day being their recommendation for touring work.

Table 15.2 The Musicians' Union guidance for performers pay in the UK. The table refers to session musician pay for artists who have recording contracts. The union also published pay scales that have been negotiated and agreed by concert orchestras and broadcasters

VENUE TIER	INDICATIVE CAPACITY	DAY RATE
5	>300	>£200
4	>1000	>£250
3	>2000	>£300
2	>5000	>£350
1	Arenas, stadiums, festival headline slots	>£400

The rates are recommendations, but it is not mandatory for any touring organisation to recognise them. However, union members are unlikely to be keen on working for less, and the member that does, runs the risk of upsetting their union colleagues and having their union membership revoked.

DANCERS AND EXTRAS

Dancers are a common sight during large-scale, pop concerts and bring with them a unique set of financial challenges.

Dancers are numerous, adding to transportation and hotel bills. Warming up takes up lots of space backstage and dancers will require heating in those areas as their costumes are often flimsy. The costumes themselves get ripped and dirty, and so another job – that of wardrobe assistant – must be created. The wardrobe assistant's job is to attend to the cleaning, pressing, and repair of the dancers' stage clothes, with more expense on laundry and millinery consumables. Finally, dancers consume a great deal of food. The food must be highly nutritious, and so is probably best prepared "in-house" (at the venue). The promoter will have agreed to pay for catering for cast and crew and may balk at the extra cost for dancers thus transferring the expense back to the artist.

NON-PERFORMERS

Non-performing tour personnel assist the artist in technical roles (audio engineering for instance), support (wardrobe, catering), or management. These people are collectively called the crew (or road crew) and are hired by the artist, either directly or as part of the service provided by a supplier (the PA rental will send a crew with the system, for instance). The number of crew working for an artist on tour can be as small as one (a tour manager for a DJ or emerging artist, for instance) up to 50 for a stadium-level production tour (Table 15.3).

You have seen that the artist's touring costs are dictated by venue type. This is reflected by the number of crew an artist hires. An artist touring non-production (<700-capacity) venues will not be travelling with a rented PA system – each venue has its own PA – and

Table 15.3 Tour personnel on mid-level and arena/stadium tours

DEPARTMENT	ROLE	NUMBER	DIRECT EMPLOYER
PRODUCTION MANAGEMENT			
	Tour manager	1	Artist
	Production manager	1	Artist
	Production assistant	1	Artist
AUDIO			
	FOH engineer	1	Artist
	Monitor engineer	1	Artist
	Audio system technicians	3	Audio rental company
	Backline technician – drums	1	Artist
	Backline technicians – guitars and bass	2	Artist
	Backline technician – MIDI/ playback	1	Artist
LIGHTING			
	Lighting designer/operator	1	Artist
	Lighting system technicians	2	Lighting rental company
VIDEO			
	Video operator/director	1	Artist
	Video system technicians	2	Video rental company
PRODUCTION			
	Caterers	2	Catering supply company
	Wardrobe/dressing room assistant	2	Artist
	Personal security/close protection	1	Artist
	Rigger	1	Artist
	Set technicians/carpenters	2	Set supply company
TRANSPORT			
	Truck drivers	2	Trucking company
	Bus drivers	3	Bus company
MERCHANDISE			
	Merchandising manager	1	Merchandising company
	TOTAL TOURING PERSONNEL	**32**	

so will not have the expense of "system techs" (technicians supplied by a rental company) on the road. Non-production venues will supply technicians to help mix sound and operate the lights, and these salaries are a cost to the promoter.

Road crew personnel are freelancers who will charge a set daily or weekly rate. You shall look at pay rates and conditions for other tour crew later in this section and two roles need further examination here:

- Concert tour manager
- Production manager

CONCERT TOUR MANAGER

The concert tour manager (CTM, also known as a road manager) is hired primarily to travel with the artist on-the-road to act as a liaison between the artist, the venue, the promoter, and the booking agent. The CTM will collect the performance fee and take care of other duties as they arise on the day. However, an artist can benefit greatly from the experience and knowledge of a CTM well before the tour starts, and this is when a CTM typically becomes involved.

The concert tour dates are submitted to the artist manager by the booking agent and the artist manager may attempt to draw up a budget and look at the logistics of the proposed tour. Hopefully, the manager is too busy with other aspects of her artist's career and so will hire on a CTM to take charge of this period of touring activity called "pre-production".

PRE-PRODUCTION

Once involved, the tour manager will look over the date sheet and assist the artist's team with the logistics and budgeting of the proposed tour. The CTM will have the experience to understand the many issues and challenges of touring – especially if international concerts are involved. During the pre-production period, areas where money can be saved and – more importantly – where it needs to be spent (paying for little-known, but necessary good and services, for instance) will be identified. You shall look at the pre-production process later in this section.

REMUNERATION FOR PRE-PRODUCTION WORK

An issue for the CTM at this stage is remuneration for their services. Tour planning and pre-production can start some months before the start of the tour, but the CTM will have a daily or weekly touring rate and will be unable to charge that rate to the artist for months on end during pre-production. The work itself is desk-based, knowledge work, interspersed perhaps with meetings and site visits. Such work does not require five days a week, 9–5 attendance, yet the constant refining of budget, travel schedules, and attending to incoming email requests is a significant amount of work for a professional CTM. The artist and the CTM must agree on how the CTM will be paid for the pre-production period. Emerging artists may view this work as part of the service the CTM provides to command their daily rate and not pay any fee for pre-production on top. Sophomore and superstar artists may have some ability to pay something towards a salary for pre-production work, perhaps based on a one-full touring day's rate per week, for instance. Even so, planning a tour that will be logistically and financially successful generates a considerable amount of work, not helped by participants working in different time zones than the CTM. A CTM based in the UK may be engaged in pre-production for a tour that will visit the US (5 or 7 hours behind UK time), Japan (nine hours ahead) and Australia (11 hours ahead). Email can be sent and read regardless of the time zone of the participants, and some queries may be urgent, or require phone and video calling, in which case someone will be working in their pyjamas to take the calls.

PRODUCTION MANAGER

A production manager (PM) will be hired on for touring of production venues (>5000-capacity) to oversee the production elements of the show. The artist will be travelling with rented production and the heads of each department (sound, lights, video, backline, set, stage, and transport) will look to someone to plan and coordinate daily schedules. The tour manager could do this work, but managing the day-to-day activity of the artist as well as the production is too much work for one person. For instance, the artist may have an important interview and recording session at a local radio station which is scheduled for the same time as the load-in at the venue. The tour manager should rightly be overseeing both activities – the load-in can only commence once a touring representative has ensured the venue is safe for the touring crew to enter and do their work, for instance. Splitting the roles over two people therefore makes sense and this is what happens on production-level tours. The production manager is responsible for the production elements (the "steel and wood") and the tour manager oversees the production manager and is more directly involved with the artist and their day-to-day schedule.

As with tour managers, the artist is hiring the PM's experience as well as their skills. No one person can have mastery of all the disciplines necessary to produce a concert. A good PM will rather have a relationship with suppliers and crew and draw upon collective knowledge and experience to anticipate issues and challenges.

The PM's relationships with suppliers are of paramount importance to instil a culture of safety for all touring personnel. Some countries do have prescriptive standards for health and safety at work (the UK, for instance), but no amount of legislation can prevent accidents occurring because of people who have no appreciation for risk to themselves or others. It is therefore vital that the PM, as well as adhering to any local legislation, also encourages a robust attitude towards a culture involving health and safety.

PAY AND CONDITIONS

The hiring of crew for a tour or for festival appearances must be a budget-led process. The artist's wage bill will be her biggest expense, and that assumes she has money in the bank or a successful application for tour support in progress. An emerging artist will have little money to fall back on, and the tour support offered by the record company may be dependent on seeing a return from chart positions and streaming numbers. Yet the hiring of experienced crew (such as tour manager) can reap dividends down the line, assisting the artist to realise their potential from performing live.

So, what to do if the artist cannot afford to hire from the top-level? And what does the top-level charge anyway?

Pay rates for touring crew are not set and there is no union or federation representing road crew who could recommend and negotiate touring pay rates (see *IATSE and BECTU*). This is unfortunate for the technicians and tour managers and is probably to the advantage of the artists. Much touring, especially of non-production venues is done on a "shoestring budget" with very little performance income. Artists and their managers reply on the good-will of road crew people, especially new entrants to the concert production industry, to work for a low day rate. The deal will include a promise of higher salaries and better conditions when the artist has "made it" (become more successful and earned money from touring). Unionising or federation-backed recommendations for daily rates might discourage this practice and will also prohibit young people and new entrants from ever finding touring work.

IATSE AND BECTU

Unionisation of touring activity may be difficult. There are organisations that recognise the work of touring technicians in part and offer recommendations about pay and conditions.

BECTU (UK) is a union for technicians from the film and TV production industries and has some inclusion for sound engineers.

IATSE, in the US, is a strong union of theatre and other entertainment technicians.

Concert touring practitioners at the top level may be approached by an emerging artist about working on an upcoming tour. The practitioner, say a CTM, may suggest and hold out for what they consider to be a reasonable salary. The artist team may counter with an offer for pay that is considerably lower than the CTM's preferred rate. Yet, faced with the prospect of a month's work at a low rate or tuning down the job and not working at all, the CTM will probably accept the rate to get hired on. This scenario takes place for real every day, dictating that pay rates in the concert production industry have not increased significantly in the last 20 years.

CHAPTER 16
TRANSPORT

CHAPTER OUTLINE

The second largest expense in a tour budget will be that for transport. The very activity itself (moving from one city to the next) requires robust transport modes for cast, crew, and equipment.

ROAD

Most of the touring is accomplished by road (with the exception, perhaps, of tours undertaken by DJs). The early days of the "traditional bands" saw them loading up their backline into a rented or borrowed cargo van, the band members sitting on the equipment in the back, and driving through the night to get from one concert to the next (Figure 16.1).

Touring of this type continues to this day in the US. Musicians of all genres are raising the necessary funds to rent or buy vehicles suitable to convey them and their equipment across the country. These vehicles are second-hand and cheap to buy because of their age. The economic drain on running old vehicles can be considerable, and there is no backup if the artist's 20-year-old van breaks down somewhere. A broken-down van will likely result in a missed concert and unforeseen repair and lodging bills. Artists who have access to record company funding, or have built up sufficient revenue from performance income, will therefore move to renting dedicated touring vehicles.

There are two types of vehicles used for touring in the US and Europe – the splitter van and the sleeper bus.

DOI: 10.4324/9781003019503-18

SPLITTER VAN

The splitter van provides a legal and comfortable alternative to renting a cargo van and having to sit on top of the equipment. The splitter van is adapted from a design used to convey construction workers. The base model (usually a Mercedes Sprinter) features a passenger compartment with a bulkhead at the rear to create a dedicated space for the artist's backline and luggage (Figures 16.2 and 16.3).

Splitter vans are available to rent from companies that have a vested interest in keeping their vehicles on the road. Broken down vehicles cost money to repair and purvey an image of unreliability to customers. Rental fleets are therefore modern, with vehicles being replaced every three to four years. New vehicles are reliable and economical, also complying with low-emission regulations in some city centres.

Figure 16.1 Cargo vans are ubiquitous and inexpensive, making them popular for low budget touring. They are less than ideal though, being both uncomfortable and dangerous in the event of a crash. Image from Adobe Stock

Figure 16.2 A splitter van can transport 9 people including the driver. Image courtesy of the author

Figure 16.3 The cargo compartment of a splitter van. The artist's equipment can be stored safely here. Image courtesy of the author

Renting a late model splitter van gives the hiring artist peace of mind. The vehicle will be safe, comfortable, and there is backup in the form of a replacement vehicle if something goes wrong.

The rental of a splitter van is similar to that of renting a car. The contract is for self-drive; the renter is responsible for fuel, oil, and road toll costs. These items will have to be calculated and included in the tour budget.

LEGAL CONSIDERATIONS

The weight of the vehicle when operational needs consideration. Many countries have regulations concerning the laden weight of vehicles on the road, with good reason. A heavy vehicle is difficult to steer and requires a great deal of room to break from speed. The modern splitter can accommodate up to nine people including the driver. That combined weight, along with the backline in the cargo compartment, means splitters can be over the permitted laden weight. The tour manager must ensure that every item the artist proposes to take with them on tour is necessary, leaving behind anything that will contribute to the van being overweight. A popular solution is to discard the hard cases ("flight cases") that protect the equipment while in transit. Removing this protection may seem counter-intuitive – the cases are designed for this very purpose – and the resulting weight reduction from removing these cases can bring the vehicle back under the permitted laden weight, saving on the cost of fuel, possible fines, and injury and death in case of a sudden breaking stop.

Splitter vans are the backbone of non-production venue touring in Europe (and increasingly in the US) and are ubiquitous at European festivals (Figure 16.4).

Figure 16.4 Splitter vans parked backstage at a festival in the UK. Image courtesy of the author

SLEEPER BUS

A sleeper bus (sleeper coach, or entertainer coach) is a specialised music touring road vehicle with beds ("bunks"). The inclusion of beds facilitates travel overnight for cast and crew, saving travel time during the day and providing a comfortable travel experience.[1]

A bus is converted (or manufactured) with 8–16 bunks arranged in berths (a 10-berth bus has ten bunks, for instance. The artist and crew get on the bus after a concert and are driven overnight to the next concert. All being well, they will wake up to find themselves parked outside of the next venue, ready to start a new day.

The tour budget is influenced by venue type and distance between concerts. The use of a sleeper bus reflects the second influence. A typical tour of the US will be made up of concert stops that are 200–400 miles apart. The distances involve a great deal of time on the road each day. Travelling by splitter van, for instance, would entail leaving the city of the previous night's concert at 9 a.m., at the latest. This would be followed by a 4–8-hour drive, to hopefully arrive for load-in and soundcheck at a time appropriate to the schedule of the concert. Factor in the late night/early morning finish of work for the touring cast and crew, and it is easy to see how quickly dangerous fatigue can set in.

Travelling by sleeper bus hopefully eliminates travel-induced fatigue. The touring artist should be able to get to bed almost immediately after the concert (the sleeper bus being parked right outside the venue), and the crew straight after loading out the equipment. In both cases there is no waiting around for other people to finish work, driving to a hotel, checking in, finding parking for the van, taking equipment into hotel rooms to prevent theft, and all the rigmarole that can add another hour to everyone's workday.

The sleeper bus rental company will supply the bus with a dedicated driver. The quote for the rental will usually include all driver wages fuel, oil, and road toll, costs. The bus rental company will also arrange for payment of ferry crossings, and all these costs are based on the proposed tour routing.

LEGAL CONSIDERATIONS

The use of a sleeper bus mitigates the effects that a long workday will have on the cast and crew. The touring party will go to sleep on the bus and wake up at the next venue, a driver having safely conveyed them there. The workday of the driver needs consideration so as to avoid accidents caused by fatigue.

Regulations in Europe and the US stipulate how long the driver of a commercial vehicle, such as sleeper bus, can drive. The regulations vary and can be complex. The artist tour manager should consult with the sleeper bus rental company as to the limitations of the regulations and how they affect travel for the potential tour. The regulations may necessitate that another driver ("double driver") is brought in for legs (sections) of the tour as the distances are too great to be completed within the driving hours regulations. The second driver will take over from the first driver, who continues to travel with the tour but must not drive for set times. (Some regulations stipulate the first driver must not be travelling while on their driving break, necessitating them staying behind in a hotel and flying to rejoin the tour when their mandatory rest break is finished.) The provision of double drivers costs a great deal of money. There are the extra crew wages for a start. The second driver will be joining the tour after it has set off and so will need to take a train or plane from their hometown to the city where they are needed to join the tour. There are other accommodation and catering costs, plus the associated costs of the first driver not being allowed to travel while on their break. These costs all add up and can be significant.

Having to use a double driver is an indication that the tour routing is not economically efficient. The routing of the tour is arranged mostly by the booking agent and, in fairness, it may have been difficult to find the right promoters, with the right offers, to add in more stops closer together. Less distance between concerts would negate the need for double drivers for some sections of the tour.

PRACTICAL CONSIDERATIONS

There are also practical considerations to touring via a sleeper bus.

PARKING AND ACCESS

Sleeper buses were originally designed to expedite touring in the US where distances can be great. Superstar artists used the buses initially, performing in large theatres and arenas with ample parking for buses. Indeed, most of the US is designed around the automobile, and access by road to venues is rarely an issue.

Today, sleeper buses are used throughout Europe as well as the US, although access to some venues in Europe is not so easy. The UK can also be problematic for concert touring – accessing and parking next to <500-capacity non-production venues in some UK towns is impossible. Venues on the continent have restrictions regarding any vehicle parked nearby and other venues are inaccessible to high-sided vehicles (such as double-, or twin-, deck sleeper buses), due to low bridges and tram electrification infrastructure.

The driver of a bus in such cases has no alternative than to "drop and run" – disgorging the cast, crew, and equipment into the venue at load-in and driving off to a bus/coach parking place for the day. The cast and crew no longer have their temporary home for the day and must ensure that they have retrieved everything they need for the performance from the bus before it goes away. The bus may be parked some kilometres form the venue and retrieving forgotten in-ear monitor moulds (a common occurrence) will result in time-wasting and expensive taxi journeys to and from the bus park.

Access to the venue to "drop and run" may be out of the question, due to overhead cables, or weight restrictions on the access roads. Promoters of such concerts must arrange for the bus and trailer to park at an agreed parking place. Vehicles that comply with the local regulations (less heavy and smaller than a tour bus) are used to "cross-load" the people and equipment from the tour bus and convey everything to the venue for load-in. The process must then be repeated after the concert. Cross-loading of this type is conventionally the cost of the promoter. Cross-loading is a common practice at open-air, green-field festivals. The bus parking areas at such concerts are kept away from the noise of multiple stages. These parks are far away from the performance areas, and so any artist equipment must be cross-loaded from the buses in the bus park and transported to the relevant stages using cargo vans or construction vehicles with trailers.

BUS POWER

Sleeper buses are fitted out to a high standard to reflect the "VIP" nature of the clientele. The facilities, such as in-bunk entertainment systems, require power that is supplied by the engine when the vehicle is moving. This power is not available when the bus is parked up, so "bus power" (AKA "landline" or "shore power") must be available for the bus (Figure 16.5). This 16A or 32A power consists of a cable run from the venue

Figure 16.5 32A and 16A power supplies for sleeper bus power. Image courtesy of the author

that powers the buses internal inverter system, ensuring that the entertainment, comfort conditioning, and kitchenette facilities all continue to work. Providing bus power is not a problem for production touring venues (>5000–100,000) but is problematic for open-air festivals and for <500-capacity non-production venues.

AIR

The distance between venues or the time required for travel may require flying to the next show. Using aeroplanes for concert touring presents its own issues and challenges.

As with road transport there are different modes available for consideration:

low-cost carriers
commercial carriers
air charters

LOW-COST CARRIERS

So-called low-cost ("budget") airlines have proved a big hit with passengers. The no-frills approach means low fares and a plethora of new destinations for the traveller on a budget. Touring artists can take advantage of low-cost airlines to reach concert destinations, but there are disadvantages to this type of air travel for the professional touring artist.

Low-cost airlines are "point-to-point". The terms and conditions of the air ticket are for the airline to get the passenger to the destination, using only their equipment at the times that they specify. The low-cost airline has no obligation to get you onto another flight should their original one be cancelled or delayed. Low-budget airlines often fly to a destination twice a day – once in the morning and again in the evening. The airline will try to get the passenger on the evening flight if the morning one is delayed or cancelled, regardless that other airlines flying from that airport may be offering flights to the destination throughout the day.

Another issue with low-cost airlines is the fees for luggage ("baggage"). Low-cost airlines triumphed in their early days, offering fares as low as €0.99, with baggage being accepted for free. That situation has now changed. Low-budget airlines need fast turnarounds of their aircraft on the stand; eliminating hold luggage helps with this. Passengers on low-cost airlines are subject to high fees for checking luggage into the hold. These fees are bad enough for a family going on holiday with a suitcase each but can be prohibitive for an artist touring with an assortment of guitars, keyboards, pedal boards, MIDI controllers, personal luggage, and everything else they need for a festival performance. Planning to fly on a low-cost airline is a false economy – the cost of the baggage fees will outweigh the potential savings of an equivalent fare on a commercial, scheduled carrier.

Finally, the culture of low-cost airlines does not allow for flexibility. Aircraft must leave on time, full of passengers, who should not have much luggage between them. Check-in and baggage handling are often automated and are not designed to deal with the touring artists who present themselves at check-in with three baggage trolleys piled with guitars, for instance.

COMMERCIAL CARRIERS

Commercial flights of the type offered by a nation's flag carrier, such as British Airways, are traditionally seen as expensive for emerging artists and DJs but offer the flexibility and guarantees missing from low-cost carriers.

There are other advantages to flying with a scheduled airline. The touring artist has more choice of departure and arrival times when choosing to fly with a commercial carrier. Destination airports are usually the major airport serving a city, and not an ex-military airfield 70 km from the city as favoured by the low-cost carriers. Luggage allowances can be generous, although these are being cut back on some routes by some carriers. Tickets for business and premium cabin seats include extra baggage allowances, and the higher ticket cost may offset fees for additional baggage.

Most importantly for the touring artist is the guarantee of travel that comes with a commercial airline ticket. The national carriers have the capability to get passengers onto flights subsequent to a delay or cancellation, even if that is with a competitor. The chances of missing a concert due to a delayed flight are less if flying with a scheduled carrier than with a low-cost, point-to-point airline. This fact must be a consideration for anyone looking at the logistics of a touring artist.

A welcome by-product of a busy touring schedule conducted on aeroplanes is the accumulation of frequent-flyer points and awards. Airlines offer loyalty programmes that enable passengers to accumulate points each time they fly as a member of that programme. An artist undertaking a year's touring that includes a handful of business-class flights can quickly move up the tiers of the rewards programme, accruing enough points for cut-price, even free, flights in the future. Of more use is the access to fast-track check-in and baggage reclaims rewarded at certain tiers and access to private departure lounges. These lounges offer complimentary food, drink, and wi-fi and are appreciated by the busy touring artist in claiming back some valuable quiet time.

AIR CHARTER

Commercial airlines offer a service that will be suitable for most touring artists, and there may be occasions when commercial flight schedules do not match the needs of the touring party. Private chartered flights are an answer to the problem (Figure 16.6).

The perception of the "private jet" is of millionaire rock stars zooming around the planet in a luxurious, leather padded tube, flying high above us all, sipping expensive champagne, and spending a fortune on this mode of travel. The reality is that chartering a private aircraft is as cost-effective for ten people as it would be if they were flying business or premium class on a commercial carrier's flight.

Figure 16.6 Renting a charter jet can be cost-effective for mid- to superstar-level touring. Image by Adobe Stock

Private charter companies operate a variety of sizes of aircraft that can carry from 8 to 32 passengers. Interior decor can be as ostentatiousness as the example above but is usually a bland, corporate look that reflects the primary use of such aircraft – shuttling executives to business meetings. Private charter aircraft operate from the same airports as commercial planes, and operators can apply for flight time outside of the usual times allocated to the international carriers.

As well as flexibility in flight scheduling, private charter companies can arrange for all the necessary examination of travel documents. Passport check and security scans can be done in private in a dedicated area away from the travelling public. This arrangement is not designed necessarily to ensure an artist's privacy (although that can be a welcome by-product); private check-in facilities have no queues thus saving the touring artist from having to spend time hanging around queueing in airports.

TRANSPORTATION OF EQUIPMENT

The transportation modes discussed so far have concentrated primarily on the transport of humans. However, touring artists travel with their own personal musical instruments and, in the case of production tours, with rented sound, lights, video, set, and stage.

The concert production industry has evolved to offer specialised means of making sure that equipment gets to the next stop of the tour.

TRAILER

You looked at sleeper buses earlier in this section. Modern sleeper buses are finished to a high standard, with air-conditioning (even when stationary), satellite TV, on-board console gaming systems, and fully appointed kitchenettes all included. A trade-off in supplying all these mod-cons is that sleeper buses have very little storage space available for the backline. Bus rental companies therefore supply trailers for any equipment that must travel with the artist.

Pulling a trailer adds more expense to the cost of hiring a sleeper bus. The rental company will charge a daily rate for the hire of the trailer itself, and then the extra money is conventionally paid to the driver for the inconvenience of having a trailer attached to the bus (pulling a trailer makes driving a bus more difficult apparently). And the fuel cost is greater, as the bus is pulling more weight and restricts the top speed at which a bus can travel.

Artists on a tour of production venues will still have backline and are probably carrying rented sound and lights in trucks – their backline will go in these trucks, and a trailer on the artist bus would not be needed.

TRUCKS

Trucks ("lorries") are needed to transport rented sound and light equipment on production tours. Convention and common-sense dictates that like equipment is carried in its own truck – sound and backline in one truck, lights in another, and so on. A tour of mid-size production venues (5,000 – 10,000-capacity) can typically be achieved using tow trucks to carry the necessary production. The allocation of the trucks would be as follows:

Truck one: Lights, video, rigging, and catering equipment
Trucks two: Sound, backline, production office equipment.

The trucks contain the equipment that is necessary at certain times of the day, helping speed up the load-in and load-out processes each day. Truck one in the example would unload first, with the catering equipment being packed at the rear of the truck, ready to be unloaded first. Rigging (chain hoists and controls used to suspend lighting and sound elements) goes into the venue next, followed by the video and lighting equipment.

The sound equipment is not needed straight away and keeping it on a separate truck means that flight cases full of sound equipment are not being unloaded before they are needed, and the cases are not blocking loading bays and venue access.

The truck allocation described above is standard at mid-level production touring, which is therefore called "two-truck touring".

The renting of trucks is the responsibility of the artist (or their production manager), and the truck rental supplier is decided by the production vendors. The sound rental company may have a relationship with a particular trucking company and so may prefer to use them. They will ask the trucking company to provide a quote for their services, and this quote would be included in the quote for sound services that the sound company presents to the artist. The preference for a particular trucking company must be examined by the artist's team as a competing trucking company may be offering a better deal.

Finally, the driving of trucks is subject to similar regulations concerning drivers working time, and the trucking company would advise of any issues and challenges when quoting for their services. Double drivers, or longer rest periods, may have to be built into the schedule if distances cannot be covered within mandated time periods.

FREIGHT SHIPPING AND TRANSPORTATION

Trucks and trailers on buses are applicable to moving the concert production equipment around by road. There are circumstances when the artist must travel by air (see "Air" in this section) and some or all of their production equipment must travel with them. Checking a few guitars into the hold of a commercial aircraft is standard for an artist flying abroad for a promotional tour of radio stations for instance. This means of transport is not applicable for moving PA, lights, and stages, around the planet.

Goods transported by road, rail, sea, or air are called freight, and concert production equipment becomes freight when it is transported. Transportation of freight can involve road, rail, sea, and air (freighting is also called "shipping" even though this is not always by sea.) The logistics and mode change when air travel is required for the artist.

A sophomore or superstar level artist will have accumulated a substantial amount of equipment for use in their concerts. The equipment may be the backline, and this will now include their instruments, amplifiers, keyboards, computers, UHF transmitters and receivers, and all stands, as well as "production cases" and "work boxes", containing spares and workstations for the touring technicians. This amount of equipment is too much to present at check-in as part of the baggage allowance for the artist and the crew and is designated as freight and loaded on the aircraft as such. Moving freight on commercial flights requires specialised knowledge concerning carnets and other customs regulations, and specialised concert production equipment freighting companies are available to assist the artist with moving their equipment for fly-dates. For instance, an important aspect of freighting equipment is total weight of the equipment ready for transportation. A freighting company can attend a concert or rehearsal by the artist with portable weighing equipment, prior to travel. The weights and sizes of production equipment can be ascertained easily saving the artist's team having to weigh the equipment using domestic tools. This is one aspect of the specialised freighting companies work, and their expertise and experience is vital for large-scale production tours visiting different continents.

Freighting large-scale concert production equipment is a massive expense and the preserve of the superstar and heritage act. Equipment that needs to be freight is typically heavy, big, and expensive – all factors that drive up the cost of flying it around the world. The artist with commitments abroad must weigh up the cost (both financial and environmental) in freighting their production. The artist may be keen to present a fantastic stage set and blinding lightshow to all their fans, regardless of where they live, but is the cost to do so worth the price?

STACKS AND RACKS

An artist does not necessarily have to freight their entire production by air or sea. Some of the equipment may be available for rent at the destination.

PA speaker cabinets and the amplifiers are large and heavy. However, there are only three major PA manufacturers currently competing for first-class touring contracts, and any large-scale production touring today is likely to use one of these three manufacturers in their concert production design. The manufacturers sell their equipment to PA rental companies around the world and maintain good relationships with those customers. This relationship has developed into "rental partner networks" – databases of PA companies who stock a particular manufacturer's speaker system. The partner networks facilitate the cross-rental of standardised systems throughout the world. For instance, an artist from the US can rent a Meyer (US) PA system from the manufacturer's rental partner for touring in the US. The artist may then have a tour taking in Australia and New Zealand. Meyer can assist the artist by contacting a rental partner in Australia and arranging for the rental of the equivalent Meyer system when the artist arrives there. This so-called "racks and stacks" (sourcing the standardised components locally) gives the artist consistency in their production for all their fans and eliminates the need to freight large, heavy boxes across the planet.

"Stacks and racks" can be applied to any of the production elements except for stage set pieces. Such elements are custom-made for a particular tour – they do not exist elsewhere – so freighting them from the originating continent is the only choice.

THE CAORNET

A carnet (pronounced kar-nay) is referred to as a "passport for equipment" and permits tax- and duty-free import and export of an artist's touring gear (Figure 16.7).

The carnet stipulates that the equipment is covered by a bond and that the bearer of the carnet is not going to sell the equipment while in another country, and if they do, they will pay the resulting tax due on the sale.

The carnet itself is a series of importation, exportation, and transit "vouchers", in a booklet. A voucher is a single page in the booklet, and the booklet must be inspected and approved by the customs (or equivalent regulatory body) of each country listed in the carnet document. The vouchers display a manifest of the artist's equipment. The manifest lists the size, weight, and identifying marks (such as serial numbers) of every single price of equipment – including cases and carrying bags – that will be transported into each country on the tour.

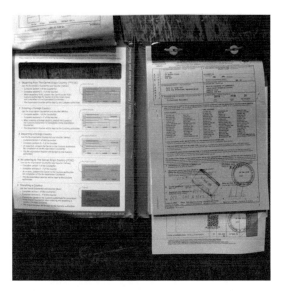

Figure 16.7 A carnet issued by a British Chamber of Commerce for travel into Europe.
Image courtesy of the author

The following is the procedure involved in using a carnet for concert touring:

Creating the manifest

The artist must assemble all the equipment that will be used on the tour. All items must be measured, weighed, the serial number noted, and the information entered into a spreadsheet. The manifest should include all sound and lighting equipment (in the case of a tour of production venues) as well as the artist's own backline.

Raising the carnet

The carnet is "raised" (organised) by a member of the International Chamber of Commerce (ICC). The ICC has federated members in all trading countries and the artist will need to find a local chamber of commerce (COC) to raise the carnet. The artist submits the manifest, along with a list of the countries to be visited, and the COC creates the necessary vouchers and bonds.

Specialised freighting companies

The artist may elect to use one of the specialised music freighting companies to raise the carnet instead of finding a local chamber of commerce. This is a common activity, as these companies deal with the importing and exporting of touring equipment as a profession and will have a working relationship with a COC.

Leaving the home country

The artist must have the carnet inspected and authorised by the customs authority of the home country when leaving for the tour. The authorisation is signified by rubber-stamping the first exportation voucher – hence you will hear the term "stamping the carnet" from touring crew and tour truck drivers.

Entering the first country to perform

The artist will present the first importation voucher to the border authorities of the first country. If arriving by air, this will be in a separate office in the arrival airport. Specialised customs points deal with the inspections of carnets at road borders.

Leaving the first country

After performing the concerts in the first country the artist must present the exportation vouchers to the border authority of that first country to be inspected and approved by stamping.

Entering the second country to perform

The artist will present the second importation voucher to the authorities in the second country. Again, this entry could be air or land. It is worth noting that the presentation of carnets and the resulting waiting time can be considerable, especially if crossing land borders in the early morning hours.

Transiting a country

The carnet vouchers system also considers that the artists may have to drive through a country to get elsewhere and may not be performing in that "transit" country. For instance, touring in Europe may well necessitate transiting through Switzerland. In this case, the artist will present export vouchers to the country they are leaving (France, Germany, or Italy) and then present transit vouchers to the Swiss authorities. The carnet must then be stamped again when leaving Switzerland and stamped again going back into the next country.

Returning home

The artist must have the carnet "closed" (inspected and stamped by the domestic authorities) when arriving back home after the tour. The closed carnet is then sent back to the COC as the bond is no longer valid.

NOTE

1 You may view the interior of sleeper buses by visiting supplier sites. https://nitetraincoach.com/ and http://www.beatthestreet.net are a good place to start.

17

CHAPTER 17
ACCOMMODATION

CHAPTER OUTLINE

The third budget category is that for accommodation. The cast and crew need some-where to rest and sleep, and the tour budget should include the cost of doing so.

HOTELS

Hotels are the common form of accommodation for touring artists. The cost for a hotel is the artist's cost unless the promoter is contracted to supply the hotel as is often the case with DJ deals.

Hotel types include:

bed and breakfast or "pension" guest house
budget travel hotels near interstates and motorways
budget hotels in cities
business hotels in cities
luxury hotels in cities
luxury retreats outside of cities

Artists booking and paying for their own hotels will be keen on a hotel as close to the venue of that night's performance as possible. Proximity to the place of work cuts down on travel time and creates flexibility. The artist is more likely to be able to return to her hotel if she can walk there after soundcheck, as opposed to sitting in rush hour traffic travelling to a hotel on the other side of the city from the venue.

ROOMING TYPES

Hotel rooms are available in different configurations:

Single/Double for Single Use (DSU) – one-person occupancy
Double – two people sharing a room in one bed
Twin – two people sharing a room with two beds

DOI: 10.4324/9781003019503-19

Putting two people in one room together is less expensive, and each person should be aware they are sharing a room with someone else before the start of the tour. Sharing is common for low-budget, non-production touring where a party of eight band and crew can be accommodated in just four hotel rooms. There may be a situation where the touring group that is sharing rooms has a gender minority – one woman touring with seven men for instance. Convention dictates that the woman gets her own single/DSU room unless she is in a relationship with someone else in the touring party and would then be in a double room with that other person. Although not a problem, the extra room in this case means the artist must pay for five rooms, instead of four.

DRIVER ROOMS, SHOWER ROOMS, AND DAY ROOMS

Hotel rooms are used by touring artists for other purposes than sleeping in after a concert.

The drivers of sleeper buses based in the US are accommodated in a hotel after they have finished driving for the night. (Sleeper bus drivers in the UK and Europe sleep on the bus during the day). The room for the driver is a cost to the artist. The room is booked as a "day room" for a 12-hour period – 8.00 until 20.00 for instance. The driver gets a taxi to the hotel in the morning, sleeps all day, and then returns to the bus, which is parked at the venue, that evening.

Artists touring by sleeper bus will want a shower once a day. Sleeper buses have no showering facilities on board. Convention sees the promoter or venue agreeing to supply showering facilities as part of the contracted deal. Shower facilities are not always available in the venue, especially in <500-capacity non-production venues. The promoter will rent hotel rooms nearby for the cast and crew to use for showering in this case. A canny promoter in the US can mitigate the cost of these rooms by doing a deal with the artist. The artist already must pay for one room for the driver and this room is free after the driver has left for the evening. Promoters will often contribute an amount to the cost of this room as it can be then used as a shower room for cast and crew.

The use of hotel rooms as day rooms is accepted practice for non-production touring. Venue facilities at this level of touring can be grim, and two clean, warm (or air-conditioned, depending on the season) rooms with hot water and clean towels can help maintain morale on a long tour of grimy venues. The artist's tour manager may book day rooms if they have previous experience of a particular venue and know how bad the facilities are or may book day rooms once every four days. Consider though, the bus is serving as accommodation, and any booking of hotel rooms is a somewhat extraneous expense.

OTHER CONSIDERATIONS

Budgeting for accommodation in hotels must factor in ancillary costs. For instance, city hotels have little or no parking. Artists touring non-production venues in a splitter van find it difficult to park the van where they are staying. On-road parking is also usually prohibited, so alternatives must be found for parking the van securely each evening. Parking for commercial vehicles, such as splitter vans, is expensive compared with car parking.

The price of hotel rooms often includes complimentary breakfast. Unfortunately for touring artists, breakfast is served at the hotel very early relative to the working times of the touring party. The tour manager looking to save money in the budget will therefore book hotel rooms at a room-only deal with no complimentary breakfast (which will be less expensive) and then arrange to pay the breakfast bill for any member of the touring party who does stagger down to eat before the end of service. The amount saved could be considerable over five rooms for a 20-date tour.

Hotels usually have some type of luggage storage facility. This is primarily used for the bags of guests who arrive too early to check in, or check out on their day of departure and are not leaving the city until the evening. In either case the hotel can store the luggage in a room, sometimes for a fee per bag. Artists on fly-dates, or those not wanting to leave instruments in the van overnight, will also need to use the luggage room (unless they want to man-handle all their gear into their separate bedrooms). Hotels are not used to dealing with mountains of musical equipment in big, heavy flight cases, and consideration should be given to checking in advance if the hotel will accept backline into their luggage room.

OTHER ACCOMMODATION TYPES

The popularity of home-sharing sites has provided alternative forms of accommodation for travelling artists. Properties listed on home-sharing sites can be inexpensive compared with hotels and are worth considering. An artist who is performing several shows in an area may consider renting an apartment through a home-sharing site and using that as a base for the duration of the concerts in that area.

Accommodations booked through home-sharing sites can be inexpensive, but the experience tends not to be as flexible as staying in a hotel. Complicated check-in and check-out procedures, dealing with self-catering, spurious claims of damages from the host and other restrictions, can offset the appeal of the low expense.

TRAVEL AGENTS

Tour managers and artist teams do not have to contact each hotel required to book rooms. Specialised music touring travel agents operate to assist with entertainer travel. These companies offer comprehensive transport and accommodation organisation for artists at all stages in their career. The agents receive commissions from accommodation and travel services they book, as with other business travel agencies.

18

CHAPTER 18
PRODUCTION

CHAPTER OUTLINE

The fourth budget category – production – describes the equipment and processes for which the touring artist is responsible. The artist is the "producer" of the concert, and the resulting entity (equipment, people, and processes) is the "production". Any cost associated with production is paid for by the artist.

DOI: 10.4324/9781003019503-20

The person responsible for budgeting for the touring activity of the artist should include costs for the production elements, and some may not be relevant to a particular artist's situation – the artist may be touring non-production venues and so may not need to pay for anything to do with PA for instance (the PA is usually installed in non-production venues).

"Production" can be divided into seven sub-categories:

PA
backline
lighting
video
set
stage
other production considerations

PA

The PA system is fundamental in the production of modern amplified music.

The components of concert sound reinforcement systems are small, light, and efficient, enabling artists and concert organisers to deliver clear and consistent sound to audiences.

A PA system comprises the same general components regardless of whether the PA is an installed system in a 200-capacity bar, or a system rented in for a stadium (>25,000-capacity) concert. The modern PA comprises:

AUDIENCE LOUDSPEAKER SYSTEM

The loudspeakers seen in the venue are what are generally thought of as the "PA". The loudspeakers are powered by amplifiers and controlled by loudspeaker management systems (Figure 18.1).

Figure 18.1 A line-array speaker system being assembled and ready to be suspended ("flown") above the performance area. Image courtesy of the author

Figure 18.2 The FOH audio console is situated where the audience will sit or stand. The image shows the console, along with devices for measuring sound pressure level (SPL). This measurement is required to ensure the FOH audio engineer does not exceed any volume limits set by local regulations. Image courtesy of the author

FRONT-OF-HOUSE MIXING CONSOLE

The levels and tone of the sound sources on stage are mixed to create a sound for the audience through the front-of-house (FOH) mixing console (aka "mixing desk"). The console is situated where the audience sits or stands (Figure 18.2).

MONITOR LOUDSPEAKER SYSTEM

Monitor speakers are placed on stage, facing the performers, enabling them to hear themselves. Monitor speakers are referred to as "wedges" (the profile of the loudspeakers is wedge-shaped). Loudspeakers situated either side of the stage are used to flood sound across the stage and are called "side fills"; drummers may have a dedicated loudspeaker stack, named a "drum fill". All monitor loudspeakers must be connected to dedicated amplifiers via a loudspeaker management system. Artists also use in-ear monitors (IEMs) which comprise earbuds connected to portable (belt-worn) UHF receivers. Artists using IEMs often have no wedges or side fills on stage, receiving the required pitch and timing information directly from the IEMs (Figure 18.3).

MONITOR CONSOLE

The monitor console is used to mix the levels and tones of the sound sources on stage and to create individual mixes of these sources for each musician on stage (see *Stage monitoring systems*) These mixes are sent to the wedges, side fills, drum fill, or IEMs, as required. The monitor console is situated at the side of the stage (usually stage left).

Line system. The line system connects all parts of the PA, sending audio signals from the stage to the FOH console, and the audience mix back out of the FOH console to the PA

Figure 18.3 A monitor wedge can be seen on the floor facing the guitar stack on stage right. A drum fill can be seen behind the drum kit. Floor wedges, drum fills, and side-fills all help the performers hear themselves on stage. Image courtesy of the author

speaker management system, for instance. Line systems were based on copper cable "multi-cores" (multiple audio signal cables combined into one large cable). Analog multi-cores are expensive to manufacture and heavy and cumbersome in operation. Digital systems based on computer networking technology, running on CAT-5 or fibre cable, are now common. Such systems are unobtrusive compared with copper cables – and quick to deploy.

RIGGING

Suspending ("flying") a PA has advantages over stacking the system on the ground. The audio coverage can be far greater when a system is suspended, and the audience line of sight is not impeded by piles of PA speakers on either side of the stage. Rigging consists of chain hoists ("motors"), a chain hoist control system, brackets and fixings (needed to suspend the speakers from the chain hoists), and safety restraints for all the suspended equipment (Figure 18.4).

MICROPHONE AND CABLES

The artist can assume a PA system will come with the necessary microphones, direct injection (DI) boxes, and cables necessary to introduce their sound sources into the system.

THE SCIENCE OF SOUND

The speed (velocity) of sound in air is approximately 344 meters per second, 1,115 feet per second, or 770 miles per hour at room temperature of 20°C (70°F). The speed varies with the temperature of air, such that sound travels slower at higher altitudes or on cold days. Sound waves also refract (bend) downward as they travel away from their source.

Sound waves produced by an artist in a cold empty room, such as a venue during soundcheck, will slow down and dip in height as they reach into the room. A lack of clarity results in the high frequencies (>5000 Hz) and a "dampening", or lack of resonance for the low and sub-bass frequencies (<250 Hz). The resulting sound will be "smeary" and lacking in perceptible bass, even if extra of those frequencies are boosted by the artist's engineer on the mixing console. Venues often have reflective surfaces, such as polished dance floors or walls of mirrors, as well. Being empty, there is nothing to stop the sound waves in the venue from striking these surfaces unchecked and being reflected and refracted. Reflected frequencies can be "picked up" by the microphones on stage. The signal will be amplified again and the combination of the original signal with the reflected signal can cause "feedback" – the howling, screeching sound associated with bad sound.

An experienced engineer will be knowledgeable about the properties of sound at different temperatures and humidity. She should not try to create the perfect mix in the room during the soundcheck. Any adjustments made to add more bass, or calm the screeching high frequencies, will be negated when the audience is allowed into the room. The temperature will then rise, and the fans' clothing will absorb the reflected signals.

Figure 18.4 Production elements for concerts are suspended ("flown") using chain hoists to lift the equipment into the air. The image shows a chain hoist being prepared by the rigger. Image courtesy of the author

STAGE MONITORING SYSTEMS

The stage monitoring system enables the performers to hear themselves while on stage. The individual sound sources from stage are sent to the monitor console. The operator ("monitor engineer") then creates a separate "mix" for each performer. Each mix comprises a balance of the stage sources in accordance with the taste of the individual. The singer, for instance, will want to hear their own voice and some of the backing instrumentation. The bass player may not want to hear the singer at all, favouring a mix of drums and their bass instrument, and so on. Concert production also involves playback elements and "click tracks" (a metronome sound played out to the performers on stage for timing purposes); each of these also requires balancing and sending to the relevant performer's mix. The resulting audio patching is complex; the numerous channel count (up to 60 inputs), the intricacies of the individual's require-ments (making sure drummers have the click track in their IEMs for instance), and the number of mixes themselves (several for the performers and the same number again for backline techs, stage callers, lighting operators, etc.) take time to recreate every night on the tour. Figure 18.5 shows a typical monitor mix configuration.

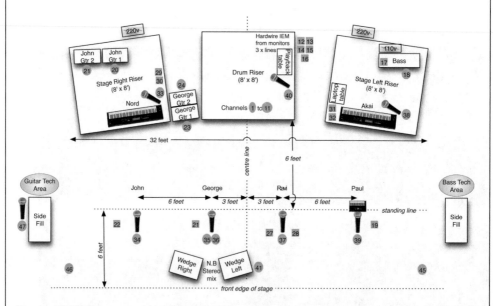

Figure 18.5 The stage plan for a touring artist. The monitor engineer must provide mixes to wedges, side fills, drum fills, wireless in-ear monitor receivers (IEMs) for the performers, hard-wired in-ear feeds for the drummer, and wireless IEMS mixes for the two backline technicians. The numbers on cir-cles represent the input channel numbers on the consoles. Image courtesy of the author

DIGITAL CONSOLES

The technology of sound reinforcement has advanced considerably, embracing the benefits of digital transmission of audio. These benefits can be most clearly seen in digital mixing consoles that are now platforms with capabilities far more advanced than their predecessors.

The consoles used to mix FOH and monitor sound were traditionally based on analogue technology, where each sound source ("input") required a channel strip in the console. The channel strip contained all the necessary controls (input gain, EQ, and output volume) to sculpt and level the sound of a source. The more inputs there were on stage, the more channels were needed in the console. A production tour of mid-level venues (10,000–20,000 capacity) would require at least one 48-channel console at FOH and another "on monitors" (for the onstage monitor sound). A console containing this many input channels would be large and heavy. More importantly, there was no way to store or recall settings and adjustments made on each channel strip. The controls on the console would have to be "flattened" (reset to zero, or no change) if the console were to be used by another artist – the opening acts on the night of for instance – that, or else multiple consoles would be required, each expensive to hire and taking up valuable audience space. The settings would then be returned to the original settings of the headline act for the performance. Settings on analogue consoles can never be recalled with 100% accuracy, so consistency of the sound between soundcheck and performance could not be guaranteed. Likewise, the settings were not likely to remain on the console during transportation from one concert to the next.

The problems of size, weight, and recall of settings, have been eliminated with the advent of digital consoles. Digital consoles rely on the power of the processors within the system, not multiple channel strips, to process sound sources from the stage. The digital console is a small control surface and does not need multiple channel strips to accommodate large channel accounts. That is a good thing, as artists performing in arenas (5,000–20,000 capacity) often have upwards of 60 input sources from the stage, with opening acts having another 20–30 each. Each function and its setting on the console can be programmed, stored, and recalled perfectly, enabling the one console to be used for any number of acts during a concert (Figure 18.6)

PRACTICAL CONSIDERATIONS OF USING DIGITAL CONSOLES

Reduced size and weight, instantaneous recall of complicated adjustments, and the ability to process numerous channels of audio are some of the reasons that PA rental companies have invested in digital consoles. Digital consoles are ubiquitous in non-production venues, and are supplied as standard equipment at open-air, green-field festivals. This ubiquity has benefits and presents challenges.

CONSOLE ARCHITECTURE

Analogue consoles from different manufactures were all laid out and operated in much the same way. The sections of an analogue console were similar from manufacturer to manufacturer, and the operator (the artist's sound engineer) could quickly get working on a console, even one from a previously unknown manufacturer.

Figure 18.6 A digital console, made by Solid State Logic, seen here at the FOH position during setup for a concert. Image courtesy of the author

Digital consoles follow no set layout or internal "architecture". Console manufacturers design and write software and graphical user interfaces (GUIs) based on what they consider best-practice for concert audio. The consoles consist of a control surface with faders and encoders and there the similarity ends to an analogue console. Digital consoles are menu-driven (functions being accessed through pages in a software-based hierarchical system) with no two manufacturers using the same software. The operator who is unfamiliar with a console will have to spend time learning the software and becoming familiar with the GUI before being able to do meaningful work.

LATENCY

Digital audio systems, including mixing consoles, suffer from "latency" – a "lag" or delay in the audio signal path. Latency is caused by the analogue to digital (AD) (and vice versa – DA) conversion that allows the sound sources on stage to be processed by a digital device. The AD and DA in digital consoles are powerful, therefore fast, and latency is imperceptible to most humans in a simple digital audio setup – a microphone plugged into a digital console and amplified through a loudspeaker system, for instance. Latency can be a problem though in a complex concert production system, where various digital components are all processing the audio signals. In-ear monitoring is especially problematic. The digital console has latency, and the performer using IEMs may notice a slight "doubling" of her voice when she hears it in the earbuds. Digital stage microphones compound the problem adding more latency into the audio signal path and increasing the perceived delay for the performer.

SHOW FILES

"Show files" are the settings for a console, and can be moved from one console to another, providing the consoles are the same make and model.

Digital consoles have the unique ability to be programmed (adjustments and settings stored into an onboard memory) and for those settings to be recalled when needed. An example would be a headline artist's sound engineer making all the necessary adjustments during soundcheck for a concert (see "day-to-day schedules" in appendix 5 and 6). The engineer can store the settings for each instrument, and the mix of the sources, into the onboard memory of the console after the soundcheck is finished. The resulting file is called the "show file" as it pertains to that show.

The console may be used subsequently to mix the opening acts, and the settings of the headline act will be changed and overwritten. However, the headliners' engineer can recall the show file to the console before the headliner's set, and the sound for the audience should be as it was left at the end of soundcheck (differences in temperature and humidity in the venue permitting).

The engineer also has the option to save the show file to a USB hard drive (or send it somewhere via the internet). The show file is carried with the engineer on the USB drive and can be loaded up the next time the sound engineer uses a console of the same make and model – perhaps at the next venue on the tour. The settings from the previous show using that type of console will be recalled, providing consistency in sound and saving the sound engineer time making manual adjustments.

Show files are not compatible between consoles from different manufacturers, although show files are somewhat compatible between the different models from the same manufacturer.

PRE-PRODUCTION PROGRAMMING

Show files make it easier for the artist engineer to ensure consistency of sound and quicker to set up a console at soundcheck – in theory. The reality is, that as show files are not compatible between consoles from different manufacturers, the touring sound engineer must create and travel with show files for all the consoles she is likely to encounter on tour.

The artist may be touring production venues and renting and transporting a console, in which case the engineer will have the same equipment to operate at every show. However, the artist may be touring non-production venues (with in-house consoles) or appearing at a string of festival dates with different consoles being provided by the festival organisers.

The engineer can save the settings of a console from a previous show to use as a starting point for each concert in a non-production venue. Over the period of a tour she will amass show files for each console type and be able to deploy them at concerts accordingly. However, the artist may be looking for more consistency of sound, especially for their onstage monitor sound.

The show files for a monitor console contain a "mix" for each performer on stage (and also for backline technicians and others who need to hear the performers onstage sound). Having the "right" sound in the monitors (wedges, IEMs, etc.) is vital for the performer – a good sound on stage will make the performers comfortable and more able to deliver a "killer" show. Open-air festivals do not allow any time for soundchecks before the performance, however, and it is not possible to "dial in" the monitor sound until the artist hits the stage. Digital desks do allow for dialling in, as the console and the backline can be set up in a pre-production facility before the tour (or festival run) and the setting for the complex monitor patch can be set up, adjusted, and stored as a show file. Come show day, the artist's monitor engineer simply needs to load in her show file to the console at the festival, make a few small adjustments if necessary, and be confident that the sound the artist hears when they step on stage will be almost the same as they heard in the rehearsal facility.

There are issues with the practice of pre-programming monitor consoles for festival shows. Show files are not compatible between consoles. The artist who wants to ensure they have a show file ready for every console that might be supplied during a summer festival run must complete pre-production programming on each console. This activity takes time (a day for each console) and is expensive – a model of each console must be rented in, along with all the necessary microphones, cables, IEMs, etc.) as well as the cost of renting the room, crew wages, etc. The result will hopefully be a consistency of sound at each festival show but comes at a cost.

The cost and time taken to program show files for each console type ultimately leads the artist to renting their own digital console for their use at festivals. The side stage of a festival stage will often have multiple consoles set up and waiting, as many artists ensure consistency of stage sound by electing to bring in their own console.

RF

The term "RF" (radio frequency) is used to describe the wireless transmission and reception of audio signals in concert production. RF equipment includes handheld microphones (which are transmitters), in-ear monitors (receivers), and dedicated instrument transmitters. RF microphones and monitors allow performers to walk (and run) around a performance area without being inhibited by cables. Not being attached to a cable is not only an aesthetic consideration – the inclusion of numerous dancers or a choir on stage is only possible using RF equipment. Running cables to 20 or so choir microphones is impracticable, for instance. Modern concert production is dependent on RF; the high-end productions associated with superstar and legacy artists could not take place if forced to use cable and copper wire to connect microphones and monitors.

RF equipment for concert production operates in the UHF spectrum, typically 400–700 Mhz. The transmission of a microphone, for instance, must be on a frequency that is "clear"; there is nothing else transmitting on that frequency in the venue or the surrounding area (usually 1 km²). All sorts of horrendous noise can result from two transmitters operating on the same frequency.

The concert production industry faces a problem. Parts of the UHF are also used for the transmission of digital television (DTV) and mobile data (4G and 5G), and this space is becoming crowded as more capacity is needed by the telecom operators. The governments in some countries have sold large parts of the UHF spectrum to the telecom companies, resulting in less of the spectrum being available for program makers and special events (PMSE) use. The remaining spectrum is used for DTV transmission, with unused (clear) frequencies referred to as "white space".

A tour of mid-level (5,000–10,000 capacity) production venues may require 20 or so "channels" (specific UHF frequencies) in the white space for its RF equipment. Finding clear frequencies can be an issue, especially when vising cities that have a major TV broadcast centre, such as Koln (Germany) or New York (US). Open-air festivals and large-scale music awards shows (such as the European Music Awards (EMA) and the BRIT Awards in the UK) require hundreds of RF frequencies for their events. Accommodating the RF requirements of the visiting artists, their dancers and backup singers, special guests, and the presenters themselves is a major administrative headache.

The use of the UHF spectrum for PMSE is regulated in most countries, with different countries allocating different parts of the spectrum for concert production. The UK has a robust licensing system for instance and PMSE users can discover and purchase clear channels on an event-by-event basis.

The country-by-country variation in available channels means that RF equipment originating from one country (the US, for instance) may not be legal in another (Japan, for instance). Artists undertaking world tours must investigate RF licensing regulations in their intended destinations, and will probably end up renting their wireless transmitters and receivers for each country stop of the tour.

DATA AND NETWORKING

Audio for concert production moved into the digital world following the introduction of digital mixing consoles. Converting audio signals into digital ones and zeros enabled more audio (higher channel counts) to be captured at a higher quality and distributed beyond the constraints of a typical analogue line system (See "PA" earlier in this section). The distribution of digital audio relies on networks. Consoles, speaker management systems, audio playback, sound measurement tools, communication, and other devices can all be joined into a network using technology found in IT, such as switches, routers, and network bridges. Much of this equipment has been adapted for the demands of seamless audio transmission.

Protocols for audio signals have also been developed and unfortunately there are now competing protocols from different manufacturers. Some protocols are unable to talk to others, creating issues for audio engineers with a preference for certain equipment. Fortunately, some protocols have emerged as being more suitable for high-speed, reliable transmission of audio than others, and these protocols have been adopted by manufacturers to create unofficial standards. There is a long way to go though, and implementing an audio network for large-scale events still requires specialised knowledge of IT networking and audio protocols.

BUDGETING FOR THE PA

An artist touring non-production venues should not have to spend any money on PA rental. The sound system will be already installed in each venue, or the promoter will rent a system if no installed system exists in a particular venue. The artist can also assume that the supplied PA will have the necessary number and type of microphones and DI boxes, and appropriate enquiries should be made as part of the "advancing" process. In any case, there should be no cost to the artist – the promoters agree to supply PA as part of the contracted deal.

Artists may elect to rent (or purchase) an in-ear monitoring system and microphones (especially wireless equipment) for their touring activity, as this equipment will continue to serve them when they move into production venues and open-air festivals. The budget must reflect the cost of this rental, or purchase, as well as the cost of consumables – batteries for wireless microphones and belt-packs, for instance.

Promoters also agree to supply PA at their sole cost when organising concerts in production venues (no in-house sound equipment in the venue – see "Venues" earlier in this part). Artists should not have to budget for PA when performing in production venues, and that is usually the case unless the artist is undertaking a tour of such venues.

PROMOTER'S CONTRIBUTION

You saw in "*Chapter 13: Planning a Tour*" earlier in this part that artists may elect to carry a rented PA system with them when touring mid-level (5,000 – 10,000 capacity) production venues. The understanding is that the promoter pays for the PA (as part of the contracted deal for those concerts). The promoter will have allocated an amount for PA hire in their show costings. The artist wants to rent and transport a system; the promoter pays the artist the amount agreed in the show costing towards that PA rental as a "contribution". The contribution should in theory equal the amount the artist is spending on rental for the evening. The reality is that the artist will have specified a far more expensive system than the promoter would have paid for, and so the contribution is less than the rental amount. The artist is therefore paying for PA rental, even though the contract stipulates the promoter pays the bill! Take the first city on the tour shown in Figure 18.7. The promoter is DF Concerts, who are promoting a show for the artist at Barrowland in Glasgow (1950 capacity). A local PA rental company has quoted £600.00 to supply audio equipment for the concert, and DF Concerts will have included that amount in their costings for the show. However, the artist wants to hire and transport one PA system for all four dates on the tour. This will cost £4500.00. DF Concerts pays the artist £600.00 as a contribution to the cost of the PA. This leaves the artist with a shortfall, which, if divided between the four shows, would be £525.00 for the Glasgow show.

CHARGING FOR SYSTEM TECHS

Artists who are opening for a national touring band in production venues may have a PA-related expense they did not consider.

To explain: non-production venues (<1000 capacity) have in-house sound systems and supply technicians to operate those systems. The artist does not have to pay these

VENUE	GLASGOW	MANCHESTER	CAMBRIDGE	LONDON
	BARROWLANDS *DF CONCERTS*	O2 APOLLO MANCHESTER *SJM CONCERTS*	CORN EXCHANGE *CROSSTOWN CONCERTS*	O2 ACADEMY BRIXTON *CROSSTOWN CONCERTS*
QUOTE TO PROMOTER FROM LOCAL AUDIO SUPPLIER	EFX (ADLIB) - £600	ADLIB - £650	AUDIOLEASE -£650	BRITANNIA ROW PRODUCTIONS - £800
COST TO BAND FOR PA	£0	£0	£0	£0
	BAND WANT BRIT ROW TO SUPPLY PA FOR ALL FOUR SHOWS. COST = £4500			
COST TO BAND PER SHOW.(TOTAL COST OF PA MINUS CONTRIBUTION FROM PROMOTER)	£525	£475	£475	£325

Figure 18.7 The promoter agrees to supply (pay for) the PA rental. The artist specifies equipment above the price agreed by the promoter, and the artist loses money. Image courtesy of the author

technicians for their work on the evening and the technicians will assist in setting up and operating equipment – the stage monitor sound console for instance.

There are no in-house technicians in a production venue. The rental company supplies technicians to set up and assist the headliner's own audio team. These "system techs" are also available to assist opening acts. Strictly however they are being paid to work for the headline act as part of the PA rental – they are not obliged to operate the equipment on behalf of opening acts. An unsavoury convention is for the system techs to charge money to opening acts in return for the system techs operating the equipment. Common practice is for the PA crew chief, or headliner's production manager, to seek out payment for the system techs from the opening acts before soundcheck can commence. The charge may be $10 per tech per evening, which although a small amount, is a shock to the opening acts if they are not aware of the practice.

The recourse for opening acts is to contact the promoter. The deal between the opening artist and the promoter is the same as that for the headliner – the promoter agrees to supply PA at the promoter's sole cost. The term PA does not explicitly reference any technicians necessary for operation of the PA equipment, and it can assume that it does. The wording should imply the artist opening on the night should not have to pay for someone to operate the monitor console.

THE SUPPLIER'S QUOTATION

An artist is undertaking a tour of production venues. Each promoter of specific concert dates has been made aware that the artist will be renting and transporting their own PA, so each promoter does not have to organise this locally and will pay the contribution set out in their show costings to the artist.

Someone from the artist's team (usually the tour manager or production manager) will then contact audio rental suppliers and request a quotation to supply an appropriate system (Figure 18.8). The artist audio team will be involved in this process as they will

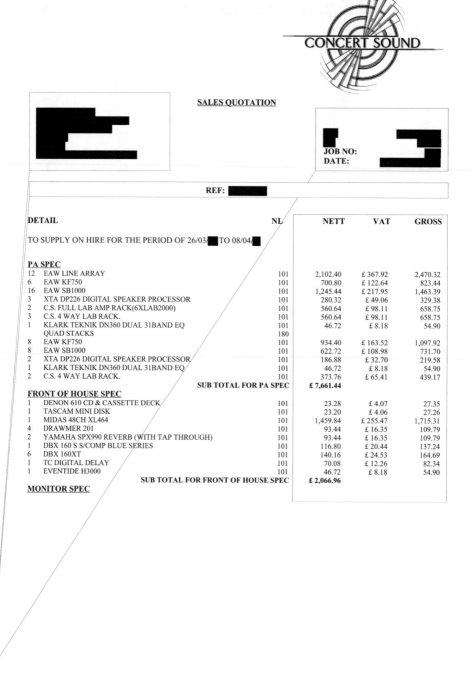

CONCERT SOUND

SALES QUOTATION

JOB NO:
DATE:

REF:

DETAIL	NL	NETT	VAT	GROSS
TO SUPPLY ON HIRE FOR THE PERIOD OF 26/03/ TO 08/04/				
PA SPEC				
12 EAW LINE ARRAY	101	2,102.40	£ 367.92	2,470.32
6 EAW KF750	101	700.80	£ 122.64	823.44
16 EAW SB1000	101	1,245.44	£ 217.95	1,463.39
3 XTA DP226 DIGITAL SPEAKER PROCESSOR	101	280.32	£ 49.06	329.38
2 C.S. FULL LAB AMP RACK(6XLAB2000)	101	560.64	£ 98.11	658.75
3 C.S. 4 WAY LAB RACK.	101	560.64	£ 98.11	658.75
1 KLARK TEKNIK DN360 DUAL 31BAND EQ	101	46.72	£ 8.18	54.90
QUAD STACKS	180			
8 EAW KF750	101	934.40	£ 163.52	1,097.92
8 EAW SB1000	101	622.72	£ 108.98	731.70
2 XTA DP226 DIGITAL SPEAKER PROCESSOR	101	186.88	£ 32.70	219.58
1 KLARK TEKNIK DN360 DUAL 31BAND EQ	101	46.72	£ 8.18	54.90
2 C.S. 4 WAY LAB RACK.	101	373.76	£ 65.41	439.17
SUB TOTAL FOR PA SPEC		**£ 7,661.44**		
FRONT OF HOUSE SPEC				
1 DENON 610 CD & CASSETTE DECK	101	23.28	£ 4.07	27.35
1 TASCAM MINI DISK	101	23.20	£ 4.06	27.26
1 MIDAS 48CH XL464	101	1,459.84	£ 255.47	1,715.31
4 DRAWMER 201	101	93.44	£ 16.35	109.79
2 YAMAHA SPX990 REVERB (WITH TAP THROUGH)	101	93.44	£ 16.35	109.79
1 DBX 160 S S/COMP BLUE SERIES	101	116.80	£ 20.44	137.24
6 DBX 160XT	101	140.16	£ 24.53	164.69
1 TC DIGITAL DELAY	101	70.08	£ 12.26	82.34
1 EVENTIDE H3000	101	46.72	£ 8.18	54.90
SUB TOTAL FOR FRONT OF HOUSE SPEC		**£ 2,066.96**		
MONITOR SPEC				

Figure 18.8 A quote to rent a PA system for a tour. Although this is a quote from many years ago, it is relevant as the quote details the equipment, people, and extras the rental company will send out on tour with an artist. Image courtesy of the author

SALES QUOTATION

JOB NO:
DATE: 28th January

Continued.....

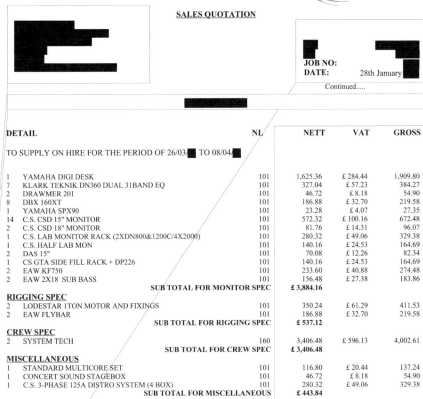

DETAIL		NL	NETT	VAT	GROSS
TO SUPPLY ON HIRE FOR THE PERIOD OF 26/03/ TO 08/04/					
1	YAMAHA DIGI DESK	101	1,625.36	£ 284.44	1,909.80
7	KLARK TEKNIK DN360 DUAL 31BAND EQ	101	327.04	£ 57.23	384.27
2	DRAWMER 201	101	46.72	£ 8.18	54.90
8	DBX 160XT	101	186.88	£ 32.70	219.58
1	YAMAHA SPX90	101	23.28	£ 4.07	27.35
14	C.S. CSD 15" MONITOR	101	572.32	£ 100.16	672.48
2	C.S. CSD 18" MONITOR	101	81.76	£ 14.31	96.07
1	C.S. LAB MONITOR RACK (2XDN800&1200C/4X2000)	101	280.32	£ 49.06	329.38
1	C.S. HALF LAB MON	101	140.16	£ 24.53	164.69
2	DAS 15"	101	70.08	£ 12.26	82.34
1	CS GTA SIDE FILL RACK + DP226	101	140.16	£ 24.53	164.69
2	EAW KF750	101	233.60	£ 40.88	274.48
2	EAW 2X18 SUB BASS	101	156.48	£ 27.38	183.86
	SUB TOTAL FOR MONITOR SPEC		**£ 3,884.16**		
RIGGING SPEC					
2	LODESTAR 1TON MOTOR AND FIXINGS	101	350.24	£ 61.29	411.53
2	EAW FLYBAR	101	186.88	£ 32.70	219.58
	SUB TOTAL FOR RIGGING SPEC		**£ 537.12**		
CREW SPEC					
2	SYSTEM TECH	160	3,406.48	£ 596.13	4,002.61
	SUB TOTAL FOR CREW SPEC		**£ 3,406.48**		
MISCELLANEOUS					
1	STANDARD MULTICORE SET	101	116.80	£ 20.44	137.24
1	CONCERT SOUND STAGEBOX	101	46.72	£ 8.18	54.90
1	C.S. 3-PHASE 125A DISTRO SYSTEM (4 BOX)	101	280.32	£ 49.06	329.38
	SUB TOTAL FOR MISCELLANEOUS		**£ 443.84**		

Figure 18.8 Continued

CONCERT SOUND

SALES QUOTATION

JOB NO:	
DATE:	28th January 2▮

Continued.....

REF ▮▮▮▮

DETAIL	NL		NETT	VAT	GROSS

TO SUPPLY ON HIRE FOR THE PERIOD OF 26/03/0▮ TO

This quote does not include crew transport,hotels,catering or the services of a tour rigger.
I have been talking to ▮▮▮▮▮▮ and have agreed the spec for this tour.
This quote does not include any extra equipment or transport to the ▮▮▮

TOTAL QUOTE			£ 18,000.00	£ 3,150.00	£ 21,150.00

TERMS : PAYABLE UPON RECEIPT OF INVOICE - E&OE
NO BOOKING CAN BE CONFIRMED UNTIL AFTER RECEIPT OF A VALID PURCHASE ORDER. THIS
QUOTATION IS VALID ON PRICE FOR 30 DAYS FROM QUOTE DATE. DISCOUNTS OFFERED ARE FOR
PAYMENT WITHIN THE SPECIFIED TERMS. WE RESERVE THE RIGHT TO SUBSTITUTE EQUIPMENT. THIS
QUOTATION IS SUBJECT TO OUR TERMS OF HIRE, COPIES OF WHICH ARE AVAILABLE ON REQUEST

CONCERT SOUND LTD VAT ▮▮▮▮▮▮

Concert Sound Ltd, Unit C Park Avenue Industrial Estate, Sundon Park Road, Luton, Bedfordshire, LU3 3BP
Tel: +44 ▮▮▮

Figure 18.8 Continued

have a clear idea as to specific requirements of the system – the input list and channel count, for instance, as well as preferences for console and loudspeaker makes and models.

The rental company will provide a quote, and this will include a price for these items:

- *rental of the PA itself* – loudspeakers, consoles, line systems, rigging, and cables to suit the artist's specifications. The supplier may not stock certain items as requested by the artist, so these would have to be "dry-hired" from another supplier when the order is placed
- *transportation of the PA*. This will be a quote for trucks and The PA rental supplier may have a relationship with a trucking company
- *system techs*
- *consumables* – PVC and gaffa tape, recordable media

The quote will also advise the renter about:

- the electrical power required to run the proposed system
- the weights and sizes of the proposed system. The artist may elect to provide their own transport or may be freighting the system abroad
- stipulations for crew working conditions – bunks on artist buses and contribution towards system crew meals, for instance

Figure 18.8 shows a typical quotation for a PA system.

BACKLINE

The second production element is backline – the instruments and musical equipment used by the performers on stage. The term "backline" is probably derived from referring to the traditional drum kit, guitar amps, and keyboards, used by musicians – this equipment was set up behind the musicians on stage, creating a "backline" of equipment.

Traditional backline equipment is still used by musicians. Technology-driven music-making methods are also common on stage, and contemporary performance is a mixture of the two.

The artist should own their music-making instruments and devices, and there is no "standard" backline set up – every band and performer uses completely different combinations of music equipment.

The initial concert performances will involve figuring out ways to transport instruments and technology. Artists that use "traditional" backline (such as the drum kits and guitar amps mentioned above) may benefit from being able to share or borrow equipment from other artists on the bill. Singer/songwriters who perhaps use a guitar and a "looper" (an effect box for the guitar that samples one phrase and loops it) would be able to travel on public transport to a gig if needs be.

The amount and complexity of an artist's backline will increase over the course of their career. Reproducing studio-recording experiments may lead to more instruments and devices on stage, for instance. This, and the need for instruments and technology to be working and in good repair, makes the hiring of backline crew necessary.

PLAYBACK & MIDI CONTROL

"Playback" and MIDI (see *MIDI*) control is now an accepted part of live music performance.

The term "playback" is associated with miming to a pre-recorded piece of music, or lip-syncing (mouthing the shape of words to pre-recorded vocals played out live). Modern concert production rarely employs such techniques but elements of playback are still required.

Producing music requires no more than a reasonably powerful computer, a digital audio workstation (DAW), such as Live or Logic, and a pair of headphones. Artists that have success with music produced in this way face the challenge of translating their music to the stage. Setting up a computer on stage and pressing buttons is all that is required for the musical output itself and is hardly a compelling performance.

You saw about the work of the musical director (MD) earlier in this part. The MD will be responsible for making that translation of the recorded music into parts for numerous singers and musicians. Parts may be allocated to human beings on stage and certain elements must still be reproduced by the DAW to recreate the feel of the recorded material. This is the role of playback.

A simple playback "rig" (setup) may be a laptop running a copy of a DAW, typically Live by Ableton (Figure 18.9). Elements of the original recorded session can be played out. These elements may include electronic drumbeats and sub bass – elements that are difficult for a human player to reproduce effectively. The DAW may also generate the click tracks needed for the performers to keep time with the playback elements (see "stage monitoring" earlier in this part). Playback and MIDI control systems are simple or

Figure 18.9 A simple playback rig built around dual-redundant computers running Ableton Live. Image courtesy of the author

become complicated. Systems for productions in arenas and festivals are built to generate program changes for lighting and other cues and have dual-redundancy AB-systems where the backup B system will take over if A fails for any reason.

MIDI

MIDI stands for Musical Instrument Digital Interface. MIDI is a communication protocol used by all music-making devices and allows them to be connected to send and receive music note-based data. DAWs, for example, use MIDI to capture and store musical performance – the resulting MIDI information can be used to send the notes to internal sound sources and external modules that generate sound. The modules receive the midi note information and play sound at the appropriate time, pitch, and volume. MIDI can also be used to send and receive system information, such as program changes and controller changes (CC).

The modern stage playback system will consist of computers that replay audio (recordings of vocals or orchestras, for instance) and MIDI data that is used to generate beats and melodies from electronic sound sources. The MIDI can also change effects patches on a guitarists foot pedal board at the right place in a song, saving them from having to make the change manually.

PLAYBACK AND SET LENGTH

Playback or MIDI control of material can be controlled on-the-fly to a certain extent. Songs can be started on command, and the order of the songs changed during the performance of the set. Some DAWs allow sections of songs to be repeated (or skipped) in real time, in the same way as musicians may improvise the structure of a song. However, the artist may not be using such robust playback technology or be controlling other elements that do not respond well to such mid-set changes. The stage set length (the amount of time allocated by the promoter for that artist's performance) is therefore required information. The number of songs and the overall length of the set, can be programmed before the show, ensuring the artist does not under or over play. Set length is no so important for the artist's own hard-ticket or headline shows but makes all the difference for festival appearances. The artist appearing at a festival may have programmed the playback system to deliver a 45-minute set, only to find out on the day that the allocated time on stage is 30 minutes. Songs will have to be cut from the set in this case, to make sure the big ending number can still be performed. Depending on the technology the artist is using, cutting songs may not be possible on-the-fly. Knowing the set length in advance is always a good thing.

TOURING ABROAD

An artist will hopefully be touring abroad as their career and appeal progresses. They will need to take their backline with them or rent it locally on arrival. An artist touring by road in a splitter van or on a sleeper bus with a trailer can take all their backline with them, with no need to rent.

FLY-DATES

Flying to a concert presents challenges for the artist. They need to take their backline with them and may not be able to fly with certain elements due to size, weight, or number of the instruments and devices they usually use.

Artists that use mainly traditional backline – drum kits, guitar amps, etc., will be able to rent (or have supplied by the promoter) equivalent equipment in most countries in the world. Artists that incorporate specialised, or cutting-edge, technology and devices may struggle with renting the equivalent in some parts of the world.

The "fly-date" dilemma requires consideration. Countries that start to embrace a concert-going culture as personified in the US, UK, and Europe, may not have the infrastructure to be able to supply the necessary production equipment to the artist's specifications – that includes the backline. Any offer for a festival in a country not known for its concert production experience must be considered with technical limitations in mind. Would the resulting cost of freighting the artist's backline outweigh the performance fee the festival is offering?

DJS

All artists use different combinations of music instruments and devices and so there is no accepted standard of instruments, makes, and models, for performers – except DJs. Most DJs will specify, or be happy to use, Pioneer DJ products (Figure 18.10).

Figure 18.10 Pioneer DJ equipment, especially the NXS range of CD players and mixers shown here, is ubiquitous. Image courtesy of the author

CONSUMABLES

The tour budget should include a line for backline consumables. This term refers to the drum sticks, guitar and bass strings, reeds, picks (plectrums), 9v batteries, USB sticks, and the countless other items that break or need replacing after each performance. Musical instrument consumables are not cheap – a pack of electric guitar strings is currently $8.99. A guitarist changing the complete set of strings for guitar on a 20-date tour would spend $179.00 just on strings. The need for these items to be included in the budget is highlighted when additional guitars and musicians are factored in.

LIGHTING

The technology and techniques of concert lighting have developed since the early experiments by alternative rock bands in the late 1960s. Artists such as The Grateful Dead (US) and Pink Floyd (UK) adapted existing theatre lights and experimented with projection shapes using coloured-oil wheels to enhance their music when performing live. Today's touring artists have a vast array of fixtures and controllers at their disposal that enable them to create dazzling "light shows" that become as much a discussion point as the artist's music itself. The artist and her team must be aware of the possibilities of concert lighting to complement and enhance the music.

Well-designed and sympathetic lighting "looks" can enhance the music at all stages of an artist's career (Figure 18.11).

Figure 18.11 Concert lighting should be effective at all stages of the artist's career. The image is of testing a lighting scene in a 300-capacity club. Image courtesy of the author

A concert lighting system is made up of:

fixtures – the lamps and lamp housings
control desk
dimmers – power distribution
rigging

FIXTURES

Lighting technology was based on incandescent lamps – tungsten or tungsten halogen – similar to domestic light bulbs and requiring much more power. A by-product of this power consumption is heat generation. Performing under a simple lighting "rig" comprising parabolic aluminised reflector (PAR) lamps is hot work – each lamp radiates heat into its housing, as well as in the direction the lamp is facing. Modern concert lighting is increasingly based on LED technology which requires a lot less power, and the individual fixtures do not emit heat on the scale of a PAR lamp.

Incandescent lighting fixtures must be "focused" – set in place, pointing at the part of the stage that needs to be illuminated. The colour of the lamps can be changed by placing a coloured "gel" over the lamp, and once set and focused, that fixture can only project that colour light. The operator must set up and focus many lamps if they want many different colours. Several lamps with blue gels, several lamps with yellow gels, and so on, must be set and focused to create the "looks" or lighting "scenes" for different points in the concert.

Setting and focusing incandescent lamps and fixtures created the traditional lighting rigs of the 70s and 80s. These rigs are an impressive sight in photographs from the era, and took considerable time to set up and focus, as well as occupying many trucks during transportation.

The 80s saw the development of the "moving head" fixture, followed by the "moving mirror" type lighting instrument. Moving heads are fixtures that can be instructed to pan, tilt, and change the colour of the lighting beam. Motors in the fixture control the movement, and dichroic filters enable the lamp to emit different colours. Advances in lamp technology, involving metal halide lamps, meant that fixtures could be set into a lighting rig and then controlled to move around and change colour – during the concert itself.

Moving heads work well but are inefficient. The fixture does not need to be moved to aim a beam in a different direction – the light source itself needs to move. Moving mirror fixtures do this by redirecting the light beam, using motor-controlled mirrors in the fixture, resulting in faster, more precise movement of the resulting light.

CONTROL DESK

As with a PA system, the lighting "show" is controlled using a console that is situated at the FOH position. The console can be programmed – different lighting scenes set up and stored ahead of the concert or tour. The operator can program scenes and scenes-within-scenes – "snapshots" – for each song (or part of a song) in advance and then recall those scenes and snapshots at the appropriate point during the concert. These scenes help to create the exciting light shows we very much take for granted.

Although the artist may be touring with a rented lighting rig, and all the fixtures are in use every evening, the operator may have to compromise in the exact portioning of fixtures. A venue may be smaller, narrower, or the "trim height" (the height at which the fixtures are suspended) may be lower than ideal. The operator will have programmed the show based on a certain size of performance area – the lighting beam focuses and position will have to be changed in venues that do not adhere to that certain size. The operator will have to undertake a certain amount of reprogramming at each venue, and this takes place in the afternoon, concurrent with the artist's soundcheck.

The console controls the brightness, on/off state, pan, tilt, iris, and beam colour of each fixture in a lighting rig through a control protocol called DMX512, which is often shortened to just "DMX" (Digital MultipleX). DMX512 "talks" to individual moving head or moving mirror fixtures and can control the brightness and on/off state of incandescent lamps through the "dimmers" (see below).

DMX512 can transmit 512 channels of communication. A moving head fixture can consume ten or more channels, as each command for pan, tilt, focus, colour, iris size, etc., uses one channel. The operator can quickly run out of available DMX channels when designing and operating a rig with many fixtures. To this end, the DMX512 system operates on a principle of "universes" – each universe incorporating 512 channels of DMX. A concert-ready lighting console will have the capability of running two or more universes (most consoles can run four universes), giving DMX channel counts in the thousands!

DIMMERS – POWER DISTRIBUTION

As mentioned, incandescent lamps require lots of power to work. That power must be controlled, especially if the operator wants to be able to dim lamps, or even turn them off, at certain points during the concert. Dimmers enable the operator to do that (Figure 18.12). Named after the function most needed, dimming the brightness of the lamp, dimmers using silicon rectifiers and triacs (a type of auto-controlled transformer) to reduce the incoming mains power signal to modify the resulting light intensity. The dimmer receives its commands via the DMX512 protocol which is sent from the operators lighting console.

RIGGING

The final element in the lighting system is the "rigging" – the chain hoists, truss, and other suspension points, used to place the lighting rig.

Most lighting elements are suspended ("flown") in the same manner as the PA. In fact, lighting and video elements are usually suspended first, as these elements require many more suspension points and chain hoists. The chain hoists (Figure 18.4) will lift up

Figure 18.12 The dimmers and other lighting controls, stage right for a concert at the O2 Academy Brixton, UK. The dimmers control the power to the incandescent lamps, allowing dimming of the light beams. Image courtesy of the author

sections of "truss" – aluminium frameworks from which fixtures are hung by hooks (Figure 18.13). A typical lighting rig will have three trusses – front, middle, and back, corresponding to the front, middle, and rear of the performance area. The trusses themselves span the width of the stage, and the fixtures are attached at intervals along the truss, depending on the design of the system.

BUDGETING FOR THE LIGHTING SYSTEM

The lighting system can complement and enhance the music and can be used to create impact. This impact many be necessary if the artist's music is lacking somehow, or the artist is unknown to the audience. This will certainly be the case in a showcase environment, where tastemakers are being introduced to the artist's live show for the first time. It is often deemed necessary to make a statement in these situations by including or adding lighting.

Lighting equipment is not necessarily as bulky or heavy as PA equipment, and there are certainly more individual elements that must be planned, budgeted, and paid for.

DESIGN

The "lighting designer"(LD) will the first port of call when considering a lighting rig for a tour or one-off event. The LD may also be the operator for the final performance, and they are retained to design a suitable look for the concerts, based on consultation with the artist team and their own unique vision.

Figure 18.13 Sections of truss have been bolted together to create a "box truss" that will be suspended above the performance area. You can see three fixtures that have been fixed to the truss already. Others will be attached and cabled before the truss is "flown" to its operating height. Image courtesy of the author

The LD is able to visualise and plan a lighting rig using specialised computer aided design (CAD) packages. These packages can produce highly detailed renderings of the resulting design to show to clients, as well as creating rigging "plots" and inventory manifests.

Designing and implementing a lighting rig for a showcase or other marquee event will be expensive – roughly 2.5 times the price of a PA system for the same event.[1]

VIDEO

The use of video (projection or display of moving images) is a response to advances in sound reinforcement and is as much a part of the concert experience as lighting. The advances in sound reinforcement have resulted in clearer sound that can be delivered to larger audiences using smaller and lighter audio equipment. The fact that the sound can reach a larger number of people in an area has a trade-off – many fans are further away from the performers on stage and cannot necessarily see what is happening up there. At the same time, the popularity of electronic music that often has no performance element to it (no vocalists, drummers, or guitarists) has resulted in video being used in the same way as stage lighting. Moods and highlights in the music can be accentuated using content shown on screens near the performance area.

Video in concert production consists of two elements:

- image magnification (IMAG)
- content

IMAG

Image magnification (IMAG) uses cameras to capture performances in real time and projection or display technology to magnify the performances so any member of the audience can see the result. IMAG output is real-time and responds to the mood of the performers and the audience.

IMAG is costly to produce. The camera people, broadcast cameras, live vision mixers, directors, and the display technology (projection screens of LED panels) that are needed are expensive to rent (Figure 18.14). A concert production that incorporates IMAG should ideally have some period of camera rehearsal – either preceding the tour or before the event. Extra days of equipment rental and wages are also expensive.

CONTENT

"Content" refers to any non-IMAG elements that are projected or displayed and are not real-time. Content may be pre-recorded film, computer-generated images, or text for announcements or displaying lyrics. Content is stored as digital files in media servers which are controlled by dedicated software. This software allows the operator to cue up the digital files and display them on command. Complex, rhythmic, sequences can be generated in this way, enhancing the performance of the music.

TECHNOLOGY

Concert video production has arguably seen the most technological advancement. This sector of the concert production industry is linked with the wider events industry where the use of video in product launches, trade shows, industry keynote

Figure 18.14 IMAG needs broadcast-quality cameras to capture the performance. Image from Adobe Stock

Figure 18.15 A video wall being built as part of an outdoor event. The "wall" is made up of individual panels – the more panels, the bigger the wall. The image shows the cladding that will cover the steel structure, and the part of the PA system (top right). Image courtesy of the author

presentations, and on televised awards shows has excited and inspired manufacturers. The result is higher-definition capture and a more vibrant and larger display of the resulting images.

The LED panel is an example of technological advancement and its use in concert production. LED panels are used to make up the screens, or "video walls", used to display IMAG and content. The panel themselves are available in all sizes, and several panels are fitted together to make a screen (Figure 18.15). The LED in the name refers to the individual light sources in the panel. More LEDs, closer together, result in a higher-definition image when viewed at an appropriate distance. Advances in technology have resulted in more LEDs being fitted into a panel with minimal changes in weight or power requirements. Cutting edge panels now have a "pitch" (the distance between the LEDs) of 2.6mm. Panels can also be flexed, enabling them to be used in curved configurations – ideal for incorporating scenic elements on stage.

VIDEO FOR LIVESTREAMING

Camera-based IMAG video may have been associated with concerts of >10,000 capacity, but the popularity of livestreaming has changed that perception. The live music business has demonstrated its ability to adapt, innovate, and execute quickly, with a myriad of new companies and innovations contributing to create a unique online experience for any participant in an event.

Livestreams employ the same technology as a multi-camera concert IMAG deployment, and companies and individuals with touring experience have been able to utilise their talents to create seamless livestreaming experiences.

BUDGETING FOR VIDEO SYSTEMS

Budgeting for video is not only for superstar and heritage acts touring in arenas and stadiums. Emerging artists and DJs will have video production expenses.

Festivals have screens and display technology in their major performance areas. These are used for advertisements, announcements, and the occasional showing of sports events. The screens are also made available to visiting artists who can display their own content during their performance. The festival organisers will advise artists as to the size and pitch of LED screens, as well as the shape and orientation of the panels (the resulting video screens are not always in the traditional 14:3 rectangle).

Producing content for display is a specialised creative process, just like producing music. Video content can highlight a particular artist performance and differentiate them from other performers on the same bill. Creating striking content is not easy. The artist will not have the skills, or the time, necessary to create motion graphics or film to the standard expected by audiences. Professional motion graphic producers should be used, and these people will charge professional rates for their services. The cost is well worth it and should be figured into the budget as soon as possible.

SET AND STAGE

"Lavish stage sets" is a cliche associated with concerts by superstar acts. Concert production at the arena- and stadium-levels will indeed see the design and construction of incredible stage sets incorporating elements including rainfall and water fountains.[2] The pinnacle of stage set design in recent years was the 2009–2011 "360°" tour by Irish rock band U2. The concerts were staged "in-the-round" with the performer in the middle of the stadium, surrounded by fans on all sides. The stage itself consisted of a structure 51 metres (167 feet) tall, nicknamed "The Claw".[3]

The design of stage sets reflects the need for performers to differentiate themselves from other artists at the same level of success. Set designers will want to incorporate the latest structural and display technology.

Artist touring in non-production venues and appearing at festivals may also have the need to budget for set and stage elements. An example might be the artist who has a DJ/turntablist in their line-up. They may rent a dedicated DJ "table" for their tour, for instance (Figure 18.16). The DJ table would traditionally be draped with cloth to hide the cables and the DJs legs. The artist may instead commission a collapsible surround for the DJ table, perhaps printed with their logo or album artwork.

Another example of set items at non-production and mid-level touring is the design and manufacture of enclosures for instruments and devices on stage. Keyboard players may want to give the impression of using a vintage instrument for instance. A carcass in the shape of a piano or vintage organ can be manufactured to incorporate a digital equivalent, giving the impression the player is vibing the authentic, analogue sound, on stage.

Figure 18.16 A DJ table made from Lite-Deck, and modelled by a willing stagehand. The Lite-Deck components can be easily rented for a tour, ensuring the DJ has a consistent platform each night. Image courtesy of the author

Such elements are common for festival appearances and on televised music awards shows like the EMAs (Europe) and the BRIT Awards (UK).

BUDGETING FOR SET AND STAGE

The cost of set and stage design and manufacture may be unnecessary, and it is true their use can help to differentiate the performance by an artist on a busy festival bill. Their inclusion should be considered by the artist for this reason. Consideration should also be given to lead times for design and manufacturer of set pieces in the event the artist decides to place an order. Only a handful of reputable set fabricators operate, as with many suppliers in the concert production industry. These suppliers will hopefully be busy in the lead-up to festival season and the fall touring period and may not be able, or willing, to fulfil orders of basic decorative stage panels ("flats") for an emerging artist on a shoestring budget.

The emerging artist should also consider the size and weight of any set elements they rent or purchase. The DJ table in the example above would probably be made of an industry-standard decking element such as Lite-Deck. Lite-Deck comes in standard sizes; 8' x 2' would be a good size for a DJ table. This is obviously a large piece of equipment, and the artist must make sure this will fit in any transport they are using for the tour.

NOTES

1 Based on the author's experience.
2 "Aphrodite: Les Folies Tour".(2021) *Wikipedia*. Available at: https://en.wikipedia.org/wiki/Aphrodite:_Les_Folies_Tour
3 "U2 360° Tour",(2021). *Wikipedia*. Available at: https://en.wikipedia.org/wiki/U2_360_Tour

CHAPTER 19
OTHER PRODUCTION CONSIDERATIONS

CHAPTER OUTLINE

DOI: 10.4324/9781003019503-21

Taking production on-the-road involves the six elements described in the previous chapter, and these in turn create a myriad of activities and services that need to be organised, rented, or purchased.

REHEARSALS AND PRE-PRODUCTION REHEARSALS

Modern concert production is too complex to stage without rehearsing the elements. Even the artist touring non-production venues and not carrying any of their own production will still want to get all the instruments, devices, musicians, and crew in one space prior to the tour or festival appearance. In this case, the musician's will want to rehearse their parts and decide an appropriate order for the songs (the "set list"). They may even have to program a playback and MIDI control system in response to an allocated set time at a festival.

Artists can rent dedicated music rehearsal facilities. These spaces vary in the level of facilities and comfort they offer and be rented by the hour or blocked out for a 12-hour day. The state-of-the-art facilities offered by the professional production rooms will be unnecessary for simply practising their songs and will be of use when the artist wants to move to full pre-production rehearsals later. Figure 19.1 shows a typical band practice/rehearsal room.

Once together in the rehearsal space the artist will want to concentrate on these activities:

Figure 19.1 A typical band practice/rehearsal room. Image from Adobe Stock

- deciding on walk-on music
- organising the set list
- deciding on points in the set for talking, instrument changes, special guests
- playing through the set, at least twice
- organising spares
- sourcing vital equipment
- creating "looms" from cables. A loom is several cables that all run to the same point on stage and can be fastened against each other to create one, larger, cable.
- testing and repairing broken equipment

These activities will hopefully take a full day, and that will incur costs for transport to and from the rehearsal room, the rehearsal room itself, and wages for the crew members for the day.

An artist can incur major expenses during the festival season. The artist may be booked at a series of festivals over the summer and may, quite rightly, want to rehearse before each festival concert. Most festivals take place at weekends, and the artist may have one show each weekend for the summer. Rehearsing before each appearance entails rehearsing almost once a week – with full band, crew, and everything else required. The expenses involved can be significant and must be acknowledged in the budget for the season.

PRODUCTION REHEARSALS

You should now have an idea of the scale and complexity of a production tour setup from examining the six production elements of audio, backline, lighting, video, set and stage. Bringing these elements together before the first date of the tour (or festival appearance) is necessary. Issues with size, weight, power requirements, and other considerations are best resolved when all the equipment and departments heads are on-site and able to work together.

A simple production rehearsal may see the artist renting in the necessary equipment to program the sound consoles and to run through the set using the playback/MIDI control system. Production rehearsals for larger venues (theatres and arenas of 5,000–20,000 capacity) will involve assembling the equipment from each of the six elements in a suitable space. Programming and adjustments can then be made under the watchful eye of the artist.

There are few options when deciding on a space that is suitable for an arena-size production rehearsal. The production can either move into the venue that is the first date on the tour a few days early or move into one of the dedicated concert production rehearsal facilities that exist. Going into the tour venue can be a good idea, and the first date of the tour needs to be as close to the home of the production suppliers as possible. Organising production festivals in Stockholm (first date of the tour) will present challenges for a UK-based artist with UK suppliers, for instance. Renting a dedicated, arena-size, facility, although more expensive, offers the production team numerous advantages, the main one being proximity to suppliers.

Facilities that can accommodate arena and stadium-sized productions were typically limited to film studios, but now several specialised concert production facilities exist.

Touring productions can occupy these spaces and perfect the concert sound and visuals, in secret, behind closed doors. Production crews can practice, and make note of the time spent time on, the load-in and load-out of the resulting production. As well as ironing out any issues, this activity enables the production manager to estimate the number of stagehands required for the load-in and load-out and the duration of the call for each. This information will be useful for the promoter who may be able to save money by cutting the number of stagehands originally entered in the budget for the show.

VISAS AND WORK PERMITS

The cast and crew may need visas or work permits to perform and work in some countries on the tour.

Appearing at festivals is a major part of any successful artist's work schedule, and some of those festivals will be abroad. Arranging the necessary permits and permissions to enter a country to perform can be expensive and time-consuming; the expense may be disproportionate to the performance fee or potential exposure offered by visiting a country for one day. Festivals need international talent to create a diverse and exciting event, however, so visa and permit restrictions may be relaxed to encourage artists from overseas to visit and perform. The UK, for instance, has declared certain music, literary, and other performing arts, festivals to be "permit-free" – artists and performers who are invited to perform at these festivals do not have to apply for an entertainment visa in the same way they would for a concert tour of the UK. The festivals on the list must meet certain criteria and other conditions of entry apply to the performers. There is no doubt that the waiving of the usual regulations avoids the potential bureaucratic bottleneck each summer.

HEALTH, SAFETY, AND SECURITY

The safety and security of all cast, crew, venue staff, and the audience should be utmost in the minds of everyone involved in concert touring. The artist, tour manager, and production manager, are therefore involved – from simple reminders regarding safety and mental health for touring crew members to evacuation plans in case of an emergency.

A "SAFETY" CULTURE

Observing sensible procedures for health and safety should not be a "box-ticking" exercise where certain activities are completed to satisfy a manager's directive or local regulation. Everyone on tour, from the artist down, needs to be part of a culture of safety – looking out for themselves as well as everyone else on tour with them. Clear expectations should be set, and all tour personnel invited to feel comfortable and informed as to the purpose of instilling such a culture.

ACCREDITATION

Touring personnel are given passes to allow them access to certain areas of the venue. These passes are in the form of laminated A6 cards ("laminates") worn on a lanyard around the passholder's neck and are valid for the duration of the tour (Figure 19.2). Temporary day workers (such as stagehands) and venue staff will be given disposable adhesive passes ("stickies") that are valid only for the day of the performance. All visiting VIP guests, photographers, press, record company personnel, local opening acts, and other temporary help must be issued a sticky pass for the day. These passes will be colour-coded and worded to indicate the relevant permissions. "Pass sheets" (Figure 19.3) are produced by the production team to assist stewards and door staff to understand the validity and access level permitted by each pass. These pass sheets are then posted at all venue access points.

Tour laminates are an artist's expense, and the cost of stickies is usually split between the artist and the concert promoter.

Figure 19.2 Laminates are issued to touring cast and crew. Image courtesy of the author

Figure 19.3 A pass sheet contains images and information of all the laminates and stickies that have been issued for the concert. The sheets are posted at access points and enable stewards and security staff to check the validity of passes as people enter. Image courtesy of the author

PERSONAL SECURITY/CLOSE-PROTECTION PERSONNEL

An artist may elect to hire close-protection personnel for the duration of the tour. These people are part of the touring staff and are paid for by the artist. The close-protection staff may also act as security director for the tour. This role involves them liaising with venue door staff and stewards and conducting in-house security briefings before the opening of the doors. Security briefings are useful for locally hired casual stewards' staff – information about the audience demographic, maturity, and general mood can be gained from a well-run security briefing. Stewards and venue staff can adapt their approach to crowd control for each new audience based on these briefings.

SET BUILD AND ASSOCIATED COSTS

The set pieces carried on a tour of production venues must be assembled each morning and disassembled and loaded onto the trucks each night. Tour "carpenters" are responsible for this activity. The numbers of carpenters required to assemble the set will be decided during production rehearsals, with two carpenters being required for a theatre or mid-sized arena tour (5,000–20,000 capacity) and up to ten being hired on for large-arena and stadium tour (20,000–100,000 capacity). The carpenters work with locally hired stagehands, and the number of those required is also decided in the production rehearsal.

Assembling the set may require the hanging of "drape" – heavy, black cloth that is suspended to block off sections of a venue. Drape is heavy and cumbersome – the tour may carry it as part of the production inventory, and this adds to the trucking requirements. Drape is rented locally wherever possible, and coordinating the draping company and crew is the job of the head carpenter on tour.

STEEL CREW

The infrastructure of a stage set designed for stadiums (15,000–100,000 capacity) is referred to as the "steel". The erection of the set steel takes two or three days, with another two days to dismantle. Production cannot hold a concert while the set steel is being built, dismantled, or transported between stadiums, and there is no revenue from ticket sales during this time. Multiple steels are therefore fabricated, and these structures leapfrog each other around the world. One steel is in use in a concert, whilst another is being built elsewhere. Three sets of steel were used on the 360° tour by Irish rock band U2 in 2009–2011[1].

Multiple steels require multiple construction crew members, as well as site managers, portable power, extra transport, accommodation, and other services necessary to ensure the steel is safely built.

SHOW AUTOMATION

Concert production has borrowed technology from theatre. There is a blurring of disciplines between theatre and large-scale concert production, and elements, such as show automation, are now used to create the illusions seen in plays and musicals.

Automation refers to the control of hydraulic winches and hoists. Truss, lighting, video screens, and other elements can be suspended from the hoists which can then be raised, lowered, and moved horizontally, using automation control software (Figure 19.4).

Show automation enables set designers to create powerful moving effects and set pieces (called "gags") which are played out during the artist's performance. Show automation on tour requires an operator.

Automation is also used to control staged "reveals" – elements of the set or stage that were covered and are revealed on command. A "kabuki drop" is the most well-known reveal gag. A curtain falls on cue to reveal the stage (or part of it) at a particular section in the set. Kabuki drops can be affected by stagehands pulling the curtain down by hand (the curtain is attached to a set element with special clasps), or by using a kabuki-drop system that is controlled by the show automation engineer.

FX & PYROTECHNICS

The term "gags" also refers to special effects (SFX), such as pyrotechnics (pyro). The use of pyro in concert production has increased, with EDM DJs and promoters making much use of flames, confetti, and CO2 cannons to punctuate and accentuate the music (Figure 19.5).

Figure 19.4 Controllers for a Kinesys motion control system. Kinesys software and chain hoists allow show designers to automate large-scale movement of suspended production elements. Image courtesy of the author

Figure 19.5 Compressed air cannon used for launching confetti. The confetti is blown out of the large vertical tube at the rear of each cannon. Image from Adobe Stock

Fireworks and stage explosions are inherently dangerous, and forward planning should be made. Pyro is also expensive. The control and delivery systems are inexpensive to hire, but the operators and consumables contribute to significant costs. Confetti "shots" are particularly expensive. The individual price per shot runs into hundreds of dollars. The resulting covering of all surfaces creates extra cleaning for venue staff. Venues now charge artists who discharge confetti during their performance, with cleaning charges of several hundred dollars being the standard.

COMMUNICATIONS

Production crews working in arenas (5,000–20,000 capacity) or at open-air, green-field festivals are reliant on communication equipment – hand-held transmitter/receivers known as "radios" or "walkie-talkies" (Figure 19.6). The handsets and charging stations can be rented from specialised suppliers. Each member of the crew is issued a radio for the duration of the tour.

Radios are suitable for day-to-day communications and a dedicated communication net is required for the performance itself. Large-scale productions incorporate instructions from a show caller who issues "cues". The cues are commands to initiate the gags – kabuki drops or pyro firings, for instance. Hearing these cues is vital for the smooth and safe running of the show, so a "shout" or "show call" system will be devised, usually in cooperation with the PA department. The PA engineers will be able to create a dedicated audio chain for the shout/show call and supply the necessary microphones, speakers, and headsets.

IT & DATA

"Is there wi-fi?" A common question on tour and one that highlights the modern musicians' need to stay connected via the internet. While most venues will have some wi-fi provision, the production staff on a tour of large theatres or arenas cannot work effectively if relying on a domestic-grade internet service. The tour will therefore carry its own IT infrastructure and engineer, and ad-hoc networks for laptops, printers, web

Figure 19.6 Radios ("walkie-talkies") are necessary for >5000-cap touring and for working at festivals. Effective communication is difficult without them. Image courtesy of the author

cams, and other devices, can be created in each venue solely for the visiting production team. These data networks are separate from the audio–visual data networks described in "PA" earlier in this part.

Livestreams require high–speed and stable internet connection, an aspect often overlooked when scouting locations for high–impact online concerts. As stated, public access wi–fi networks are not suitable for livestreaming concerts and many "interesting" locations (warehouses, churches, etc.) have no existing internet infrastructure. Temporary internet networks can be rented for short–term installation and operation, and are available as:

- cellular (mobile) 4- or 5G wireless (similar to public wi-fi networks)
- temporary cable or fibre-based networks
- satellite links on dedicated trucks or vans (upload speeds can be very low)
- point-to-point microwave links

Planning must allow for installation of any cable–based solution, as these networks cannot be installed in the same short time frame as a 4– or 5G mobile network.

Venues looking towards the post-pandemic recovery would do well to look to installing fast and stable internet access to encourage rental of ancillary livestreaming spaces and equipment by concert promoters.

COSTUME AND WARDROBE

The artist may have dancers. There may be costume changes. Wardrobe assistants travel with the artist to maintain, adjust, repair, clean, and press costumes as necessary.

Consideration must be given to the incorporation of RF receivers for performers IEMs. Belt packs are now small and light and the costume must be made to allow quick access to the belt packs for battery changes for instance. RF reception is adversely affected by contact with the human body – the antennae of belt packs should not touch the skin if at all possible.

FESTIVALS (OTHER PRODUCTION CONSIDERATIONS)

You have looked at the pros and cons of festival performances earlier in this section. Many of the drawbacks are caused by the limitations and procedures imposed when performing at multi-act, open-air festivals. Artists and their technical teams need to anticipate these procedures and limitations, which may have an impact upon costs for the artist.

These limitations and procedures include:

- changeover time
- the use of rolling risers
- the use of floor packages

CHANGEOVER TIME

"Changeover" is the time allocated to get one artist offstage, and the next one on, ready to perform. Artists do not soundcheck for festival performances (except for headliners), and the first time the artist steps onto the performance area is when they go on to perform. The average changeover time at open-air, green-field festivals is 20 minutes and is sometimes as short as 10 minutes (Figure 19.7)). The previous act's people, crew, and

FESTIVAL	Vendredi 24 aout 2018 portes 14:00							
	Bands	Get-in	Load-in	Set up	C/over	Line-check	Show time	Length
GRANDE SCENE	ATTAQUE 77	10:45	12:15	12:15	13:15 / 13:30	13:30 / 14:00	**15:30 / 16:15**	45
	FIRST AID KIT	12:45	14:15	14:15	16:15 / 16:30	16:30 / 16:55	**17:00 / 18:00**	60
	MIKE SHINODA	14:30	16:00	16:00	18:00 / 18:15	18:15 / 18:40	**18:45 / 19:45**	60
	DIE ANTWOORD	09:45	11:15	11:15 / 13:15	19:45 / 20:00	20:00 / 20:30	**20:45 / 22:00**	75
	PNL	08:00	09:00	09:00 / 11:00	22:00 / 22:15	22:15 / 23:00	**23:15 / 00:30**	75
	Bands	Get-in	Load-in	Set up	C/over	Line-check	Show time	Length
CASCADE	JOSMAN	10:30	12:00	12:00		13:15 / 14:00	**16:15 / 17:00**	45
	DIRTY PROJECTORS	13:30	15:00	15:00	17:00 / 17:15	17:15 / 17:45	**17:50 / 18:40**	50
	NICK MURPHY	15:10	16:40	16:40	18:40 / 18:55	18:55 / 19:25	**19:45 / 20:45**	60

Figure 19.7 The stage times, set length, and changeover times for the artists appearing at a festival. The time given for changeover and line check is generous in this example – some festivals operate on a ten-minute changeover schedule!

equipment must be removed from the performance area; the following artist's equipment, performers, and crew members pushed onto stage; the monitor speakers, microphones, stage boxes and cables reset, plugged in, and tested; and the performers ready to rock, all in that changeover time. If an artist is not ready to perform at the end of the changeover (something is not working, someone leaves something in the dressing room and has to go back for it, or the microphones are plugged into the wrong channels, for instance) then the time to rectify the situation and for them to perform is deducted from their allocated set time. A 40-minute allocated set could be reduced to 30 minutes or less if the changeover goes badly. The stage manager has responsibility to ensure all artists keep to the allocated set times – festival promoters face large fines for running over times agreed for the end of live music for the day – and will be strict in asking performers to leave the stage when they overrun.

Artists and their technical team should appreciate the pressure caused by the changeover system. The artist may perhaps "drop" (remove) songs that require intricate or one-off instrumentation, for instance. Doing so will reduce the amount of equipment that has to be set and struck. The artist's manager should also consider employing technicians with plenty of experience in festival changeovers to assist with initial festival performances by a new artist.

THE USE OF ROLLING RISERS

Rolling risers are platforms on wheels and are used to facilitate short changeover times. Artist's equipment is pre-built backstage directly onto rolling risers (Figure 19.8). The equipment can then be mic'd up, supplied with power, plugged into the PA system, and

Figure 19.8 A drum kit built on a rolling riser. The image shows all the microphones and cables set up and connected to a "floating" remote stage box. The riser will be pushed on stage when changeover commences, and the remote stage box will be patched into the sound system. The whole procedure should take a minute (or less). Building the drum kit directly onto the stage, setting up the microphones, and cabling up each component would take considerably longer. Image courtesy of the author

made ready to push onto stage at the start of the changeover. For instance, the artist's drum kit will go on one riser, the keyboard players electronics will go on another, and so on. Stacks of guitar amplifiers are placed on smaller, mobile, risers called "skids". Artist's equipment can be also easily removed from the stage after the performance and the next artist's equipment wheeled on ready for their stage time.

Festival organisers will require artists to supply rolling riser requirements as part of the advance process, and this information is usually supplied as part of an updated stage plan in the technical rider.

Rolling risers are large (either 8' x 8' or 8' x 6') and take up a lot of room back stage. Artists will typically use at least one riser (for the drum kit); bands that have lots of "tech" (keyboard/electronics stations, extra percussion set ups, etc.) may need four or five rolling risers each. These requirements will cause problems for the stage manager. Consider a typical festival bill: there may be six to eight artists appearing on each stage, each day. Space backstage can be an issue if all the risers are available to every artist before they go on – some twenty 8' x 8' risers would occupy an extraordinary amount of space. Rolling risers are therefore usually limited in number, three or four sets, used in a sequence.

A typical riser sequence would be (Figure 19.9):

- artist A is on stage on one set of risers
- artist B, coming on next, gets their gear built on another set of risers
- the artist that has just finished performing (artist C) and is offstage, is packing down their gear from a third set of risers
- the stage crew then give the risers from artist C to artist D, who are onstage after artist B

Such a routine enables stage managers to limit backstage build space to a bare minimum. Only three sets of risers are needed at any one time: two behind stage, being prepared, and one for the artist currently performing. Minimising backstage space is essential – building extra preparation and storage space is an added cost to the promoter.

Again, artists should plan out the instrumentation required to perform every song in the set. The simpler the backline needed, the less risers are required and the easier (and quicker) the resulting changeover time.

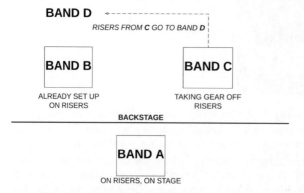

Figure 19.9 A sequence for using three sets of rolling riders on a festival stage

THE USE OF FLOOR PACKAGES

You saw earlier that artists are not usually permitted to "bring in production" – the festival supplies all the PA, lighting, video, and sometimes even backline for all artists. Artists must differentiate themselves from other acts on the bill though, and individual set elements, video, and lighting, helps them to do that. Although large scale production elements are not allowed, artists can bring in "floor packages" – lighting and set elements that can be pushed or rolled (not suspended) onto the performance area. The floor package may be as simple as a few "floor cans" (lighting fixtures on the floor), or as complex and visually striking as elevated platforms and banks of video panels with dedicated content.

Floor packages allow an artist to have some control over the look of her performance, and this is important: the performance may be broadcast (either as a livestream or by a TV broadcaster) and will be snapped and shared on Instagram (a photo-sharing social media app).

The artist's team should evaluate the potential impact of floor packages, weighed up against the cost of designing, fabricating, and renting the necessary equipment.

CATERING

Touring caterers are hired to ensure consistency of food and service for the duration of a tour of production venues (see "catering and pre-shop" earlier in this part). Promoters on each tour date have one less thing to organise – they simply need to make the necessary financial arrangements for the dedicated tour caterers.

Hiring on a tour catering company is also of benefit for production rehearsals. Such activity will see all the touring cast and crew coming together and working for full days. Health and welfare are just as important during this period; dedicated chefs and access to constant supplies of coffee and tea does wonders for morale and well-being. Figure 19.10 shows the backstage beverage station at a concert venue.

Figure 19.10 The beverage station that supplies hot and cold drinks for production crew and artists. The station is set up in the area designated for catering activities and can provide a much-needed focal point for rest and relaxation. Image courtesy of the author

DRESSING ROOM/AMBIANCE

Providing "home-cooked" food does wonders for the morale of touring cast and crew away from home for months on end. Setting out communicable areas with homely touches and a welcoming ambiance can also boost morale. Venues such as arenas and stadiums are function-based buildings not known for their creature comforts. Soft furnishings and lighting, entertainment centres, and flowers can make all the difference to cast and crew who rarely get to see daylight. The job of providing these touches often falls to the caterers and, on tours of stadiums, dressing room and ambiance coordinators join the touring crew.

Providing soft furnishings and other homely touches costs money, and promoters of festivals cannot justify turning temporary cabins into a comfortable lair. Dressing room facilities at open-air festivals are often spartan affairs (Figure 19.11).

MEET AND GREET

VIP packages were discussed in *"Revenue Streams from Live Music – Promoters and Organizers"* in Part One. Organising the access, times, and space within the venue creates a significant amount of work. The baby artist's tour manager may take on these responsibilities initially. Artists touring at the arena level (5,000–20,000 capacity) may be meeting up to 30 VIP-package holders a night and it therefore makes sense to employ a dedicated VIP/meet and greet coordinator to oversee this activity.

FINANCE AND ACCOUNTING

Someone on the artist's team must ensure sufficient funds exist to pay for all services and products that are needed, especially those required before the tour. Sleeper buses, rehearsal

Figure 19.11 A dressing room at a major European open-air festival. The promoter has many costs; creating a homely ambience in artist dressing rooms is not one of them. Image courtesy of the author

facilities, and crew transport are all examples of expenditure before a tour or event – expenditure that cannot be avoided. Consider as well that there is no income until after the first concert has been performed. Keeping an eye on funds and cash flow is vital.

BUSINESS MANAGEMENT

The sensible artist will retain some form of business management or financial services.[2] Part accountant and part payroll department, such companies administrate the financial aspects of the artist's career. Activities of the business manager include:

- raising and arranging payment of invoices
- crew and session musician payroll and workers' contributions
- liaising with banks on behalf of the artist
- bookkeeping and accountancy
- organising and administration of funds, including credit cards
- tour accounting and reconciliation

The business management team will have been closely involved in the budgeting and tour support application (if relevant) and will be aware of bills that need paying before the start of the tour.

Business management can liaise with the booking agent to arrange the release of any money held as deposits from promoters. It may be the case that tour support from the record company has been agreed, and only a percentage is available before the start of the tour. Business management must work closely with the tour manager and the artist manager to ensure money is available for all expenses.

FLOAT

Cash money or a spending amount on credit cards to pay for sundries (taxis, incidental charges in hotels, etc.) will be useful for the tour manager. The amount of this "float" will be decided by the tour manager, and the business management will arrange for cash or a credit card amount to be made available.

CREDIT CARD

Society is moving away from the use of cash. The tour manager will need access to credit cards or payment methods, such as Apple Pay and Google Pay. Specialised tour accounting companies can supply multi-currency credit cards for use on the road, able to support up to 15 currencies. The backend software also helps to keep the financial management team up-to-date with card balances and transaction reports.

BOOKKEEPING

Any on-the-road expenses must be tracked and a receipt kept. These expenses should be in line with what has been budgeted. The tour manager is responsible for operating a bookkeeping system on the road, ad this can be as simple as amounts entered into a spreadsheet. Sales and expenses for merchandising operations are usually kept separate from the main tour bookkeeping unless merchandising is included in a tour support option in a multi-rights deal, for instance.

Specialised tour accountants may be hired as revenues increase from ticket sales in arenas and stadiums. The business manager may provide such as person, or the artist may ring in a third party to oversee the bookkeeping and accounting of the tour.

RECONCILIATION

All expenses and income must be accounted for, and reconciliation showing the actual profit or loss should be made available to the artist, management, and record company. The record company will need the accounting and reconciliation before they release the remaining tour support money.

INSURANCE

The artist will require insurance to cover them in these areas:

- cancellation/non-appearance
- public liability
- employee liability
- instruments and equipment
- vehicle insurance
- medical and travel

Specialised entertainment insurance brokers have been able to obtain policies that recognise the needs of the live music business. Comprehensive coverage is not cheap. Insurance of this type is in addition to the insurance that the promoters and organisers are obliged to have in place as part of the contract for any show.

Insurance for live activity can be bought for the touring period (summer festivals, say) or for a year (Figure 19.12). The broker will want to see a list of the proposed concert dates, along with the capacity of each venue, before deciding on a suitable policy for the artist.

ADVANCING AND THE TOUR BOOK

Convention dictates that the schedules for each day of the tour are set out in a printed document called the "tour book" (itinerary). The information for the tour book is obtained in a process named "advancing".

ADVANCING

Advancing takes place during the pre-production phase of tour planning with the artist's team (the tour manager) contacting all relevant promoters and organisers. Advancing is an opportunity for the two parties to obtain more specific information from each other

A MUSIC INSURER, LONDON. W1.

Quote No: 7████

PREMIUM INDICATION

RISK DETAILS (SCHEDULE)

TYPE:	CONTINGENCY NON-APPEARANCE AND CANCELLATION INSURANCE
PROPOSAL DETAILS:	No Proposal Form
ASSURED:	████████████
MAILING ADDRESS OF ASSURED:	Care of Live Music Business UK address to be advised
INSURED PERFORMANCE(S) OR EVENT(S):	████████████
INSURED PERSON(S):	████████████ and/or Band
PERIOD OF INSURANCE:	From: *A date to be agreed* To: 9th November ████
INTEREST:	This Insurance is to indemnify the Assured for their Ascertained Net Loss and Additional Costs as set out in 1.1, 1.2 and 3.1 of the Certificate Wording
COVER:	Beyond the Control of the Assured and each and every Insured Person
LIMIT OF INDEMNITY:	GBP 23,130.00
DEDUCTIBLE:	Nil
LOSS PAYEE:	Not applicable
CLAIMS NOTIFICATION TO:	Robertson Taylor Insurance Brokers Limited
CHOICE OF LAW:	English **JURISDICTION:** England and Wales

See overleaf for any ADDITIONAL TERMS CONDITIONS LIMITATIONS AND EXCLUSIONS THAT APPLY

Figure 19.12 An excerpt from an artist's tour insurance cover document. The policy will cover non-appearances and cancellations caused by injury, illness, or death

and to address any challenges or issues. Most of the conversation will be focused on the contract rider, which has hopefully been accepted and agreed by the promoter.

The tour manager will want information on the following:

Has the promoter/promoter's representative seen the rider and, if so, is everything agreed and understood?

What parking for tour vehicles is available? Can the vehicles stay there until the next morning?

Can tour vehicles be supplied with landline/shore power?

Are there any low bridges, bollards, or other restrictions for high-sided vehicles near the venue?

What time is the venue open for showers, breakfast, etc. (if relevant)?

What time should the artist load-in their equipment?

Are their steps, stairs, or elevators, to get from the load-in doors to the stage?

Times for soundchecks (including opening acts)?

Is there any limit to soundcheck times? Some venues operate within commercial buildings and office blocks, and there can be a "no noise before 17:00" restriction. Venues can also operate "dark stage" policy – a time period when no work can be done in preparation for the concert. Dark stage is put in place to ensure venue workers get a break after soundcheck and before the show begins, and usually lasts for one hour.

Is there any type of audio volume limit? Switzerland, for instance, has a nationwide limit on sound pressure of 100dB(A)/Leq60, which means an average of 100dB over one hour.

What showering facilities are available (relevant to touring on a sleeper bus)?

How many dressing rooms are there?

Is there a dedicated office or room for the visiting production (production office)?

Can the artist access the stage without walking through the audience?

What time are "doors" (the time the audience is let into the concert room)?

What time is the live music curfew?

Does the venue turn into a night club immediately after the concert? Many venues run such events in the same room as the previous concert, and require visiting artists to pack down and load-out in 30 minutes or less. This process is nicknamed "disco load-out" and is universally hated by road crews.

Is there a concession fee for artist merch sales?

Where is the merch area, or where do artists usually set up their own merch tables?

Does the venue have strong, reliable wi-fi?

Can the promoter/promoter's rep please send over information about the PA, lights, and other production elements? (This information is relevant to non-production venues and festivals.)

Has the promoter been able to source backline as per the specification in the rider? This question would be relevant for a fly-date where the promoter agreed to supply backline.

Who will be the venue or promoter contact on the day (if not the person the advancing is taking place with)? Who will be responsible for the settlement at the end of the concert?

How is the show selling? A sold-out show is good for the promoter's bottom line, will make the artist happy – and a warm, full, room will sound better than a cold, empty one (see PA earlier in this part).

The promoter's rep will in turn want to know:

Where is the artist travelling from the day before?
Does the rider contain the same information, or have there been significant changes?
What is the length of the artist's set? (For headliners; opening acts are allocated a set
    time, and must make their material fit.)
Does the artist have merch to sell, and do they have a seller with them?
Does the artist anticipate requiring large numbers of guestlist tickets?
Where is the artist travelling to after the show?

Let's examine the last question. Asking about the artist's pre- and post-travel is useful for
a couple of reasons. For one, it gives the promoter or venue staff an idea of whether to
anticipate the late arrival of the artist due to traffic or sheer distance. The potential for
delay accumulates with distance. Secondly, a busy venue, especially a festival, will have
artists arriving and leaving every day, with numerous arrivals and departures in the case
of a festival. One artist may have left something behind after performing at the festival;
the festival will want to know that another artist is making the same journey the next
day and could perhaps take the lost item with them.

Advancing can take place by phone or email. Venues and promoters will often have prepared information "packs" (PDF documents) that contain answers to frequently asked
questions and information that the visiting production may find useful. Routes avoiding
low bridges and access codes to pedestrian-only areas are examples of the type of information that promoters and venue managers send out.

CASCADING INFORMATION

You may have thought that much of the process of advancing is unnecessary – surely the
contract has been signed, the promoter has received the artist rider, and, apart from the
venue's technical specifications, the artist should expect everything to be as they wish
when they arrive. However, as discussed in "regional and sub-promoters" in part one,
it is often the case that the person who made the deal and signed the contract is not
always the same person who deals with the concert on the day. There is an information
"cascade" that does not reach all the participants. The advancing process in such cases
is pretty much starting from scratch, with neither "side" (artist and venue) having full
details of the deals and sub-deals in place.

TOUR BOOKS

The tour book is a printed A5 booklet that contains all the schedule for the cast and
crew for each day of the tour. The schedule information is collated as part of the
advancing process. Addresses, contact names and details, and notes on specific challenges and issues (soundcheck curfews or sound pressure limits, etc.) are all listed in the
tour book. The resulting books are printed and distributed, not only to cast and crew,
but also to friends and family of the artist and tour-related offices such as the record
companies marketing and promotional departments. PDF copies are distributed for this
wider set of recipients to save money and reduce environmental impact. Figure 19.13
shows a tour book page for a concert at the O2 Academy Brixton (4921 capacity).

SATURDAY 16TH OCTOBER 2021	**FARRY KISHER**
SHOW DAY - LONDON, UK	**GMT**

VENUE:	Brixton Academy	**FORMAT:**	Indoor
		CAPACITY:	4921
	211 Stockwell Road		
	Brixton		
	London		
	SW9 9SL		
	England		
TEL:	+44 20 7555 3000		
FAX:	+44 20 7555 4427		
PROD TEL:	+44 20 7787 5555		
PROD FAX:	+44 20 7787 5556		
PROMOTER:	A Promoter		
TEL:	+44 (0)20 7555 6800		
FAX:	+44 (0)20 7555 6849		
PROMOTERS REP:	Barry Reliable		
MOBILE:	+44 (0)7555 222547		
EMAIL:	reliable@prom-rep.com		

TRAVEL:	
BAND DEPART:	14.00 from hotel. Please check out
BAND ARRIVE:	Venue 15.00
CREW DEPART:	07.30 from hotel. Please check out
CREW ARRIVE:	Venue at 08.30

SCHEDULE:		*PROMO:*
ACCESS TO VENUE:	08.30	
PA & LX LOAD IN:	09.00	
BACKLINE LOAD IN:	13.00	
SOUND CHECK:	16.00	
DINNER:	17.30	
DOORS:	19.00	
SUPPORT 1:		
SUPPORT 2:	19.50	
FARRY KISHER:	**21.00**	
FINISH:	22.45	
CURFEW:	23.00 STRICT? Yes	

AFTER SHOW:	
BAND:	On bus overnight to Bristol. 193KM, 120M. 2.5 hours
CREW:	As band

TOMORROW:	**Show in Bristol**

NOTES:	Please check out of hotel today! We may not have buses outside venue - TM will advise.	*LOCAL MONEY:*	
		£1=	£1
		$1=	0.64p
		e1:	0.72p
		LONDON:	Same
		LA:	- 8 hours
		NYC:	-5 hours

Figure 19.13 A page from a tour book, detailing the schedule of a concert at the O2 Academy Brixton. This concert is part of the tour and you can see the notes regarding travel after this performance

SATURDAY 16TH OCTOBER 2021	FARRY KISHER
SHOW DAY - LONDON, UK	**GMT**

PRODUCTION INFORMATION	
VENUE:	Brixton Academy
	0
	211 Stockwell Road
	Brixton
	London
	SW9 9SL
	England
TEL:	+44 20 7555 3000
FAX:	+44 20 7555 4427
PROD TEL:	+44 20 7787 5555
PROD FAX:	+44 20 7787 5556

TRANSPORT:	
PARKING:	Limited. Wandsworth Road lorry park is an alternative
PERMITS:	No
LOAD IN TYPE:	Flat roll to stage
LANDLINE:	Yes

FACILITIES:	
DRESSING ROOMS:	5 - 2 ensuite
SHOWERS:	Yes
CATERING:	Facilities. Stage right

PRODUCTION:	
STAGE SIZE:	74' x 52'
CLEARANCE:	65'
PROSCENIUM:	Yes.
PA WINGS:	
FLYING POINTS:	Yes, 13 fly bars 12 ton load in total

POWER:	

SOUND:	
HOUSE PA:	Hire In
DESK:	
MON. DESK:	
MIXES:	
FOH MIXER AREA:	Platform on dance floor
S/C CURFEW:	No
RESTRICTIONS:	None

LIGHTING:	
HOUSE LX:	Hire In
DESK:	
DIMMERS ETC:	
HOUSE SPOTS:	
SMOKE ALARM:	No

GENERAL:	
BARRIER:	Fixed
MERCH AREA:	Four booths in foyer
MERCH FEE:	25% of gross +VAT.
PERSONNEL:	

Figure 19.14 A page from the tour book showing the production information related to the concert at the O2 Academy Brixton from figure 19.13. The tour manager will have gleaned this information in the advancing process and highlighted any issues or challenges the crew might face on the day

Details regarding schedules and accommodation are useful, and the touring production crew will benefit from information regarding the infrastructure of the venue itself. Figure 19.14 shows the production information for the same concert shown in Figure 19.13, only this page details technical information, such as weight limits of the suspension points in the venue roof, access points for equipment, and the venue's power supply. The production crew may have worked in the venue before and being reminded of the issues and challenges of each venue by highlighting them in the tour book saves time and frustration on the day.

Tour books need to be finished and printed before the start of the tour; this presents challenges when producing such documents for a long tour (two or three months). The promoters and organisers for concerts at the end of the tour are unlikely to have organised themselves that far in advance – information for a tour book of a three-month tour requires contacting promoters about events four months in the future, so pages for these end dates may be lacking in information at the time they are printed.

Although less permanent, online tour books can be created and these can be updated and amended, even as the tour progresses. Day sheets (a page indicating the particular day's schedule) can be generated by the tour manager each morning and distributed to everyone concerned by email or social messaging systems. Schedules and activities change all the time during a concert tour, and an online system can instantly reflect those changes, informing everyone in good time.

NOTES

1 "U2 360° Tour",(2021). *Wikipedia*. Available at: https://en.wikipedia.org/wiki/U2_360_Tour
2 This information from http://www.willtaylor.cc/

APPENDIX 1

Concert Production Personnel

The following pages contain a brief list of the roles of the various people involved in creating a modern show or tour.

ARTIST MANAGEMENT

The artist manager is responsible for overseeing every aspect of the artist's career. This is not a recognised "touring" position, as such, but the manager will probably accompany the artist as they start out performing live. The manager will appoint a "tour manager" to oversee the concert performances as the artist becomes established, then "visit" the tour as it plays in key markets and more important cities.

Level of tour:
Bars to stadiums.
Qualifications or training available:
Yes. Artist management, music management, and live event management degrees and training courses are available.
Employment status:
Usually, self-employed. Successful artist managers will then employ full-time junior managers and assistants.
Skills and personality:
- Total understanding of every aspect of the music business – record company deals, publishing deals, synchronisation deals, copyright law, radio and TV promotion, touring, and offline and online marketing and branding opportunities.
- Office productivity software skills – Word, Excel, email client.
- Self-motivated.
- Established industry network.
- Good business acumen.
- Calm under pressure.
- Passionate about their artist.

Equipment needed:
Telephone, laptop or desktop computer, and a reliable internet connection.
Comments:
The manager's income is dependent on the earning potential of her artist: good artist managers will, therefore, set clear boundaries when it comes to responsibilities – spending all day sorting out her client's laundry or ordering taxis is not an effective, or income-generating, use of the manger's time.

BOOKING AGENT

Finds paid performance work for the artist. Not a touring position as such.

Level of tour:
Bar to stadium.
Qualifications or training available:

Not specifically. Live events management and music management courses may touch on some aspects of becoming an agent. Most agents learn from mentors or from on-the-job training.

Employment status:
- Self-employed initially or may join an established company as a junior booking agent.
- *Skills and personality:*
- Total understanding of the live music business – concert promotion, contracts and riders, foreign artist taxation, visas and work permits, ticketing, and merchandising. Some knowledge of tour production would also be very useful.
- Office productivity software skills – Word, Excel, email client.
- Must be able to establish and grow a network.

Equipment needed:
Telephone, laptop or desktop computer, printer, and an internet connection.
Comments:
Booking agents may have to attend gigs 4 or 5 nights a week to observe new talent and
    see existing clients in concert.

CONCERT PROMOTER

Level of tour:
Bar to stadium.
Qualifications or training available:
Yes. Live event management and show promotion courses and degrees available.
Employment status:
Self-employed initially or may join an established promoter as a junior promoter or
    assistant.
Skills and personality:
- Total understanding of the live music business – concert promotion, contracts and riders, foreign artist taxation, visas and work permits, ticketing, and merchandising. Some knowledge of tour production would also be very useful.
- Office productivity software skills – Word, Excel, email client.
- Talent-spotting skills.
- Good financial acumen.

Equipment needed:
Telephone, laptop or desktop computer, and an internet connection.
Comments:
Promoting is a financially risky occupation. Competing events, the weather, and transport problems can all affect the amount of people who turn up at a show. A successful promoter must promote as many events as possible and be ruthless in cutting costs – which sometimes is to the detriment of the artist and audience.

PROMOTER'S REP

Level of tour:
300-capacity and upwards.
Qualifications or training available:
None that is specific to this role. Live music management or events management courses may be useful.
Employment status:
Freelance.
Skills and personality:
- Total understanding of the live music business – concert promotion, contracts and riders, and foreign artist taxation.
- Self-motivated.
- Responsible.
- Excellent financial skills – show settlements, taxation, etc.
- Show production knowledge is very useful.
- Office productivity software skills – Word, Excel, email client.

Equipment needed:
Telephone, laptop, a device capable of sending and receiving emails on the move (cell phone, tablet, etc.), portable printer, car.
Comments:
A promoter's rep has a great deal of responsibility. They represent the concert promoter and not only have to make sure the show runs smoothly but also must oversee the collection of ticket money and undertake accurate concert settlement (see Chapter 5, *Creating the Deals*).

TOUR MANAGER

The tour manager does not book the shows but is responsible for all aspects of the planning and logistics of the tour. Travels with the band and oversees the day-to-day running of the shows.

Level of tour:
300-capacity and upwards.
Qualifications or training available:

There are no specific concert tour management courses (yet), but degrees and training are available in live event management and music management.

Employment status:

Freelance. The tour manager is usually hired by the artists themselves.

Skills and personality:

- Total understanding of the music business – concert promotion, contracts and riders, foreign artist taxation, visas and work permits, ticketing, merchandising, radio and TV promotion.
- Office productivity software skills – Word, Excel, email client.
- Financial responsibility and training.
- Self motivated
- Excellent people skills.
- Calm under pressure

Equipment needed:

Cell phone, laptop with office productivity software, a device capable of sending and receiving emails on the move, a portable printer, flashlight, and a bottle opener.

Comments:

Even though the tour manager is expected to have an encyclopaedic knowledge of concert touring, it is probably more important that they know which specialist to ask in case of an issue or challenge. The tour manager will act as tour accountant on smaller level tours (200–5000-capacity venues) dealing with the payments and show settlements; this role may be taken over by a dedicated tour accountant on larger tours (see below).

PRODUCTION MANAGER

The production manager is responsible for the production elements of large-scale touring: sound, light and video equipment, staging, power, and associated transport.

Level of tour:

Any tour carrying its own production, usually of venues with capacities of 1500+

Qualifications or training available:

Yes.

Employment status:

Freelance. Hired directly by the artist via the tour manager.

Skills and personality:

- Complete understanding of the technical requirements of staging a modern music event.
- Employment and "working-time" regulations.
- Health and safety regulations.
- Office productivity software – Word, Excel, email client.
- Technical design/CAD software.
- Good leader.
- Stamina.

EQUIPMENT NEEDED:

Cell phone, laptop with office productivity software, a device capable of sending and receiving emails on the move, a portable printer, flashlight, personal protective equipment (hi-vis vest, steel-cap boots, hardhat).

Comments:
The production manager works alongside the tour manager and is responsible for the "wood and steel" – the production elements of the tour.

AUDIO CREW – SYSTEMS TECH

The system techs set up and de-rig the sound equipment on a tour carrying its own sound equipment. The system tech is there to help and support the artist's own audio engineers. There will usually be three system techs – a FOH "babysitter", a monitor "babysitter", and a "third man".

Level of tour:
Production level, usually venues with capacities of 2000 plus.
Qualifications or training available:
Yes. Audio and live audio training and degrees as well as manufacturer-specific training.
Employment status:
Freelance. Hired by the sound rental company. Manufacturers may also send their research and development (R&D) employees out on the road if supplying new products and technology to a rental company.
Skills and personality:
- Ability to set up and run pro audio equipment.
- Work as part of team.

Equipment needed:
Personal protective equipment (hi-vis vest, steel-cap boots, hardhat), flashlight, electrical multi-meter, tool kit.
Comments:
There are many specialisms now in concert audio, such as digital audio networking and wireless (RF) audio; anyone who has training and experience in these areas is going to stand a better chance of working permanently. Unfortunately, system techs very rarely get to mix audio at concerts.

AUDIO CREW – ARTIST

The artist's audio engineers are hired directly by the artist to mix the FOH and monitor (stage) sound for the band.

Level of tour:
Bar to stadium.

Qualifications or training available:
Yes. Audio and live audio training and degrees.
Employment status:
Freelance. Hired directly by the band.
Skills and personality:
- Ability to set up and run pro audio equipment.
- Mix audio to a consistently high standard.
- Work as part of team

Equipment needed:
Personal protective equipment (hi-vis vest, steel-cap boots, hardhat), flashlight, head-
    phones, electrical multi-meter, tool kit.

LIGHTING CREW – SYSTEMS TECH

Lighting system techs operate in the same way as their audio system tech colleagues: they set up and de-rig the lighting equipment on a tour carrying its own equipment. The system tech is there to help and support the LD and/or operator.

Level of tour:
Production level, usually venues with capacities of 2000 plus.
Qualifications or training available:
Yes. Lighting design and technology training and degrees as well as manufacturer-spe-
    cific courses.
Employment status:
Freelance, hired by the lighting rental company. Manufacturers may also send their
    research and development employees out on the road if supplying new products
    and technology to a rental company.

SKILLS AND PERSONALITY:

- Ability to set up and run pro lighting equipment.
- Work at heights.
- Work as part of team.
- Proficiency in lighting design software, (WYSIWYG, etc.) is an advantage.

Equipment needed:
Personal protective equipment (fall-arrest harness, hi-vis vest,
steel-cap boots, hardhat), flashlight, electrical multi-meter, tool kit.

LIGHTING CREW – LIGHTING DIRECTOR/OPERATOR

The lighting director (LD) creates the look and feel for the stage lighting, indicating which lamps and fixtures should go where on the stage. In the case of a small club show, this design takes place in the afternoon of the show; at production level, a pre-production rehearsal will take place some weeks in advance. The LD may then operate the show on tour or designate an operator to "run" the various scene changes.

Level of tour:
Bar to stadium.
Qualifications or training available:
Yes. Lighting for music events courses and manufacturer-led training available.
Employment status:
Freelance, hired directly by the band.
Skills and personality:
- Ability to design and operate a professional lighting show.
- Be confident and competent with emerging lighting control technologies.
- Work as part of a team.
- Work at heights.

Equipment needed:
Personal protective equipment (fall-arrest harness, hi-vis vest, steel-cap boots, hardhat), flashlight, electrical multi-meter, tool kit. Lighting design software and a powerful computer would be an advantage.

VIDEO CREW

The video crew set up, operate, and de-rig the video elements of a modern concert. This includes video screens that enhance visibility for the audience (known as image magnification or IMAG) and video-as-lighting effects. The video crew includes screen technicians, projection technicians, vision mix operators, graphics mix operators, and camera people.

Level of tour:
Production level, usually venues with capacities of 2000 plus.
Qualifications or training available:
Yes. Video and lighting for music events courses and manufacturer-lead training available.
Employment status:
Freelance, hired by the video equipment rental company. Manufacturers may also send their research and development employees out on the road if supplying new products and technology to a rental company.
Skills and personality:
- Ability to set up and run pro video projection, graphics, and camera equipment.
- Work at heights.
- Work as part of team.
- Proficiency in media server software an advantage.

Equipment needed:
Personal protective equipment (fall-arrest harness, hi-vis vest, steel-cap boots, hardhat), flashlight, electrical multi-meter, tool kit.

Comments:

Video is ubiquitous in modern concert touring. Lighting designers and operators are best placed to make the transition to this medium as they (should) understand colour theory and the craft of stage lighting. There is a bewildering range of technologies and disciplines in this one area, however. Training and competence with screen technology, LED devices, front and rear projection, media servers, and vision mixers, and camera operation, is essential.

BACKLINE CREW

The backline crew oversee the set-up, maintenance, and pack down of the artist's instruments (drums, bass, guitars, keyboards, stage computers, etc.) as well as the supervision of the artists stage environment – setting towels, water, and setlists on stage prior to the show.

Level of tour:
Bar to stadium.
Qualifications or training available:

No specific "backline technician" courses, but you could study electrical engineering for musical and consumer devices. You should also be qualified or have extensive experience of relevant software programs (Pro Tools for instance).

Employment status:
Freelance. You will be hired by the band.
Skills and personality:
- Understanding of how a gig "works".
- Encyclopaedic knowledge of musical instruments.
- Electrical safety.
- Knowledge of wireless (RF) transmission for instruments.
- Work as part of team.
- Excellent people skills.
- Calm under pressure.
- Ability to fault-find and solve problems.

Equipment needed:
Personal protective equipment (hi-vis vest, steel-cap boots, hardhat), flashlight, electrical multi-meter, tool kit, and a workbox with relevant test gear for your specialty.
Comments:
Backline technicians have the closest working relationship with the artists of any touring position.

RIGGER

The job of the rigger is to help the sound, lighting, and video system crews to "fly" (suspend) their equipment above the stage. The rigger will go into the roof of the venue to create "points" from which steel cables and chain hoists can be attached; these are used to lift the lighting and video trusses into the air.

Level of tour:
Any tour carrying its own production, usually of venues with capacities of 2000 plus.
Qualifications or training available:
Yes. There is increasing regulation in this area – any serious rigger should make sure they are qualified or union-assessed as to their competence.
Employment status:
Freelance.
Skills and personality:
- Head for heights!
- Awareness of health and safety regulations.
- Understanding of safe working weight load limits for venue structures, motors, cables, shackles, and harnesses.

Equipment needed:
Personal protective equipment (fall-arrest harness, hi-vis vest, steel-cap boots, hardhat).
Comments:
Riggers have an enormous responsibility. More rigging points and increased load-bearing components are required for shows with more staging, more video, and more lighting elements. These productions still have to load-in and be set up in the same time, and this puts increasing pressure on riggers to get the points put in and the equipment flown safely.

CATERER

Touring caterers prepare hot, tasty food for appreciative road crew and unappreciative artists every day of the tour.
Level of tour:
Any tour carrying its own production (not US) plus festivals.

QUALIFICATIONS OR TRAINING AVAILABLE:

Yes, but not specifically for on–tour catering. You should have firsthand experience of working in a very busy kitchen with very demanding customers.

Employment status:
Freelance, hired by the tour catering company. May be employed full-time in the US by a company supplying catering services to a venue.
Skills and personality:
- Good cook.
- Excellent people skills.
- Ability to improvise.
- Stamina.

Equipment needed:

Tour caterers travel with ovens, refrigerators, pots and pans, flatware, and cutlery provided by the on-tour catering company. You would want your own aprons, hat, and specialised knives though.

Comments:

There are not many opportunities for touring as a chef in the US as many venues have existing contracts with companies that provide food and beverage to the public as well as to the visiting artist and crew. This is not the case in Europe or Australia; however, tour caterers have the distinction of being "first in, last out" at any show – it is NOT a glamorous life.

STAGEHAND

Stagehands assist with the load–in, set–up and load–out of a modern concert. Not a touring position.

Level of tour:

Bar to stadium.

Qualifications or training available:

There are some stage management and production courses. Any technical (lighting, sound, etc) course will also be useful. Look for ways to expand your specialty; fork lift, Manitou operation, and rigging training, for instance.

Employment status:

Freelance.

Skills and personality:

- Work as part of team.
- Follow directions.
- Good time keeping.
- Willingness to learn.
- Work at heights.
- Stamina.
- Physical strength.

Equipment needed:

Personal protective equipment (hi-vis vest, steel-cap boots, hardhat), adjustable spanner (wrench) and a flashlight.

DRIVER

Driving of vans, trucks, or tour buses.

Level of tour:

Vans – bar to stadium. Trucks and buses are usually found on tours carrying their own production elements, i.e., in venues with a capacity of 2000 or more.

Employment status:

Freelance Drivers are hired by the trucking or busing company supplying the tour.

Skills and personality:
- Valid driving licence, no endorsements or penalty points.
- Appropriate licence for driving private, public, or freight transport.
- Excellent people skills.
- Ability to work as part of team.
- Understand tour merchandise operations (see "Comments" below)
- Ability to operate a spotlight (see "Comments" below)

Equipment needed:
The tour transportation will usually supply the bus or truck. Some owner/operators will have their *own bus or truck.*
Comments:
Bus and truck drivers can make extra money on tour by helping to sell merchandise, or by operating spotlights as part of the lighting crew during the show.

TOUR SECURITY

Tour security personnel are on tour to provide security and close protection services to the touring artist, as well as advice for the safety of the entire touring party.

Level of tour:
Whenever the artist or artist's management deem it to be necessary or perceive a threat.
Qualifications or training available:
Yes. Courses in crowd management, event security, and close protection are available. Many countries now require security operatives, at whatever level, to be licensed.
Employment status:
Freelance or maybe self-employed running your own security company.
Skills and personality:
- Relevant close protection, crowd management, and crowd safety training.
- Excellent people skills.
- Self motivation.
- Stamina.

MERCHANDISER

A tour merchandiser sells t-shirts, CDs, buttons, posters, and other tour memorabilia on behalf of the artist at concerts.

Level of tour:
Bar to mid-level production (venues of 5000 capacity).
Qualifications or training available:
None.
Employment status:
Freelance.

Skills and personality:
- Excellent people skills.
- Excellent financial skills.
- Office productivity software skills – Word, Excel, email client.
- Good organisational skills.
- Willingness to learn.
- Aesthetic sense – able to create an inviting display of merchandise.
- Financially responsible.

Equipment needed:
Personal protective equipment (hi-vis vest, steel-cap boots, hardhat), flashlight, cash
    box, Sharpies, laptop computer (to capture email addresses).
Comments:
The individual tour merchandiser becomes irrelevant at >5000-capacity venues.
    Specialised merchandising companies operate on tours at this level and use local
    labour to man the merchandise sales points. However, selling merch for a small-to-
    intermediate level band is still the best way to get to know the live music business
    and establish a network of touring contacts.

TOUR ACCOUNTANT

A specialised touring role reserved for larger tours, the tour accountant works with the
    tour manager to oversee the collection and payment of all tour-related money.
Level of tour:
Larger production tours of venues with capacities of 10,000 plus.
Qualifications or training available:
There are no specific tour-related accountancy courses, but you will need to have
    passed a relevant accountancy degree to be taken seriously.
Employment status:
Freelance or full-time as part of the artist's management company.
Skills and personality:
- Total understanding of the live music business – contracts and riders, foreign artist
    taxation, visas and work permits, ticketing, and merchandising. Some knowledge of
    tour production will also be very useful.
- A financial accountancy degree or award.

Equipment needed:
Cell phone, laptop with office productivity software, and a portable printer.

WARDROBE ASSISTANT

Wardrobe assistants (there are no wardrobe bosses!) oversee the preparation and
    upkeep of stage clothes and costumes for the artist and other touring musicians,
    dancers, and performers.

Level of tour:
Larger production tours of venues with capacities of 5,000 plus.
Qualifications or training available:
Yes, but none specific to concert touring. Theatre costume design degrees will
   impart the necessary knowledge of stage clothing, quick changing, etc.
Employment status:
Freelance.
Skills and personality:
- Costume design and upkeep in a theatre/concert environment.
- Excellent people skills.
- Ability to work as part of team.
- Work under pressure.

Equipment needed:
Equipment for haberdashery and millinery repairs, cell phone, laptop with office productivity software, and a portable printer.

STYLIST

Stylists attend to the hair care and makeup for the stage performers.
Level of tour:
Larger production tours of venues with capacities of 5,000 plus.
Qualifications or training available:
Yes but none specific to concert touring. Training in beauty therapy, theatrical makeup,
   and hair styling will be useful.
Employment status:
Freelance.
Skills and personality:
- Hair styling, beauty makeup, and theatrical makeup in a concert backstage setting.
- Excellent people skills.
- Ability to work as part of team.
- Work under pressure.
- Not "fazed" by working with very famous pop stars.

Equipment needed:
Equipment for hair styling and makeup.

APPENDIX 2

A Performance Contract

AN AGENCY

LONDON

W 1 A

CONTRACT NO:CM1303/555
FKISHER – LONDON
ISSUED 23.04.21

Between   P.ROMOTER (The Promoter)
And   FARRY KISHER hereinafter called The Artist whereby the Promoter engages the Artist and the Artist accepts the engagement to appear at the venue(s) and upon the terms set out below:

The Artist agrees to appear at 1 performance at a salary of £40,000 (Forty Thousand UK Pounds), vs 80% of the net door receipts, whichever is greater.

ADDITIONAL CLAUSES

PAYMENT
The Promoter agrees to pay the sum of £8000 (20% of the Artist's guaranteed salary) by telegraphic transfer to An Agency to the credit of their client account. This transfer is to be net and free of all bank charges:

AN AGENCY – BANK ACCOUNT
A BANK   SORT CODE – XXXXXX ACCOUNT XXX-XXX-XXXX
LONDON, W1A
ACCOUNT NAME – THAT MAN T/A AN AGENCY CLIENTS A/C (BUSINESS RESERVE)

To be sent to An Agency by 30.09.21. The balance will be paid to the Artist in cash on the night of the engagement.

DATE OF PERFORMANCE	VENUE
Sunday 16th October 2021	O2 ACADENY BRIXTON 211 STOCKWELL ROAD LONDON SW9 9SL UK

ACCEPTED AND AGREED:

_____   _____
THE ARTIST   THE PROMOTER

THE ATTACHED ADDITIONAL CLAUSES AND ARTIST RIDER FORM AN INTEGRAL PART OF THIS AGREEMENT

PROMOTER DETAILS:

P.ROMOTER   TEL: 0208 555 8233
LONDON, E15

This agency is not responsible for any non-fulfilment of Contracts by Managers, Artists or Proprietors but every reasonable safeguard is assured.

ADDITIONAL CLAUSES TO CONTRACT NUMBER: CM1303/555
FARRY KISHER – LONDON 16.10.21

1. The attached rider shall form an integral part of this agreement.

2. "Net door receipts" is taken to mean the gross door receipts after deduction of Promoter production costs, which will not exceed agreed attached costs. The Promoter will provide a full and detailed breakdown of production costs certified by individual receipts for inspection and approval by the Artist. Any increase in the production costs must have the prior written approval by the Artist.

3. The promoter will advise the Artist (in writing) when returning this contract the rate of PRS (or the local equivalent performance royalty) and will supply the Artist with a receipt for the same specifying in detail the amount paid on the performance(s) on this contract within 2 weeks of the show.

4. It is agreed and understood that the Promoter will provide the Artist with all possible assistance to avoid any deductions from the Artist's fee; that are applicable as a result of legislation by the Promoter's local or national government. When a deduction (artist tax, social insurance, or other) must be applied to the Artist's fee the Promoter will provide official documentation to the Artist showing details of the deductions.

5. The Artist will receive 100% headline billing on all advertising and promotion for the performance.

6. The Artist reserves the right to approve all artwork relating to the advertising and promotion for this performance.

7. The Promoter UNDERSTANDS Artist to supply PA and lights to their specification

8. The Promoter agrees to pay for catering costs for the Artist.

9. The Promoter shall guarantee proper security at all times to ensure the safety of the Artist, auxiliary personnel, instruments and all equipment, costumes and personal property from the time of the Artist's arrival until their departure. Particular security must be provided to the areas of the stage, dressing rooms and all exits and entrances to the auditorium and remote mixing console.

10. The Artist is to have a guaranteed guest list as agreed in advance of the show between the tour manager and the promoter.

11. The Promoter agrees to provide an itinerary of names, addresses, telephone and fax numbers for the venue applicable to this contract. Also, a time schedule (arrival, soundcheck, doors, on stage times) for the Artist and the support artist, and the venue's technical details (stage sizes, power supply etc).

12. The Promoter will ensure that no recording of any sort or description or for any purpose shall be made without the specific written agreement of the Artist, or their agent.

13. The parties to this agreement agree to submit all disputes arising under this agreement to the exclusive jurisdiction of the courts of England and Wales

14. The Artist reserves the right to appoint and approve the support artist for this engagement.

15. The Artist shall have the right but not the obligation to sell merchandise. The concession rate for this will be 25% (venue rate) unless agreed otherwise in advance of the show between the tour manager and the promoter.

16. The Artist retains all rights to electronic/Internet broadcasting of their performance. There shall be no recording unless prior agreement with the Artist.

17. If the Promoter cancels the performance (except because of the actions or omissions of the Artist or its manager or representatives) the Artist will be entitled to 100% cancellation fee and reimbursed any other costs incurred by the Artist.

18. The support act will be TBC at a salary of TBC at no additional cost to the Artist.

ACCEPTED AND AGREED:

_____   _____
THE ARTIST   THE PROMOTER

APPENDIX 3

Contract Rider

FARRY KISHER - LIVE BAND FORMAT
TOURING INFORMATION SPRING/SUMMER 2021 V1.2
EXPIRES AUGUST 31st 2021

Contents:

FARRY KISHER - LIVE BAND FORMAT
TOURING INFORMATION SPRING/SUMMER 2021 V1.2
EXPIRES AUGUST 31st 2021

1) Cast & Crew

We will be 6 or 11 people on-the-road:

Holly Wallace	Vocals		
Chris Needs	Keyboards, electronics		
James Spesh	Keyboards, electronics		
Julia Martin	Tour manager	+44 7767123456	jmartin@email.com
Rodiguez Garica	FOH audio engineer	+44 7767234123	rgarica@email.com
Gorou Adachi	Back line technician	+44 7767345234	gadachi@email.com

<u>11 people format:</u> we will occasionally travel with a 4-piece string section (plus sleeper bus driver) and I will inform you in advance if this applies to your show.

We have no monitor engineer or lighting person with us.

2) Hotel rooming list

Our contract usually specifies 6 (six) single and 2 (two) twin rooms if you are providing hotel rooms. Please allocate twin rooms as below if you are not providing the single rooms:

Twin room 1:
Holly Wallace and Julia Martin
Twin room 2:
Chris Needs and James Spesh
Twin room 3:
Rodiguez Garica and Gorou Adachi
Twin room 4:
String player 1 and string player 2 (names to be forwarded to you in advance)
Twin room 5:
String player 3 and string player 4 (names to be forwarded to you in advance)

3) Transport

6 people format: cast, crew and equipment will be travelling in one (1) Mercedes Sprinter splitter van which is 4 meters high and 7 meters long. Free parking next to the load in/out of the venue is always appreciated.

11 people format: cast, crew and equipment will be travelling in one (1) sleeper bus. Dimensions will be confirmed. We will probably arrive overnight. Please send me details

FARRY KISHER - LIVE BAND FORMAT
TOURING INFORMATION SPRING/SUMMER 2021 V1.2
EXPIRES AUGUST 31st 2021

about bus parking and location of bus power (if you are able to provide it) in advance.

4) Tour and venue accreditation

We will not have tour passes or laminates. Cast & crew should be issued with your venue/festival accreditation.

5) Set length

The set is currently 80 minutes (1 hour and 10 minutes), including encore, for our headline shows. Set time for festivals is as per our allocated set duration – please advise me of this time duration in advance.

6) Merchandise

We have merchandise to sell. We have a display board (4m x 1m high) and we would appreciate a clean, stable, well-lit table or booth from which to sell. Please advise me of any merchandise fee in advance.

FARRY KISHER - LIVE BAND FORMAT
TOURING INFORMATION SPRING/SUMMER 2021 V1.2
EXPIRES AUGUST 31ˢᵗ 2021

7) Hospitality – as per contract rider

We are a touring party of 6 or eleven people. We have two (2) vegetarians and one of the vegetarians is wheat-intolerant (needs gluten free food if possible).

Please discuss meal times with me on the day.

WHERE DINNER CANNOT BE PROVIDED A BUY OUT OF £20.00 PER PERSON (EITHER 6 or 11) WILL BE REQUIRED (AS PER THE CONTRACT).

For the dressing/band room on arrival:

One (1) kettle, six or eleven (6/11) mugs

Coffee & tea

Fresh milk

Pack of lemons

Selection of fresh fruit & vegetables

Fruit & nut mix

One (1) 70 cl bottle of dark rum

One (1) 70 cl bottle of vodka

Four (4) litre bottles natural spring water

One (1) litre bottle of ginger beer

One (1) case of premium beer in bottles or cans

One (1) litre bottle of tonic water

Eight (8) Diet Cokes

Twenty (20) 25cl bottles of still water (room temperature please)

Eight (8) nearly new towels suitable for showering

IF AT ALL POSSIBLE:

One (1) Full length mirror

Lighting suitable for make-up/ hair check

One (1) Ironing board with iron.

Stage towels and water – to be given to tour manager on request:

8 or 12 small bottles of water (room temperature)

4 or 8 medium dark, nearly-new towels

FARRY KISHER - LIVE BAND FORMAT
TOURING INFORMATION SPRING/SUMMER 2021 V1.2
EXPIRES AUGUST 31st 2021

After show bus supplies – to be provided if the sleeper bus is being used:

One (1) case of premium beer in bottles or cans

Eleven (11) 25cl bottles of still water (room temperature please)

Eleven (11) diet Coke

Selection of sandwiches or pizza, enough to feed 11 people i.e. 22 sandwiches or 5 x large pizza.

FARRY KISHER - LIVE BAND FORMAT
TOURING INFORMATION SPRING/SUMMER 2021 V1.2
EXPIRES AUGUST 31st 2021

8) Audio

F.O.H. Console:

Input list is attached. We are taking **32 inputs** from stage.

WE NEED AT LEAST 18 DI BOXES- WE HAVE OUR OWN ¼" TO ¼" LOOMS

We have show files for Digico, Avid, Midas, Soundcraft, Allen & Heath, and SSL consoles.
Our FOH engineer does not like Behringer or Yamaha digital consoles – please advise if you
are supplying this type of console. We may decide to rent in an alternative console and I will
talk to you about costs for this.
We supply the string microphones (probably DPA 4099).
Analogue is always good – Midas being the favourite. Please see the list of effects and
dynamics we would like if you are supplying an analogue console:

F.O.H. outboard for analogue consoles:

- 1 x Klark Teknik DN370, DN360 or BSS or XTA stereo 31 band graphic EQ
- 6 x compressor /limiters i.e. dBX162SL, 160SL dBX160A, or dBX1066
- 6 x noise gates - Drawmer DS201 if possible.
- 2 x effects units capable of producing reverb
- 2 x effects units capable of producing delay/echo

A CD player connected to inputs on the FOH console, is always useful!

Monitors:
WE DO NOT HAVE A MONITOR ENGINEER!
Three (3) mixes in total for the standard band format:

- THREE (3) WEDGE MIXES – PAIR ON EACH PLEASE

Five (5) mixes in total for the band with string section format:

- THREE (3) WEDGE MIXES – PAIR ON EACH PLEASE
- TWO (2) SMALL WEDGE/GALAXY HOTSPOT-TYPE MIXES

Monitor Console:

FARRY KISHER - LIVE BAND FORMAT
TOURING INFORMATION SPRING/SUMMER 2021 V1.2
EXPIRES AUGUST 31st 2021

Input list is still be finalized. We are currently taking approximately **32 - 35 inputs** from stage plus shout/comms as applicable.

9) Lighting brief

WE DO NOT HAVE A LIGHTING PERSON!

Farry Kisher would like a colorful, deep lighting look with plenty of slow movement. The music is mid-tempo, beats-based, so fast strobes and movement are not applicable. Hazing is fine. Holly, our singer, is not on stage for all of the songs and therefore needs to be highlighted when she is.

We will also have visual files (.avi and MP4) for projection/LED backdrop if applicable.

10) Club/theatre stage and riser requirements

Please have a look at the stage plan. We do not require the usual drum rider upstage centre. Please strike any existing drum riser if at all possible. We don't need risers for the electronics and keyboards.

Our set up takes up the whole stage and we will strike everything, as far as possible, after sound check in order to make way for other acts. We ideally need at least 20 minutes to change over for our own, headline, shows.

We will need 4 off chairs with backs and 4 off lit music stands if your show includes the string section. I will discuss hire and costs with you during the advance.

Festivals – stage and riser requirements

We have two (2) keyboard/electronics set-ups that ideally need to be pre-built before changeover. We may have a 4-piece string section for your show. We therefore require:

> **2** off 8' x 8' x1' rolling risers for keys/electronics
> **1** off 12' x 4' x 2' rolling riser (made from 2 off 6' x 4') for the string section

We ideally need power to the keys/electronics risers in the offstage/build area.

We will need 4 off chairs with backs and 4 off lit music stands if your show included the string section. I will discuss hire and costs with you during the advance.

FARRY KISHER			SUMMER 2021	V1.7 EXPIRES 30TH AUG 2021
#	SOURCE	RISER/POSITION	NOTES	DI?
1	Kick	RISER 1 -DRUMS		
2	Snare Top	RISER 1 -DRUMS		
3	Snare Bottom	RISER 1 -DRUMS		
4	Hi-Hats	RISER 1 -DRUMS		
5	Rack Tom	RISER 1 -DRUMS		
6	Floor	RISER 1 -DRUMS		
7	O/H SR	RISER 1 -DRUMS		
8	O/H SL	RISER 1 -DRUMS		
9	Sample Kick BOX 1-1	RISER 1 -DRUMS		DI
10	Sample Snare BOX 1-2	RISER 1 -DRUMS		DI
11	V drums BOX 2-1	RISER 1 -DRUMS		DI
12	Sub kick BOX 3-1	RISER 1 -DRUMS		DI
13	MOTU 1	RISER 2 - STAGE RIGHT/JAMES		DI
14	MOTU 2	RISER 2 - STAGE RIGHT/JAMES		DI
15	MOTU 3	RISER 2 - STAGE RIGHT/JAMES		DI
16	MOTU 4	RISER 2 - STAGE RIGHT/JAMES		DI
17	MOTU 5 Sub Bass	RISER 2 - STAGE RIGHT/JAMES		DI
18	NO INPUT	NO INPUT	NO INPUT	NO INPUT
19	Prophet	RISER 2 - STAGE RIGHT/JAMES		DI
20	Pads L	RISER 2 - STAGE RIGHT/JAMES	Output from Space Echo L	DI
21	Pads R	RISER 2 - STAGE RIGHT/JAMES	Output from Space Echo R	DI
22	Bass DI	UPSTAGE CENTRE/NATALIE		From amp
23	Bass Mic	UPSTAGE CENTRE/NATALIE		
24	Moog Sub 37	UPSTAGE CENTRE/NATALIE		DI
25	Sampler L	RISER 3 - STAGE LEFT/CHRIS		DI
26	Sampler R	RISER 3 - STAGE LEFT/CHRIS		DI
27	Nord L	RISER 3 - STAGE LEFT/CHRIS		DI
28	Nord R	RISER 3 - STAGE LEFT/CHRIS		DI
29	Guitar	UPSTAGE RIGHT/HARRY		
30	Vocal - Holly		We supply. Through FX	DI
31	Announce vocal SR (JAMES)	RISER 2 - STAGE RIGHT/JAMES	We supply,	
32	Announce vocal SL (Chris)	RISER 3 - STAGE LEFT/CHRIS	We supply.	

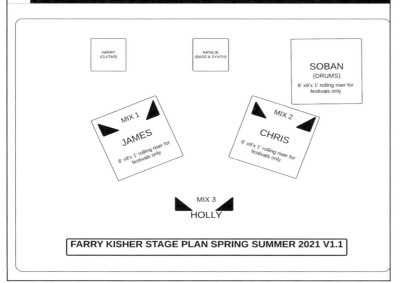

FARRY KISHER STAGE PLAN SPRING SUMMER 2021 V1.1

APPENDIX 4

Tour Budget Sheet

FARRY KISHER - UK HEADLINE TOUR BUDGET V1.2

ITEM	SUPPLIER/ SPECIFIC	NOTES	UNIT COST	MULTIPLY	MULTIPLY	TOTAL COST
WAGES						
Julia Martin	Tour manager		£350	22	1	£7,700
Rodiguez Garcia	FOH sound	Show days	£300	14	1	£4,200
Rodiguez Garcia		Travel/ off days	£100	8	1	£800
Gorou Adachi	Back line	Show days	£200	14	1	£2,800
Gorou Adachi		Travel/ off days	£75	8	1	£600
Nikola Ziolkowski	Lighting designer	Show days	£300	14	1	£4,200
Nikola Ziolkowski		Travel/ off days	£150	8	1	£1,200
Soban Singh	Drums, electronic percussion	Show days	£300	14	1	£4,200
Katie Helms	Merch	Show days	£50	11	1	£550
PER DIEMS						
Band Show			£10	4	12	£480
Band day off			£15	4	10	£600
Crew Show			£10	5	12	£600
Crew day off			£15	5	8	£600
Driver(s)			£45	3	1	£135
TRANSPORT						
Flights	Rodiguez Garcia	BCN-MCR-BCN				£275
Sleeper bus	Manchester - Southampton - Manchester		£1,125	1	1	£1,125
Sleeper bus						£0
Band/crew bus						£0
Splitter van	Tiger Tours (London)		£110	24	1	£2,640
Equipment Van						£0
Fuel			£80	12	1	£960
Ferries						£0
Trucks						£0
Trailer			£75	3	1	£225
Freight & shipping						£0
Crew - public transport			£100	2	1	£200
Parking			£10	24	1	£240
Road Tolls			£30	1	1	£30
Taxi's			£10	1	1	£10
Pick up & transfers						£0
Excess baggage						£0
Delivery						£0
ACCOMMODATION						
Manchester			£120	6	11	£7,920
Non-Manchester			£120	2	7	£1,680
Driver						£0
Day rooms						£0
Breakfast						£0
Tel & fax						£0
PRODUCTION						
SOUND						£0
Rental						£0
Equipment purchase						£0
Equipment consumables						£0
Misc.						£0

LIGHTS						
Rental	Ad Lib	Control +floor package	£975	3	1	£2,925
Equipment purchase						£0
Consumables						£0
Misc.	Ad Lib					£0

VIDEO						
Rental						£0
Equipment purchase						£0
Consumables						£0
Misc.						£0

BACKLINE						
Rental						£0
Equipment purchase						£0
Consumables		Gaffa, sticks, USB	£500	1	1	£500
Misc.						£0

SET						
Rental						£0
Equipment purchase						£0
Consumables						£0
Misc.						£0

STAGE						
Rental						£0
Equipment purchase						£0
Consumables						£0
Misc.						£0

PRODUCTION MISC						
Pre - production TM		2 x show days in total	£350	2	1	£700
Mobile phone TM			£100	1	1	£100
Administration						£0
Legal & accounting						£0
Visas & work papers						£0
Insurance	Tysers	PL, illness, cancellation	£450	1	1	£450

REHEARSALS						
Julia Martin	Tour manager		Included above			
Rodiguez Garcia	FOH sound		Included above			
Gorou Adachi	Back line		Included above			
Nikola Ziolkowski	Lighting designer		Included above			
Soban Singh	Drums, electronic percussion		Included above			
Tech	Ad Lib		£175	1.00	1.00	£175
Rehearsal studio	Islington Mill		£275	2	1	£550
Equipment hire	Ad Lib	Audio rehearsal package	£960	1	1	£960
Transport	Minibus & driver	Running around	£200	2	1	£400

OTHER EXPENSE					
Agent's commission		*10% OF INCOME:*	@£22,250		£2,225
Foreign Artist Tax					

	TOTAL	£52,955

APPENDIX 5

Day-to-Day Schedules

The concert production industry is mature, and conventions exist. The self-imposed schedules for work are known by anyone who works in the industry.

The schedule for a day on-the-road revolves around 'doors' – the time in the day when the audience is allowed into the venue, or the room holding the concert within the venue. Soundchecks must be finished, cases stowed away, suspended elements made safe, cables fixed in place, and stewards and security staff in place at this time. 'Doors' is typically in the early evening – 19.00 or 19.300 and is earlier for events at stadiums, usually 17.00 or 17.30. The early entry allows greater numbers of people to get into the venue, allowing time for security and health screening.

Figure A5.1 shows the schedule for a concert in a non-production, <500-capacity venue. The schedule is fluid and more than one activity involving the artist and touring crew occurs at one time.

Figure A5.2 is a schedule for a typical concert as part of a tour of production venues. The artist and crew are travelling overnight on sleeper buses in this case. This transport type facilitates arriving early at the next venue on the tour and this is necessary to load-in, setup, and check all the production elements before the artist arrives to perform a soundcheck. The figure shows the activities that take place throughout the day, and concurrent with each other.

	NON-PRODUCTION CONCERT SCHEDULE		
TIME	**ARTIST PERFORMING AT <500-CAPACITY VENUE**		
01:00			
02:00			
03:00			
04:00			
05:00			
06:00			
07:00			
08:00			
09:00			
10:00			
11:00			
12:00			
13:00			
14:00			
15:00	ARRIVAL AND PARKING		
16:00	LOAD IN AND SET UP	ACCESS TO VENUE	LOCAL CREW CALL
17:00			
18:00	MERCH COUNT IN	DARK STAGE?	SOUND CHECKS
19:00	DOORS (19.30)	SUPPORT ACTS ON STAGE	SUPPORT ACTS LOAD OUT GEAR?	
20:00				
21:00				
22:00	**HEADLINE ACT ON STAGE**	SETTLEMENT		
23:00	LIVE MUSIC CURFEW	AFTER SHOW CLUB?	HEADLINE ACT PACKS DOWN AND LOADS OUT. POSSIBLE 'DISCO' LOAD OUT	MERCH COUNT OUT
00:00				LOCAL CREW CUT

Figure A5.1 A typical day on a tour of non-production venues

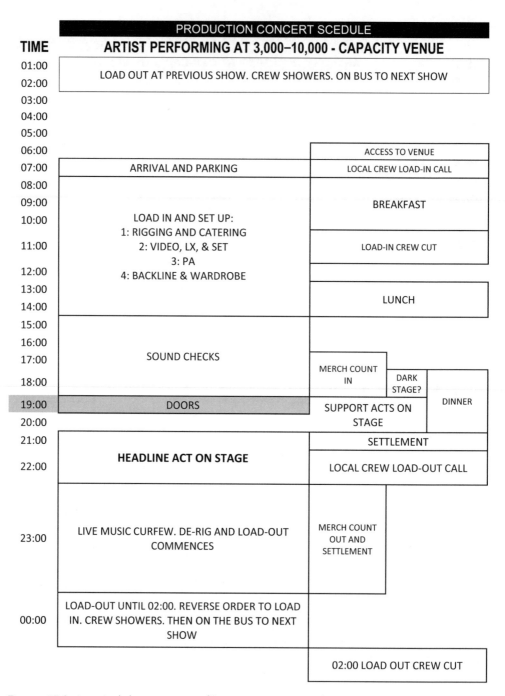

Figure A5.2 A typical day on a tour of larger-capacity, production-type, venues

INDEX

Note: Page numbers in *italics* indicate figures, **bold** indicate tables in the text.